A Hundred and One Days

Also by Åsne Seierstad

The Bookseller of Kabul

A Hundred and One Days

Åsne Seierstad

Translated by
Ingrid Christophersen

A Member of the Perseus Books Group
New York

Je suis profondément convaincu que le seul antidote qui puisse faire oublier au lecteur les éternels Je que l'auteur va écrire, c'est une parfaite sincérité.

Stendhal, *Souvenirs d'Egotisme*, 1832

Contents

Preface

This book is about a journey, a war and some of the people caught up in the war. For a hundred and one days, from January to April 2003, I tried to record what I experienced in Baghdad.

During such a journey the reporter is on duty at all times. Things can happen at any moment. Information is suddenly received or the idea for a new story comes to mind. The reader sees only the outcome; the articles say little of how they were first conceived or what has been left out.

In my ten years as a journalist reporting from war and conflict zones, I have never worked under more difficult conditions than I did in Iraq. Before the war the problem was elementary: no one said anything. Iraqis used empty phrases and banalities for fear of saying anything wrong or betraying their own thoughts.

What to do as a journalist when everyone says the same? Do they all mean it? Do none of them mean it?

I tried to move around in the landscape between

deafening lies and virtually silent gasps of truth. The sophisticated apparatus of oppression affected journalists too; sometimes it had a direct bearing on what we wrote.

In time new challenges arrived – descending from the sky, rushing through the air, crashing around our ears. There was no power, no water, no security. All the same, every day we had to file our reports, watched over by our minders.

One day the minders were gone. Then I tried to discover what happens to people when the dam bursts. What do they choose to say when they can suddenly say what they want?

My reports from Baghdad are *my* reports. They come directly from my own – not always adequate – experiences.

The events might have been interpreted differently by other correspondents. An Egyptian journalist probably saw the war in Iraq from another angle; an American might have assessed the situation in a different way again; maybe an intellectual from *Le Monde* had his own emphasis.

The truth about the war in Iraq does not exist. Or rather, there are millions of true accounts and maybe just as many lies. My remit as a journalist in the chaos of war was not to judge, predict or analyse. It was to look, ask and report.

My greatest advantage was that I *was* there. My eyes were there, my ears were there.

When I left for Iraq I had an agreement with three newspapers. *Aftenposten* in Norway, *Dagens Nyheter* in Sweden, and *Politiken* in Denmark. In time my articles were also published by *Ilta-Sanomat* in Finland, *Der Tagesspiegel* in Germany, *Trouw* in the Netherlands, *Der Standard* in

Austria, and *Tages Anzeiger* in Switzerland. In addition I was employed by several radio and TV channels.

The articles I sent home were snapshots, glimpses from the war. They belong to certain days and incidents. Some have been reproduced in their entirety, others have been integrated within a larger context. The war can never be entirely grasped or understood through instant reporting. Nor can political analysis impart the tragedy of seeing one's own child killed by a missile.

No story contains the whole story. This is just one of many and it gives a fragment of the whole, not more. Read the reports of the Egyptian, the American, or the Frenchman. But above all, try to find the Iraqi version of the war, and the time before and after the war. Together they will give us a basis for understanding what is happening, now that the acts of war are over, but before peace has arrived.

Åsne Seierstad
Oslo, 2004

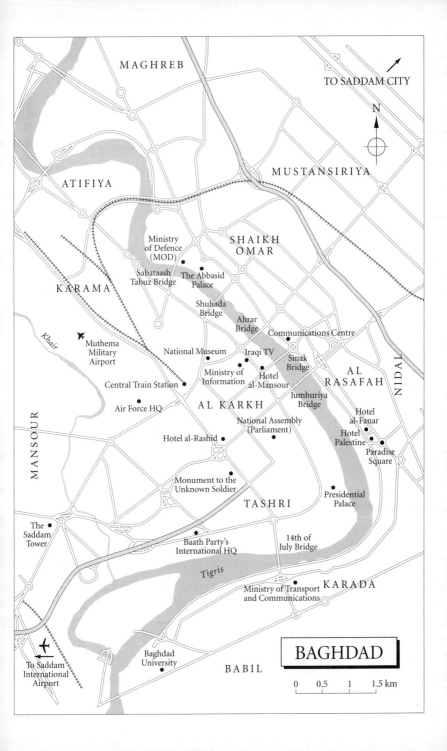

Before

First comes the light. It filters through eyelids, caresses its way into sleep, and slips into dreams. Not the way it usually does, white and cool, but golden.

Half-open eyes peer towards a window framed by long lace curtains, two patterned chairs, a rickety table, a mirror and a chest of drawers. A gaudy sketch hangs on the wall: a bazaar where shadows of women in long, black shawls slide through dark alleyways.

I'm in Baghdad!

So this is what the morning light is like here. Furtive.

The next revelation awaits behind the wispy curtains: the Tigris.

It is as though I have been here before, the view jumps out from my childhood Bible. The meandering river, the rushes, the little palm-clad islands, the trees towering nobly above their reflection in the water.

From far below the cacophony of car horns reaches me, dull roars and sharp high-pitched squeals, a snailing chaos. The road follows the river bank.

I arrived under cover of darkness, a journey of twelve hours from the Jordanian to the Iraqi capital. Night fell long before we reached Baghdad. A few scattered street lights shone palely. Without our being aware of it we crossed the river.

Euphrates and Tigris – the starting point of everything. Even the Flood had its origins here: *the land between the two rivers* – Mesopotamia. The Tigris is a treacherous river. Under layers of mud, on the river plain, archaeologists have uncovered towns. The cataclysms led to the accounts of God's judgement, the Flood that covered the whole world. The waters of the Tigris made the Hanging Gardens bloom. The Garden of Eden was somewhere near; the Tower of Babel within easy reach. From this country Abraham and Sarah were exiled.

The thickets along the Tigris are paradise no longer. The river bank is dry and barren and the only green in sight is the palm leaves swaying lazily at the top of brown tree trunks. The city too melts into brown; the contours of the houses are erased by the mists hanging heavily from the sky. Baghdad disappears into the desert.

Like so many other world cities, Baghdad's history begins with the river.

– This is the place where I want to build. Here everything can be transported on the Euphrates and the Tigris. Only a place like this can sustain my army and a large population, Emperor al-Mansour is alleged to have said in the middle of the 700s. It was summer and he was travelling around his empire. He set up camp near the village of Qasr al-Salam, said evening prayers and fell asleep. According to the legend, he was blessed with the 'sweetest and kindest' sleep in the world. When he awoke, all he looked upon he liked, and so he stayed. The Emperor himself drew up plans and allocated funds in order that the city might grow quickly. He laid the corner stone himself and said: – Build and may God be with you!

Baghdad developed on the strategic trade route between Iran in the east, the corn-growing countries in the north, and Syria and Egypt in the west. According to tradition the city was designed to express the Emperor's elevated radiance and splendour, and to keep his distance from the population. The palaces were built on the west bank of the Tigris, while the markets and living quarters were assigned to the east bank.

Like al-Mansour I too have been blessed with the sweetest and kindest sleep this first night by the banks of the Tigris. I am standing up, enjoying the noise from the ramshackle cars below. A feeling of peace spreads over me. The time has come for me to start looking; in a country where catastrophe is gathering.

On the way down the stairs I hear screams from reception. Piercing howls and scratching noises cut through the air. A skinny monkey runs crazily around inside a cage, howling, a dove coos and yellow canaries add their warble. A feeding bottle is jammed between the bars of the cage.

– Poor little guy, is all I manage before two tortuous arms grab me from behind the bars and hang on. I scream and pull away. The monkey squeals and jumps back.

– Mino steals anything he can get hold of. He can reach right down into your pockets if you get too close, the receptionist says. I glare at Mino. He should be swinging from palm tree to palm tree, eating fresh shoots or scrounging bananas.

The receptionist stuffs a few dinar notes into his breast

pocket and approaches the monkey, who grabs them.
– Look, he certainly can steal, he laughs.

In the breakfast room my previous night's travelling
companions are gathered around the oriental spread of
bread, tomatoes, olives, boiled eggs and sweet, strong tea.

– The Tigris. I turn my eyes heavenward.

– Wonderful, says Jorunn.

– Just don't drink it, Bård grumbles. His job is to purify
the water, Jorunn's to organise him. Bård is a water engineer and works for the Norwegian Church Aid, Jorunn is
the coordinator.

– We can provide clean water for hundreds of thousands
of people, Bård says. The cup of tea disappears in his large
hands. – All we need is our equipment. Much of the
machinery has been held up at the border, he sighs.

– The Bible, I suggest. Can you lend me a Bible?

Jorunn, who has been a relief worker under the aus-
pices of the church for many years, looks at me as though
I have caught her in a crime.

– Can you imagine. I don't have a Bible, she mutters,
apologetic, surprised. – I don't have a Bible.

But Jorunn can relate that Abraham lived here, in
Mesopotamia.

*Now the Lord had said unto Abraham, Get thee out of thy
country, and from thy kindred, and from thy father's house, unto
a land that I will show thee: And I will make of thee a great
nation, and I will bless thee, and make thy name great; and thou
shalt be a blessing.*

Bård was the one who got me into Iraq.

– Ali will fix it, he said when I phoned him around
Christmas. The country was more or less closed to the press;
colleagues of mine had waited for months to gain entry. The

piles of applications from news-starved journalists grew at Iraqi embassies around the world. The majority were thrown in the waste paper basket; only a few were stamped with the seal which would open the gates to Saddam Hussein's kingdom. Through Bård's excellent contacts in the Red Crescent and with the help of the local Norwegian Church Aid secretary Ali, my entry visa was granted in no time at all. On one of the coldest days after New Year we flew to Jordan.

At the Iraqi Embassy in Amman I promised to register with the Ministry of Information immediately upon arrival in Baghdad. But today is Friday.

– Everything is closed, Ali assures me. You can go tomorrow.

It will be my last day of freedom. Jorunn and I want to sightsee. Bård goes to renew his membership of Baghdad Tennis Club. He is of the opinion that some of the frustration caused by Iraq's stifling bureaucracy wears off on the court.

Jorunn, Ali and I set off for the book market, the Friday market. We leave the banks of the Tigris and join the traffic jam. Cars cough and splutter, stop and start. Like the others, our car is also patched, glued and revamped. United Nations sanctions have resulted in a lack of spare parts, leading to numerous cars breaking down in the traffic lanes and being towed or pushed to one side. Now and again we catch a glimpse of black, highly polished Japanese or German bodywork, the vehicles of the elite. Among the wrecks they look like sleek monsters. Never have I seen such a selection of American cars in worse condition; worn out Cadillacs, dented Buicks and lustreless Chevrolets. Many of them arrived as booty from Kuwait. Allegedly, few cars were left standing in the smarter areas of Kuwait after the Iraqi army withdrew and went home in February 1991.

The city where so many of the stories from the *Thousand and One Nights* are set is like any other large Middle Eastern city – noisy, pounding and fume-filled. When the stories of 'Sinbad the Sailor' and 'Ali Baba and the Forty Thieves' were written, Baghdad was surrounded by a high wall. The historical figure mentioned several times in the collection is the Caliph of all Islam, Harun al-Rashid, often portrayed in disguise, wandering around town to discover for himself what is going on: *He felt restless, he could not sleep, his chest was tight.*

Harun is said to have turned the city into a centre of culture around AD 800 and was celebrated for giving fabulous presents to poets, painters, sculptors and scientists who created something he liked. He, and later his successors, put one day aside each week for religious and intellectual discussions, and many great literary works were translated into Arabic. Baghdad was the capital of an empire which stretched from North Africa nearly all the way to India.

Internal strife drained the Empire. The headquarters of the Muslim world moved to Cairo. Turkish warlords invaded Baghdad, followed by Mongols. Hundreds and thousands of inhabitants were slaughtered. The gardens were not watered, the palaces were plundered, works of art were smashed and books burnt.

The last occupiers were the British. They conquered the town from the Ottoman Empire in 1917. The colony's rulers staked out the borders, gave the country the name Iraq and installed a pro-British king, who declared the country independent in 1932.

Little of old Baghdad remains. The rulers who took over after the British were preoccupied with modernisation. The result was that many of the alleyways and old parts of the town disappeared for good. Modern Iraqi governments might appear and disappear in an endless stream of revolutions and coups, but the renewal of the city has marched on indefatigably. Nearly all the buildings date from the twentieth century. Fabulous, mysterious palaces in narrow back alleys have become multi-storey brown, yellow or grey brick houses. Blocks of flats remind one of Soviet-style asphalt jungles, only smaller. The alleyways have been straightened and are now wide avenues. Trees have been planted around palaces and administration buildings; otherwise the roads are flanked by bumpy and, on the whole, crowded pavements.

In spite of the crowds there is no rush. No one is hurrying this Friday morning, some walk around leisurely, others pull heavy carts or drag huge sacks, swaying under the weight of their load. Shops and cafés open on to the pavements and appear relaxed and inviting. On the surface one does not notice the dark cloud of dread that is about to descend.

If the old spirit of Baghdad is still alive, it must be in the bazaars. But even they are sad reminders of the town's lost influence and intellectual strength.

The book market is little more than an accidental collection of books, displayed around a network of narrow passages in one of the town's old quarters. What was once a decadent and busy quarter is now a cluster of dilapidated houses. Past glories can only be guessed at. The books are lined up in rows, on the ground or on small carpets and tables. No one hawks their wares, rather the vendors look uneasy, surveying a collection they would prefer had remained on the shelves at home, but which decades of war have forced them to sell. Old Arab classics, the collected works of Sartre, Saddam's speeches in French, German and English. I am offered a glass of sweet tea and buy *Arabian Nights* and *By Desert Ways to Baghdad*. On the ground, in the dust, I find Gertrude Bell's *Arabian Diary*. I have promised Ali not to talk to anyone, at least to say nothing 'that can be misinterpreted'. He is my guardian today – until I am embraced by the lawful clutches of the Ministry of Information.

– You have not registered yet, you are virtually illegal, so better not get into any trouble, he explains. So I only ask about the books lying in the dust. And no one can stop me from looking at people.

The market empties of customers. It is lunch time. Ali takes us to a restaurant which lies in a garden of flowers and palm trees. Fish swim around in a pond. We pick the fattest one. The fish sparkles in the afternoon sun, a last round of the pond, a net, a blow and the cook is ready to clean, fillet, season and grill. While we follow the knife's rapid movements, salad, hummus, grilled aubergine, white cheese and chunks of bread, straight from the oven, are brought to the table. We eat with our fingers, dipping the bread in the dishes.

The conversation is stilted. It is difficult to talk with Ali. Or maybe he finds it difficult to talk with us.

There is plenty of room in the restaurant. A nearby family wolfs down starters and fish at a furious rate. In a corner two men loll about, replete. A group of big guys in leather jackets, each carrying a walkie-talkie, throw themselves like hungry bears over their meal. Mobile phones don't exist, satellite telephones are forbidden, but collaborators, the important ones, are evidently furnished with walkie-talkies.

I go out to watch the cook. He pours oil and marinade over the fish, chops some chillies and grills some more. Ali follows me, to make sure I'm behaving.

The feeling of anticipation stays with me all day. It is like being poised at the start of a maze; the answer is hidden and there is a mess of routes to choose from.

No one can reach me, the mobile phone won't work, no one knows me. Chores not done before departure will remain undone, post will remain unopened, messages will remain unanswered. The restlessness from home lets go its grip.

Back in room 707, according to the receptionist the best he has, I unpack my hoard of books and lay them out on the ochre bedspread. Like a serene island between the bathroom, where the cockroaches scurry over the broken tiles, and the evening rush-hour outside, my bed occupies the major part of the room. The noise is even shriller than in the morning. But I don't close the door to the balcony. I want the curtains to flap in the desert wind.

My eyes alight upon *Arabian Diary* and I am sent whirling into Gertrude Bell's fantastic world. Early in the last century she travelled alone with smugglers and bandits in the desert right outside my window. She was called the mightiest woman in the British Empire and was the adviser to kings and prime ministers. Gertrude Bell was the only woman Winston Churchill invited to the Cairo Conference in 1921 – the conference that was to decide the future of Mesopotamia. She was also one of the few among Middle Eastern travellers who described the life of women.

There they were, those women – wrapped in Indian brocades, hung with jewels, served by slaves, and there was not one single thing about them which betrayed the base of existence of Europe or Europeans – except me! I was the blot. Some of the women of the shaikhly house were very beautiful. They pass from hand to hand

— the victor takes them, with her power and the glory, and think of it, his hands are red with blood of their husbands and children, she writes from the Hayyil Harem on 6 March 1914. The eunuch Said has just informed her that she is a prisoner and cannot leave. She is allocated a tiny house in the harem where she waits before being released. *I sat in a garden house on carpets — like all the drawings in Persian picture books. Slaves and eunuchs served us with tea and coffee and fruits. Then we walked about the garden, the boys carefully telling me the names of all the trees. And then we sat again and drank more tea and coffee. It gets on your nerves when you sit day after day between high mud walls and thank heaven that my nerves are not very responsive. They have kept me awake only one night out of seven.*

After a long wait she is at last set free, by order of the emir. *My camels came in, and after dark Said with a bag of gold and full permission to go where I liked and when I liked. Why they have now given way, or why they did not give way before, I cannot guess. But anyhow, I am free and my heart is at rest — it is widened.*

Someone knocks on the door. Said, the eunuch with tea and exotic fruits?

A man stands outside with a yellow towel in his hand. He says something in Arabic and passes me the towel. Then he walks past me into the room. I follow. He shows me where the soap is, what the toothbrush mug is for, how the drawers are pulled out, the curtains closed and the door to the terrace shut. I smile and thank him. The man remains on the spot. I find some newly changed notes. He thanks me and leaves. A few minutes later there is another knock on the door. This time he is carrying a loo roll. I give him a few more notes. He smiles and nods and disappears down the corridor. Thus evolves our way of socialising. As soon as I return to my room I know what will happen. 'Said' will turn up with something or other – a towel, a piece of soap, an extra blanket. Nothing is replenished while I'm out, but on my return there is a knock on the door.

What did I tell you as to the quality most needed for travel among the Arabs? Gertrude Bell writes. *Patience, if you remember, that is what one needs.*

Darkness descends on Baghdad. The sun disappears behind the Presidential palace on the opposite side of the river, Saddam Hussein's most splendid palace, built to celebrate what the Iraqi's call 'The Victory in the Gulf'. The floodlit building gleams and shines among palms and gardens. It will stand peacefully for another few months.

– Why did you not come yesterday? What did you do yesterday? The man behind the desk thunders. – Who do you think you are?

I try to explain that it was Friday and all public offices were closed.

– We are never closed, our business hours are from 8 a.m. to 10 p.m. every day, and even outside those hours we still track you. If you want to stay you'll have to toe the line. There's a plane departing every day.

The man introduces himself as Mohsen. Later I am told that he is number three at the press centre.

Mohsen is so short that his legs dangle in the air behind the desk. Like many other middle-aged men in Baghdad his hair and eyebrows are tinted jet-black. In spite of his words, his face is friendly and he has beautiful brown eyes. He appears to be laughing behind the serious facade, as though he were giggling his way through the compulsory interrogation.

I tell him how I spent the previous day and fill in endless forms, so painstakingly thorough that the stout bureaucrat softens somewhat and seems to forgive my stolen day of freedom. He summons Engineer Walid, a stick of a man, who opens my satellite telephone. It had been sealed at the border. – Anyone seen taking a phone out of this building will be arrested for espionage, Mohsen grumbles.

– What are you really doing here?

– I . . . eh . . .

– Make a list of what you want to do, then I'll consider whether you can stay or not, Mohsen says. – In any case, I'll give you a maximum of ten days.

With a gesture he tells me to stay seated on the sofa. It is so soft that I am knee-high to him. Mohsen despatches an assistant to find me an interpreter. No foreigner can function without someone to monitor what we do, where we travel, to whom we speak. The assistant returns with an older, thin-haired gentleman.

– This is Takhlef, our most experienced. I am giving you the best as you are so young, Mohsen smiles.

Takhlef tiptoes around under Mohsen's gaze. He is small, skinny and dapper, dressed in a dark-blue suit, freshly ironed shirt and polished shoes. The suit is too big, as though he might recently have lost a lot of weight. The sparse hair is brushed back in a futile attempt to conceal the shiny crown. He stands beside Mohsen in a manner which shows that he works for Mohsen, not for me. – Just don't try anything, his look tells me. – We are in charge.

In order to work together we will both have to fawn, lie, conceal. Maybe that is why I dislike him from the beginning. Later I wonder whether I never really gave him a chance. Maybe he was actually quite a nice chap, squashed by the Baath Party's vice like everyone else. But at the time I thought my luck had run out, being given him.

— What interests you? is his first question, as though all I have to do is to choose. An interview with Saddam Hussein, perhaps? There is no time to think of ideas before he continues:

— Are you interested in culture?

— Hm.

— Then let's request Babylon. Let's go to Babylon. Are you interested in art? Then we'll request the Saddam Art Centre, the National Gallery, the History Museum, the Museum of Antiquity, the Monument of the Revolution. Shall we begin with Babylon? Tomorrow?

I am in no mood to go sightseeing; I want to talk to people, find out how they live. It becomes apparent that an application is needed for even the smallest thing. To visit a school, a hospital, an institution. Even to visit a family one has to apply before a name and an address will be supplied. I give that one a miss. There is no mileage in visiting a model family, hand-picked and approved by the Ministry of Information.

A special permit is required to leave Baghdad; the further away, the more difficult it is to obtain. To travel to the Shia Muslim areas of the south is virtually impossible — very few journalists are allowed to visit Basra. But the most difficult is to get to Tikrit, Saddam's home town. It is almost hermetically sealed to foreigners. The permit to Babylon takes five minutes; the town can't be of much interest.

The next morning Takhlef is waiting for me in reception, at a safe distance from Mino.

— Are you ready? he asks and glances casually at his watch. I take this as an indication that I am five minutes late.

Takhlef sits in the front seat of the car, I am in the back. I try to initiate a conversation, but every question receives a noncommittal answer, so I give up. Our newly established cooperation is based on very different objectives. I probe, he conceals. After an hour's drive on sand-blown roads the car stops in front of a high blue gate, painted with animals in yellow and white. *Ishtar Gate* is written in large letters – gateway to the legendary city. Can this be Babylon? It looks like the Disney version – all is new, shining, sleek.

We are welcomed by Hamid, the archaeologist whose job it is to show us around in what was the centre of the globe five thousand years ago. Here culture and science, literature, mathematics and astronomy flourished. Here the world's first law codes were collated. The Sumerians and Babylonians were the first to divide the circle into 360 degrees, the day into 24 hours, the hour into 60 minutes and the minute into 60 seconds. Five thousand years ago they impressed signs on wet clay-tablets and invented cuneiform writing. One of these tablets reveals that the Babylonians were aware of what later came to be known as 'the Pythagorean doctrine of right-angled triangles' a thousand years before Pythagoras.

The legendary Babylon appears in many classic tales. Most famous are the writings of the man one might call the world's first reporter, the Greek historian Herodotus. He visited the city around 400 BC. He wrote, *Babylon's splendour exceeds that of every other city in the known world.*

Ishtar, the gate with the holy, snakelike bulls' heads, led into a temple with walls of gold. At the far end was a room enclosing a seat of pure gold. *The astrologers relate, although I doubt it,* Herodotus wrote, *that the gods themselves visited the sacred room and rested on the seat.*

Gods and gold have long gone. One hundred years ago

German archaeologists removed anything of value to Berlin. In the Pergamon Museum thousand-year-old statues and sculptures are preserved. A few years ago Saddam Hussein decided that the ruins should be rebuilt. Everything was to resemble the world's first metropolis in its heyday. Thus Babylon got a new emperor. Many of the stones of the Ishtar gate are engraved with his signature. Not even King Nebuchadnezzar had thought of that.

Babylon is a tourist attraction without tourists. In fact Takhlef and I are the only ones there this morning. Everything in the showcases is a copy.

– The complete Ishtar gate is in Berlin. Other stolen items are in the Louvre or the British Museum, our guide sighs resentfully. – The originals still in Iraq are stored in vaults. You know, the war might start at any moment. It's best to hide things away. The whole of Babylon might be blown to smithereens.

The archaeologist lives alone in Babylon with his young wife and a small son. He is the guide by day and watchman by night. – The Americans want to ruin our country. First they'll get the Presidential palace, then Babylon, he snorts. – They want to destroy our culture and lord it over us, take our oil, our resources.

He halts by the model of the Hanging Gardens. Cascading down the rock face the Sumerians planted the most glorious flowerbeds. – Well, this is what we think it looked like, he says.

He is on firmer ground when talking about the Tower of Babel. The square ruins have been left standing in Babylon; the copy is in miniature. The story is told in Genesis.

And the whole earth was of one language, and of one speech.

And it came to pass as they journeyed from the east, that they found a plain in the land of Shinar; and they dwelt there.

And they said one to another, Go to, let us make brick, and burn them thoroughly. And they had brick for stone and slime had they for mortar.

And they said, Go to, let us build us a city and a tower, whose top may reach unto heaven; and let us make us a name, lest we be scattered abroad upon the face of the whole earth.

And the Lord came down to see the city and the tower, which the children of men builded.

And the Lord said, Behold, the people is one, and they have all one language; and this they begin to do: and now nothing will be restrained from them, which they have imagined to do.

Go to, let us go down, and there confound their language, that they may not understand one another's speech.

So the Lord scattered them abroad from thence upon the face of all the earth; and they left off to build the city. Therefore is the name of it called Babel; because the Lord did there confound the language of all the earth: and from thence did the Lord scatter them abroad upon the face of all the earth.

Hamid shows us out and we walk along the temple walls. They stretch ahead, straight as an arrow; there is no sign of exposure to wind and weather. A man appears amongst the rebuilt ruins. Hunchbacked and dressed in a long tunic he sweeps a large square with slow, rhythmic movements. The broom is a palm leaf twice his size. He might have been sweeping all his life. Had this been Disneyland one might have thought he was put there to represent a worker from the past. But the hunchback is real, and his task is to keep the desert sand away from the historical copies. The man and the palm leaf seem to be the only genuine articles in all of Babylon.

I tell Takhlef I want to talk to the sweep.

— Why to him? Takhlef exclaims.

— He might tell me something about Babylon.

– That one. Takhlef points and laughs scornfully. – He doesn't even know where he is, he's probably illiterate. You shouldn't interview illiterates; they don't know what's right or wrong and won't give you a correct picture of Iraq.

– But I want to, I say, and regret it immediately. I mustn't rub my guide up the wrong way so soon. Takhlef approaches the sweep after all. He towers above the skinny man, who looks up at him, terrified, and gives monosyllabic answers.

– His name is Ali. He lives close by and has worked here for many years. Was there anything else you wanted to know? Takhlef asks tersely.

– No, thank you, thank you very much, that was exactly what I wanted to know.

On a hilltop overlooking the compound is a large building. It is square, like the foundations of the Tower of Babel, but brand new. Two dark-coloured jeeps are parked outside.

– Can we go up and have a look? I ask. The sweep has returned to his customary movements and is working his way around the copy of one of Babylon's famous statues: the lion overpowering a man.

– No, says Takhlef. – That's impossible.

– Why?

– That's one of Saddam's palaces.

That's what I thought. That's why I asked. If only we could walk up the few hundred yards to the villa. We might meet one of his sons, the dreaded Uday? Or the ice-cold Qusay? Curiosity gets hold of me and almost impels me towards the building, but then I look at Takhlef and common sense takes over. I see before me the president's sons as little boys, on nocturnal wanderings around Babylon. Perhaps they climbed the lion, tamed it, fought imaginary barbarians.

Back in the dust of the present I tag along behind Takhlef to the exit. Hamid opens up the souvenir kiosk. I buy two Babylon T-shirts, a slab of ceramic depicting the holy ox, a picture book of the excavations, a bunch of postcards and stamps with images of the ruins, unaware that this little kiosk in a few months will burst into flames and become a gaping black hole. The display cases in the museum will be emptied, the ceramics smashed, the miniatures of the Tower of Babel and the Hanging Gardens broken to pieces. The light bulbs will be unscrewed from the lamps, the sockets torn out of the walls, the cords cut up and sold as scrap at the markets. Every age has its own catastrophe. But it is still some time away. In the meantime, Hamid, like most other Iraqis, lives in fear of the storm that is brewing. Will the wrath of God strike Babylon again?

Takhlef is more talkative. – Show me America's Babylon, he guffaws. – They were nothing at the time we ruled the world. They are historical upstarts. They don't build, they just tear down. It's important that you write about Babylon, show the world who we are!

Takhlef drops me off outside the hotel. Do I want him to fetch me for dinner?

I pluck up enough courage to say no.

– Saddam's Art Centre? he asks. He is planning the following day's programme.

I am here to find dissidents, a secret uprising, gagged intellectuals, Saddam's opponents. I am here to point out human rights violations, expose oppression. And I'm reduced to being a tourist.

– You have to follow the rules, Takhlef says. – That's very important; otherwise you'll have to leave. You can't wander around alone, talk to anyone or write bad things about Iraq. Believe me, trust me, do as I say.

My head is spinning.

— OK, I say. — I look forward to seeing Saddam's Art Centre. I'm very interested in art and culture.

Back in my room I throw myself on the bed. There is a knock on the door. Said and the toiletries. I thank him and pay. He straightens the bedcover, nods and leaves. I tear the cover off.

Patience. That is what Gertrude Bell recommended. Patience.

Saddam's Art Centre is a huge concrete structure in the middle of Baghdad. It consists of a few floors of Iraqi paintings from the last centuries and two floors of Saddam Hussein. We proceed quickly through the first centuries and stop at the 1970s. From there on it is all about the big leader: painted, photographed, woven, appliquéd, reproduced in graphic art and woodcut, in mosaics, in silk and cotton. With sunglasses, in a white suit, presenting arms, in an armchair, genial, or upright, mounted on a horse.

One of Saddam's official painters shows us around. He looks like a Montmartre artist: long hair swept back, sensitive fingers, casual but stylish attire. But instead of Sacre Coeur or the Eiffel Tower, Khalid is reduced to one and the same motif.

— This painting is to commemorate the victory over the Americans during the Gulf War. This one celebrates the triumph over Iran in 1988.

Khalid shows us his pièce de résistance — a fifty metre square painting representing Iraq's history. The central motif is naturally the president himself, in uniform, riding on a white horse, sword aloft. He is broad-shouldered and well-built. His eyes shine, his teeth glow; his cheeks are ruddy and healthy, the posture proud. Below him are the people, the various ethnic and religious groups represented by national costumes, the workers in Soviet-style poses by weapons-filled conveyor belts. The American threat is indicated by bombers, but there is still room for roses, palms, mountains and wild animals. Every living thing is included in Saddam's ark.

Khalid tells me how he became one of Saddam's official artists. — While I was a student at the Academy a competition was announced to paint the president from a photograph, but to use your own artistic ideas. I won, he says. — Our president is very interested in art and often announces competitions to decide who can produce the best portrait.

— Don't you get fed up with painting the same subject all the time?

— Oh no. Our president is a source of continuous inspiration.

— Wouldn't you like to paint something else?

— If I were asked to paint divine women, angels or the most beautiful roses, I would decline, because I paint the greatest of all.

— Have you met him?

— Yes, I was awarded a distinction five years ago. A great honour to my art, the greatest day in my life, Khalid assures me.

My favourite painting shows Saddam Hussein wearing Mafioso sunglasses against the backdrop of a setting sun. I feel like asking whether anyone has specialised in presidential caricatures, but I resist the temptation. My residence permit has not yet been granted.

Khalid represents one part of the complex system which feeds the personality cult of the president. The forever-appearing grotesque Saddam frescos are supposed to demonstrate his closeness to the people; several of the paintings show him kissing children or clasping the worn hands of a soldier's mother. But the portraits, both the small and the ostentatious, underline the leader's elevation – he is almost deific, and in pure goodness now and again descends to the level of the people.

Khalid no longer needs a photograph to paint from. He knows the face by heart.

The tour around Saddam's many faces continues after we leave the Art Centre. We encounter him on street corners, in restaurants, on public buildings and in squares.

– It's beautiful, isn't it? Takhlef asks.

Saddam is everywhere. On every single piece of construction, on posters, in shop windows. He makes an appearance on each of the ministry buildings. Outside the Ministry of Justice he is holding up scales. By the Ministry of Defence he sits on a tank. He stands in a field by the Ministry of Agriculture and wields a hammer and anvil by the Ministry of Industry. Outside the Ministry of Communications a large poster shows him talking on a telephone. In front of the mosques he is praying and near a teahouse he is drinking tea. The different costumes and poses accentuate the conviction that he is omnipresent. He is the descendant of the Kings of Babylon – and the man of the moment.

– Saddam Hussein has elevated Iraq to a shining world star. The Americans try to wear us down with bombs and sanctions. But we will prevail, come what may.

Takhlef does not wait for me to respond. Others might draw breath or cough; my guide proclaims, at suitable intervals, clichés about the President.

– Everything he did in the past was good and everything he will do in the future is good.

– How can you be so sure about that?

– I know it as a result of my belief in the party and his leadership.

Takhlef glares at me; he suggests we finish the tour. I am frustrated. What sort of a game is this? How long will it continue? How much longer must I praise Saddam's shining hair? How often will Takhlef boast about the victories of the revolution and how wonderful everything would be in Iraq but for sanctions? He knows he is lying, he knows I know he is lying, he knows I am lying, he knows that I know that he knows that I am lying. I keep my mouth shut. To report my questions and attitude is one of Takhlef's duties. But I want my first article home to deal with something real – how people live, how they think about Iraq, about the USA and about the war that is lurking over the horizon. I cannot just phone *Aftenposten* and ask for some space in the travel section: 'A guide to Baghdad's art scene – from Babylon to Saddam at sunset'. Bon voyage!

– Shall we do the National Museum tomorrow? Takhlef asks.

I shrug my shoulders.

– They have one hundred and seventy thousand artefacts. It is very interesting.

I do not want to see one hundred and seventy thousand artefacts.

– What about the monuments to the revolution? Or Saddam Hussein's gift collection? There are thousands of gifts from all the world's leaders. Or what about the Mother of all Battles mosque, to commemorate the Gulf War? There is a Koran inside the mosque written with the president's blood. It has six hundred and fifty pages. In the course of two years our president donated twenty-eight litres of blood in order to write the book. Or what about the Ark of the Clenched Fists? They are enlarged copies of the president's hands.

I shake my head.

– Tomorrow at eleven Baghdad's artists are marching in a peace demonstration, says Takhlef.

I might find someone who will divulge some secrets. An intellectual, an atheist, an artistic soul.

– Yes, I'd love that.

Lady Macbeth, Medea, Romeo and Othello asked for peace yesterday. The cultural elite of Baghdad, with actors at the front, were called out on to the streets to protest against what the Iraqis call the US aggression. The interpretation of the characters as demonstrators was convincing. Walking slowly, clutching pictures of Saddam Hussein, a purposeful procession wound its way through the streets of Baghdad. It was easy to learn the chant by heart: Saddam, Saddam, Saddam. In our blood and in our hearts. Saddam, Saddam, Saddam, no one must take him from us, they cried in unison.

– I hope this does the trick, said Karim Awad, one of Iraq's most famous actors. – It is our duty as actors to be good role models, we must show that we support our leader, said Awad, who was educated at a Californian school of dramatic art and has appeared in several films and TV dramas. He identifies closely with Othello, the noble warrior betrayed by his servant.

A procession of dwarves, often used in Iraqi comedies, and dancers in colourful costumes and well-known pop stars joined in the festivities.

A few blocks away, at the UN headquarters, the head of the weapons inspectors, Hans Blix, read out the new 10-point agreement.

The most significant development is that the UN is guaranteed unlimited access, to include private homes. Iraq will encourage sci-entists to speak to weapons inspectors, and will allow inspectors to interview technical experts without the presence of Iraqi officials. In addition, Iraq will establish its own team to look for warheads.

Hans Blix said Iraq had handed over several new documents, were preparing others and promised to uncover more.

— We have solved a string of practical problems, but unfortu-nately not all, Hans Blix said when he left Baghdad to report to the UN in New York on 27 January. — I am sure Iraq will honour its promises, he said and reiterated that war was not inevitable.

The UN maintains that Iraq is hiding anthrax, the VX nerve gas and Scud missiles. The country has produced no evidence that these have been destroyed.

— We have left these points to be discussed later, he promised. Iraq has put forth conflicting information about the nerve gas production programme. Last week UN inspectors found empty chemical warheads unreported by Iraq. Iraq said it was an over-sight.

After the meeting Hans Blix and his entourage left for Cyprus. Thereafter they travel to Athens to brief the UN executive com-mittee, and then on to New York.

So far 400 sites have been inspected with no proof found that the regime in Baghdad has produced weapons in contravention of UN resolutions. The inspections continued yesterday with more than 10 sites inspected.

The Iraqis might have agreed to cooperate but the country's newspapers are taking a much tougher line. Iraqi citizens must not get the impression that Saddam Hussein has given in to western demands. Al Thawra 'The Revolution', the Baath party's mouthpiece controlled by Saddam Hussein, accused the weapons inspectors of spying. — The inspections are a direct interference in our internal affairs, the newspaper reported on Monday. — They go in to the homes of normal citizens, to their bedrooms and bathrooms. *They do not respect Muslims, or our day of rest, and insist on inspecting even on Fridays and holidays, said the editorial. — Initially we thought the inspectors were neutral, now we know they are American spies. This has nothing to do with the search for weapons of mass destruction. Anyhow, we have neither chemical, biological nor nuclear weapons, so they are looking in vain, it concluded.*

The demonstration is tapering off. Satem Jassim wobbles the last few yards on sky-high heels and in tight jeans. The host of one of Iraq's most popular TV music programmes is heavily made up and her long blonde hair is bleached.

— The most important thing at the moment is to stand behind our leader. We must inspire people. In my programme we play lots of songs that support Saddam Hussein.

— Have you got a favourite song?

— Yes, all of them.

— What about songs dealing with life, love?

— The songs about Saddam are nicer. Nicer and more important, Satem assures me. She says that everyone who works at the TV station is marching in the demonstration.

— What would have happened if someone refused?

— Nothing, this is a free country.

After a few hours the spectacle is over. The clenched fists relax, shoulders sag, placards are collected. Othello and Desdemona disappear into the crowd, their paces heavy and stooping. The curtain has come down.

In the hotel reception Abdullah nods politely and receives a cheerful greeting in return. I whistle at the canaries, describe a large circle around Mino and step into the rickety lift up to 707. I sink into the grey and white speckled lump which passes as an easy chair. My first article is in the can and it said something, in spite of, or because, no one said anything. Said arrives with loo paper and a clean towel. I thank him and tip him. After just a little while there is another knock on the door.

There stands Said with a TV. He places it proudly on the table in the corner and shows me how to turn it on. There are five channels. Channel one shows Saddam talking, channel two the day's demonstration, channel three music, channel four snow and channel five sport.

Said explains the different channels and presses all the buttons so I see all the channels several times. He turns the TV on and off, on and off, to make sure I know how it works. In spite of not understanding Said's Arabic, I get it. The bit about the buttons.

I decide on a different strategy. In place of my usual little tip I give him a huge sum intended to last for some time, so that I won't have to open the door continually. Said kisses the money and leaps for joy.

The TV is on channel one. Saddam Hussein sits at the head of a long table, puffing on a cigar. Around him are men in uniform, probably the Defence Minister and various generals. I recognise the man on his right, his son Qusay, head of the armed forces.

The president talks, uninterruptedly. Some of what he says we hear, but the better part is transmitted without sound, accompanied by seductive violin music. Now and again he waves his cigar in the air in time with the music, now and again out of time. Suddenly the sound is reconnected, but there is obviously one cardinal rule: only the president's voice is heard. Whenever one of the military chiefs makes a comment, the violins take over. The sound returns when Saddam answers.

I sit in front of the TV all evening, mesmerised. It is Saddam Hussein all the way, be it news, religious or entertainment programmes. Music videos are played, one after another, between shots of the military council. There is one man and one message – Saddam!

The stars of the music videos appear only briefly on screen. Saddam plays the main role, in a variety of get-ups: uniform, lounge suit, white shirt and braces, feathered green Tyrolean hat, black beret, turban, Bedouin dress, Palestinian scarf, lambskin hat, or Argentinian tango hat; more often than not waving a rifle around.

Labourers also feature frequently in the videos, hammering and welding – the country is being built and defended for all to see. Other videos show historical ruins, camels in the desert, mighty waterfalls and beaches, followed by fighter planes, aircraft carriers and marching soldiers.

Up-to-date pictures of anti-war demonstrations from all over the world are also given prominent coverage on Iraqi TV. They even find a European wandering around with a portrait of Saddam.

Suddenly weapons inspectors appear on the screen and a Viennese waltz wafts from the TV set. The inspectors are standing outside a tall gate. They are being hassled by an Iraqi whose threatening finger is beating time to the music. Bumbling inspectors stumble around. Some are listening; some look down on the ground, others up in the air. The TV viewer cannot hear what is being said, but one thing is for sure: the Iraqi is giving the intruders a dressing down. With their rucksacks and blue berets, they remind one of a school outing where no one knows where they are or what they are supposed to look at. We never see them actually inspecting anything, we only see them being given instructions. The pictures are repeated time and again. Iraqi TV has quite simply constructed a ludicrous music video of and with the weapons inspectors – to waltz time – and they are walking out of step. Only the threatening finger keeps time – quick, quick, slow.

I have read that from time to time Saddam Hussein communicates his private thoughts to the populace. – I never have problems falling asleep. I fall asleep the moment I put my head on the pillow and I never use sleeping pills, he once said in a rare personal TV interview. At other times he relays a few comforting words and tells the viewers not to worry.

– If I am not always smiling, do not worry. The smile is there. It is there because I have chosen the right way. I smile because Americans and Zionists will have to be sacrificed. They should have chosen a small country to fight against, not mighty Iraq.

Now Saddam sits behind a desk. He talks to the camera. Is he giving us some useful sleeping advice?

– Good night. Sleep well. I am watching over you!

In slow motion he rides off the screen on a white horse – into the sunset.

The next day Hans Blix holds a press conference. It will be the last before he sets off for New York with his final report to the UN Security Council. I arrive at Hotel al-Kanal on the outskirts of Baghdad in plenty of time. I am without my minder for the first time; they are denied entry. This is UN territory. I gleefully leave Takhlef by the entrance and trot into the conference hall. Blix and his men arrive one hour late. The good-natured Swede gives a sober account of the latest developments from the weapons inspections, what the Iraqi government has accepted, what the obstacles are. He thinks the Iraqis are yielding, that they might agree to more UN demands. – But we need more time, he says.

When he has finished several hands fly up in the air. Quick-on-the-draw journalists vie with each other to ask questions. They all speak at once. – Mister Blix, Mister Blix! The answers are as noncommittal as the introduction. I wonder what he is really saying. What it implies. Does it mean war, does it mean peace, or does it merely mean a postponement of war?

– Last question, Blix says, surveying the sea of raised hands. – But it has to be in Swedish.

There are no Swedes present. The hall is silent. Surely I am able to affect something in Blix's mother tongue. But I can think of nothing, my head is empty, so empty. – So there are no Swedes around, Blix concludes. Chairs scrape the floor, the party breaks up.

– Honourable Mr Blix, a question from Dagens Nyheter in Stockholm. What did you *really* mean by all that?

That's what I should have asked. At least that's what I wanted an answer to.

– You have so much energy, Takhlef complains. I don't understand why you need to talk to so many people.

Aha, I'm winning, I think. He can't keep up.

We are at Baghdad's Stock Exchange. Takhlef thought a ten-minute interview with the boss would suffice, but I want to talk to the employees. I might have to interview ten brokers before I find one who has anything interesting to say. The ones who are prepared to share their thoughts with me are few and far between. I must go on, go on, until I have assembled a picture.

– But this is so interesting, I exaggerate excitedly. – It is important to report that quotations are hitting the ceiling, while the rest of the world thinks the country is going to the dogs.

– The last three months stocks and shares have risen by nearly fifty percent. Iraqi investors have nothing but contempt for the threat of war, the Stock Exchange chairman says. They are buying factories, banks, hotels.

I assume the appearance of a naïve and friendly journalist, energetic and enthusiastic.

– The majority speak English here, Takhlef volunteers suddenly. You'll manage on your own.

– Yippee, I think, while my minder goes and sits on a chair at the end of the room. He appears to be lost in thought, and is looking up at the boards on the wall.

The Stock Exchange is the size of a gymnasium, divided in two by a solid barrier. On one side, where the boards are, the brokers work; behind the barrier are the buyers and sellers. The closed Iraqi market operates according to its own rules. Only Iraqis can trade and only with Iraqi dinars.

Experts call the country's economy chaotic. The chaos consists of some liberalisation at the micro level and immoveable bureaucracy and planned economy at the macro level. The economy is heavily scarred by sanctions and hyper-inflation. Twenty years ago one dinar was worth three dollars; today two thousand dinars buy only one dollar. There are plenty of loopholes in Saddam's socialism. Smuggling, corruption and money laundering is widespread.

I stop next to a well-dressed man with a moustache. He speaks fluent English.

– Rising, says Telal Brahim contentedly. – Five percent in one week. They didn't get us after all!

Telal hasn't bought into any old company. He has invested in one of Iraq's chemical factories, which recently had the dubious honour of receiving an unannounced UN weapons inspection.

– Provocative, but quite fun really. I own shares in the firm so I should know whether it produces anything illegal or not. We make plastics – boxes, bags and bottles. PVC products – run of the mill plastic. A factory producing chemical weapons wouldn't be quoted on the stock market, Telal fumes, while all the time keeping an eye on the figures on the board. The quotations are altered with a felt pen and a sponge. The brokers run to and fro between the clients and the board. The swiftest is the most successful. Electronics have yet to reach the Baghdad Stock Exchange.

– A bull market. Quite unexpected! Muhammed Ali exclaims. – Most people thought shares would fall as a result of the threat of war, but the opposite is happening.

The Iraqis quite clearly *want* to believe in their economy. Anyone who gambles now might stand to gain many times over later. – Unless the war is long and bloody, Muhammed predicts. He lived in London for fourteen years, where he got a PhD in economics. – London is my second home, he says while all the time boasting about Iraqi stamina. – A quarter of a million soldiers threaten our borders. Instead of fleeing the country, people are investing in the stock market. It's impressive, isn't it? Let the Americans come. They just want our goodies, he says in his polished British accent.

Someone who was led astray by the threat of war stands gloomily in the corner watching the hive of activity. Yasser is a retired policeman who put his savings into a cycle factory. Certain that war would devalue his shares he sold them off some months ago. – When I sold, the shares were worth eleven dinar. Now they are up to eighteen, he says dejectedly. – I come three times a week to check. When they have fallen to fifteen I'll buy them back. Of course I'll end up with fewer than I had. Oh well, we can only hope they'll drop.

Beside him is an elderly lady in a white head-scarf and thick glasses. She owns one million shares in Baghdad Bank and signals continuously to the brokers. While the living standard of the man in the street has been drastically reduced during the last decade, Suham has grown richer. – I have more money now than when sanctions first began. But I don't take it seriously, this is just my hobby, she smiles apologetically. She is a doctor and owner of a clinic specialising in gynaecology.

– Most people are worse off, she admits. – They come to me with the most terrible afflictions; many of them cannot afford the treatment. This country is seeing a lot of horror.

– Goodbye Doktora, one of the brokers calls as the Stock Exchange is about to close.

– See you, says Suham, before disappearing out through the door and back into real life – to patients who cannot pay for her services. She is one of the winners; a dinar millionaire – on the board at least.

The press centre lies on the first floor of the Ministry of Information, an eight-storey monstrosity. Minister Muhammed Said al-Sahhaf sits at the top, the man who later, much later, is nicknamed *Comical Ali*. Now he's just 'the man at the top', 'the minister' and not at all comical. He's someone we never see, but who ultimately decides our destiny – how long we can stay, what we can see, where we can travel. On the ground floor is INA, the Iraqi News Agency. All Saddam's decrees and laws are broadcast from here – via television and the three major newspapers, which are confusingly similar, despite their different names and possibly different archive photos of the president on the front pages. News never originates here. It is written in the Presidential palace and phoned in to INA, where a number of secretaries and so-called journalists take dictation and pass it on to the newspapers.

Every morning a cheek by jowl stream of people rounds the corner and hastens in the door of the Ministry of Information. They are men in suits and women in high heels. Some with flowing locks, others with hair hidden under shawls and bodies under loose folds. Everyone appears to be heading for something important. Like worker ants they carry heavy bags and briefcases into and along the anthill's corridors, offices, nooks and crannies. At lunch time the building teems with people on their way out. They stop and talk by the entrance before ascending once again. In the evening they stream out once more, not quite as determined, but just as fast.

The Ministry of Information is divided into storeys according to a strict hierarchical pattern. The eighth floor commands the seventh, the seventh commands the sixth, and so on, right down to the second floor and the conference rooms where al-Sahhaf and his colleagues conduct their everlasting briefings. Anybody unlucky enough to find himself in the press centre when a conference is announced is squashed into the large hall. Kadim, Mohsen and engineer Walid, whose job it is to oversee our satellite telephones, wield invisible whips and herd us like cattle into the room. If they spot you it is too late to plead other engagements. Worst of all is when the Agricultural Minister, Trade Minister, Health Minister or any one of the others who do not speak English top the bill. They go on in Arabic, for an hour and a half, followed by questions from journalists from Arab-speaking countries. There is no translation. You can bring your interpreter with you, but having done that once you won't do it again.

The Agricultural Minister does not talk about agriculture but the strength of the Iraqi army. The Health Minister never mentions hospitals, but goes on about how wonderful Saddam Hussein is, and the Trade Minister has nothing to say about sanctions and their effect on the economy, but how the Americans will suffer should they attack Iraq. Regardless of content, the speeches all originate from the same floor – the eighth.

The ground floor – the lowest and most pitiful – is ours. Here the gruff Uday al-Taiy rules. Not as awe-inspiring as his namesake, Saddam's son, but scary enough. While the president's monster of a son is corpulent and limps as the result of an assassination attempt seven years ago, our Uday is light of foot, thin and sinewy. His brows are always knit, his shoulders heavy, his nails manicured and his suits immaculate. A cold wind blows in his wake. Even though he never deigns to greet me, I stand to attention and lower my eyes. I am always scared stiff that he will catch me doing something; that I have misbehaved, said something unforgivable.

Uday al-Taiy is one of those cold-blooded and effective pieces that every dictatorship needs. He is in charge of us; he advises the ministers as to who should stay and who must leave. This is what occupies us above all. To be allowed to stay. The rule is ten days. Only a few are smart, cunning, lucky, important or rich enough to stay beyond that period. And most of them are only granted an extra ten days. The visa and how to buy, trick or bribe to get it is the big topic of conversation among journalists. How many days have you got left? Do you think they'll extend it? Who have you paid? Wow, you got the extension! How?

These conversations are intertwined with topic number

two: When do you think the war will start? At the beginning of February, at the end of February, at the beginning of March, the middle of March, after the summer? The visa has to last long enough to enable us to cover the war, and to that end we have to enter the lion's den, Uday al-Taiy's lair.

Anyone wanting to talk to him is obliged to come between 9 and 10 in the evening. Any earlier and he will be with the minister. The result is a queue of journalists all glaring at each other. They want to be alone with the mighty man, to submit their case in secrecy. Just wait your turn to enter and listen to Uday's monologues. It must give him perverse pleasure to hear our applauding and fawning. All because of the bloody visa. We sit on the perch until we fall off while we wait for the moment when we can submit our request.

— We must combat America's imperialism before they subdue the whole world, Uday says and draws heavily on a cigarette, while a Japanese from Asahi, a pale, freckled lady from the *Guardian* and a classy TV star from France 2 nod. The beautiful but slightly moth-eaten Parisienne bobs her sky-high heels up and down. It is her way of saying she isn't getting the attention she deserves. The Japanese looks down, while the lady from London wraps a large necklace around her finger. An American TV producer sits in the corner, without applauding, without contradicting. My face is serious and humble and I wait politely for my allotted time. I am not high enough in the ranks to either applaud or protest. I don't dare nod for fear of nodding at the wrong place. The lady from the *Guardian* interrupts continually with new points. She and Uday seem to agree about most things. The TV star's heels bob ever more angrily; then she too throws in some fierce criticism of the

USA. The time is drawing to a close – the urgent matters must be dealt with. The *Guardian* wants to visit Basra; the Parisienne wants to interview Tariq Aziz. The TV producer needs permission to import one more satellite telephone. The Japanese needs an office in the building. I want to extend my visa.

– You are all flunkies of the USA. None of you report the truth, Uday screams. The air is stiff with smoke. On the wall the omnipresent picture of the president glares down at us. Behind Uday's back are stickers from newspapers and TV stations all over the world. A television in the corner plays the incessant music videos.

To repay the attention shown, Uday allows the French and the English lady to talk. The Japanese is too polite, the American too haughty. My mouth is dry from all the smoke and I sink deeper into the low sofa. I am terrified of saying something and upsetting him. Stories abound of journalists who were exposed to Uday's wrath and put on the first plane to Amman.

Suddenly the monologue is at an end and he gets up, says goodnight and strides out. I feel the eyes under the furrowed brow boring in to me, or through me. Hell, now I'll have to come back tomorrow.

I'm on my way back to Gertrude Bell's exercise in patience. Out in the parking lot Josh grabs me.

– Dinner?

Josh is an engineer with Sky News. He is responsible for the satellite system which enables the channel to report at any time from anywhere. He has the most contagious laugh and the broadest Scottish accent. Half of what he says goes over my head, but the other half usually makes me laugh. We have been bumping in to each other over the last years, at a refugee camp in Macedonia, during demonstrations in Belgrade, on a mountain top in the Hindu Kush, in the desert near Kandahar, and now in Baghdad.

Josh has been to Iraq before. During the last Gulf War he saw active service with the British Army. He was a soldier for eleven years, before being hired by Sky News.

Many TV companies recruit from the forces when they need technicians or cameramen. The one-time soldiers have stamina and war experience and bring a certain assurance to the team. They have learnt battle psychology and first aid. They know the difference between incoming and outgoing fire, and are the last to complain. Some of the correspondents also have army careers behind them.

We tumble through the door to the al-Finjan restaurant. The whole of Sky News – reporters, producers, photographers, technicians and editors, in addition to many other colleagues – are shown to a trestle table.

The British contingent are regular customers and the staff cannot be helpful enough. Rather, they know exactly what we want, and serve us beer. In cups so as not to antagonise the guests at the table nearby. Prohibition was part of the Islamisation campaign during the 1990s. Goodbye whisky, hello prayers and shawls. The former godless Saddam was suddenly being photographed in mosques, praying.

Al-Finjan is run by Alaw, a Christian Armenian who has tricked his way past the restrictions. That means contacts and patrons in high places.

We talk about the approaching war, wars we have experienced, where other wars might break out and which hotels will be safest once the bombs start falling. Al-Rashid lies right in the ministry jungle, al-Mansour between the Ministry of Information and one of the main bridges,

Hotel Palestine opposite the Presidential palace. My tiny al-Fanar, close to the Palestine, makes them all smirk. – That dilapidated building will collapse at the smallest explosion.

One dish follows another, the cups are refilled. I try to imagine the opposite situation. Great Britain is expecting a major attack from Iraq. It is feared that bombs will rain down over London. Rumours abound that Iraqis are planning wholesale takeover of many of England's larger industrial plants, oil companies and shipping. Should Iraq win the war, it is expected that its leaders will maintain power for a considerable period, until a friendly regime is in place, a regime which serves Arab interests. Right in the middle of this rumour-flood Iraqi journalists flock to London. They check in at the best hotels, rent extra rooms to house their equipment, splash money about, demand to follow their own customs and drinking habits. They have brought with them gasmasks and bulletproof vests, and buy up bottled water and tinned food which those who live there cannot afford. In the evening, they gather round the restaurant tables and await one thing: that their president will give the go-ahead for the destruction of London.

How would they have been received by the inhabitants of London? By restaurant staff? By the British Ministry of Information?

Back in 707 Said has come up with another decoration idea. A small red, yellow and black patterned rug adorns the narrow strip of floor at the bottom of the bed. How would I furnish the room of someone who had come to report on the destruction of my country?

The days pass interviewing people who won't talk, translated by interpreters who won't cooperate, in a country where eyes and ears are everywhere. Never in my life have I worked under such difficult conditions. Not because there is no water in the tap, or a threat of guerrilla warfare. Nor the difficulty in sending articles home. The problem is that there is nothing to send. The list I gave to Mohsen has come to nothing.

– Not possible.

– OK.

– Impossible.

– Of course.

– Not allowed.

– That's fine.

– No permit.

– I see.

– Out of the question.

– But . . .

– Maybe

– Oh.

– Be patient.

– Mm.

Instead I traipse around with Takhlef.

– Would you like to see the result of the sanctions in the hospitals? he asks. – Hundreds of thousands of children are dying because we are forbidden to import essential medicines.

– I have read about them everywhere.

– But you haven't seen them yourself.

– We can't all write about the same sick children, I answer stubbornly.

Takhlef gives me an astonished look. This is the first time I've grumbled. We visit a food distribution point instead. Most Iraqis are dependent on rations distributed by the government. Rice, flour, beans, lentils. In the expectation of a long war the population are being given several months' worth of rations.

For the first time I notice the sandbags, the only visible sign of Iraqi war preparations. On street corners brown sacks are stacked into little towers. The tiny forts are more comical than frightening, as if they belong to a different time.

We stop by a small shop. Every neighbourhood has an outlet which deals with rations. Huge sacks and boxes are placed on the floor next to some scales. The owner is weighing out foodstuffs when we enter.

Almost imperceptibly people freeze, turn away. Takhlef seems to take no notice. The female owner fetches large iron weights to measure everyone's portion, her gaze averted. My minder grabs a woman whose eyes are watching the gauge carefully.

Takhlef translates ponderously. About food, family, fear of war. Having watched her receive rice and flour into her bags, Takhlef asks whether I am satisfied with the answers and whether I will allow her to leave.

– She must leave when she wants! I interrupt.

Takhlef tells me that she had asked many times if she could be spared from answering the questions. – But I said no. After all, we have to finish the interview.

The woman's husband is ill and she wants to hurry home to nurse him. She fidgeted with impatience during the long interview, while I, not understanding, dutifully noted down the answers, or rather Takhlef's detailed translation.

– Then let her go, I cry indignantly.

People never say no to an interview. They always stop, nobody ever says they don't have time. Now I understand why: they are obliged to answer Takhlef's questions, as if he were a policeman. In most countries people hurry away if they are asked for interviews on the street. That is impossible in Iraq.

I feel an acute need to get rid of Takhlef. But interpreters are not exchangeable. We are. 'Hundreds of journalists are sitting in Amman, waiting for an entry permit', is the refrain if we ever complain.

— You must leave! Uday thunders.

It is the end of January and the last chance to ask for an extension. One more day and I'm illegal.

— Please, give me ten more days, I beg.

— No!

— Please!

— No!

I can't go now. I have hardly seen anything, even less understood anything.

— *S'il vous plaît, Monsieur Uday.*

Uday has a weakness: anything French. He studied at the Sorbonne and has many friends in France after years at the Iraqi embassy in Paris. Those who know him also know his passion: French cheese. Consequently he is often supplied with Camembert and Brie in exchange for a visa and a bit of goodwill. There is neither Chèvre nor Roquefort in my suitcase, but I gamble on a bit of charm à la Française.

— *D'accord, je vous donne cinq jours.*

— Only five days. That's any moment now, I protest.

— *Oh la la! Quelle Femme! Dix jours! Ca vous va?*

I scurry out of the office. Ten new days! I go to Nabil's to celebrate the extension.

Nabil's walls are pink, the sofas are soft and there is everything from Middle Eastern specialities to shrimp cocktail in Thousand Island dressing on the menu. In addition they have Lebanese, Italian and French wines, served with a carefully folded napkin round the bottle. As soon as the glasses have been filled the bottle is put under the table and removed when it is empty.

Like Alaw, the owner of al-Finjan, Nabil belongs to the Christian minority in Iraq. This evening he is scared. The weapons inspections are not going well; the American rhetoric is increasingly aggressive. Nabil is newly married, has newborn twins and says they will leave if the war starts. Maybe to London, he speculates. Close the restaurant and return when it is all over.

– Do you think there will be war?

– It will be difficult to avoid.

– When will it happen?

– Impossible to tell, but leave in time.

In the meantime Nabil does all he can to forget the clouds of war. He extends the menu and learns how to make pizza Margherita from a friend who lived in Italy.

– Come on Valentine's Day, says Nabil. We'll have a party!

Every day Takhlef propels me through the Baath Party mill, having been mashed through it many times himself. I feign compliance. However, our cooperation is starting to unravel.

One morning I make myself sound sick; I tell him I am at my hotel, in an attempt to sneak off. I am actually going out with two Norwegian child psychologists, Magne Raundalen and Atle Dyregrov. Unlike me, they have a super interpreter, a woman who takes people seriously. She is of course also hired by the regime, but she lets people speak and does not scare them off.

– We'll choose a street at random, Atle explains. – We'll knock on the first door and ask if they have any children.

— But you have to apply first, I tell them. The Iraqi bureaucracy has become part of my daily life. Obviously there are other rules for child psychologists.

We drive north and the car really does stop in a randomly chosen street. Atle takes the houses to the left, Magne and I the houses to the right. We ring the bell outside the first house. A man appears. The interpreter explains our business and the family lets us in. I am in an Iraqi home for the first time.

The family of Abu Khan — Grandfather Khan — are gathered together for holy day. Everyone assembles around him in the front room, eight children and about thirty grandchildren. They were preparing dinner when we rang the bell.

Magne's project is to establish the psychological problems or traumas present in children who live on the edge of a war. Having explained his objective to Abu Khan he asks if he may start. He is a determined guest; he asks the parents to stay in the background and say nothing and gathers the children around. — Usually I ask the parents to leave, but that is not possible here. After all, we have arrived in the middle of a family party.

— Are you frightened of anything?

— My brother is frightened of dogs.

— And you?

— I'm not afraid of anything.

Hamza looks Magne Raundalen in the eyes while fumbling with a button on his overalls. The child psychologist asks again.

— Aren't you frightened of anything?

Hamza stares defiantly at the questioning man. No one says anything. Then Hamza decides that it is permitted to be frightened when one is seven.

— I am frightened that my mummy and daddy will die, he says,

looking down. I'm frightened of being alone, that many in my family will be killed. I'm frightened that they'll shoot us. Or that they'll use weapons that will make us sick. There are some weapons like that and you don't notice at once that you get sick. Then you get very sick and it hurts terribly and then you die.

— Who has got these weapons?

— Bush and Sharon.

— Why?

— I don't know. We mustn't talk about that.

Everyone listens while Hamza speaks. Only a little girl walks around, gurgling, wide-eyed, surprised at the sudden silence. The four cousins Shahad, Hind, Sahar and Reem huddle together in an armchair. It is their turn now.

— Sometimes I can't sleep at night, I think about the bombs, eleven-year-old Shahad says. — I dream that the whole family is at home, that we can't escape. Just when the bomb falls on us and explodes I wake up. Mummy told us about all the people who were bombed and burnt alive. They were buried under lots of earth and crushed.

— We will withstand the enemy. We are strong and we will fight, says fifteen-year-old Reem. — Just like the Palestinians, we are struggling against Zionism and America. We are shut in, just like they are. We must get foreigners out of our country.

— What Reem said is typical, Magne explains. — Teenagers have been taught what to say. They use Saddam Hussein's words. But the younger children muddle everything up — fear, fantasy and snatches of conversations they have picked up.

— But I don't think they'll kill lots of children, Shahad interrupts. — No one would agree to that. I think people will show sympathy. We are peaceful and won't attack anyone.

The others don't agree. — Oh yes, they'll bomb us, I'm quite sure, says Reem. — But when Bush sees all the dead Iraqi children on TV he'll regret it.

Magne notes it all down and then asks if they can draw their insides: How much is fear, how much is unhappiness, and how much is anger. They draw circles and divide them up. Fear is the largest sector in Shahad's circle; in Reem's it is anger.

— The media is the father of fear. The children rarely discuss with their parents what has been said on telly, they just store it up and then it emerges at night or when they are alone. What they fear most is being alone, or being left alone after the war, Magne says.

As if the media has not sown enough fear already, Grandfather Khan fuels the fire.

— I was a soldier when the British attacked us in 1941. That was awful. But the Gulf War and the American bombs were even worse. This war will be devilish. And do you know why? The weapons are larger and stronger and it will be impossible to defend ourselves. The new bombs will kill us all.

He gets up from the chair and shakes his fist. — But we will fight.

The psychologist takes his leave. The grown-ups return to their cooking. The children go out to play. The Security Council meets to discuss the situation in Iraq. Bush is impatient.

Several days go by and I do not see Takhlef. I tell him I am at the hotel writing, reading or resting. In reality I sneak out at daybreak to work with the child psychologists.

One evening when my minder phones I realise I can avoid him no longer and agree to meet him next morning at nine. At the crack of dawn I leave to meet Shaima, a six-year-old who regales me with how the Americans will bury her house in sand, how all the sand will cover her, how she will rub and rub her eyes but the sand will not go away and in the end everyone will be smothered by it.

I am caught offguard by her stories and forget the rendezvous. When I appear one and a half hours late Takhlef is livid.

— What are you up to? he cries. — You sneak out without me. They'll throw you out!

My minder has done his job and has asked for me at the hotel. Abdullah told him I had left at six. Takhlef quivers with fury, but is scared at the same time. If I do anything illegal he will get the blame. I resort to a lie.

— My editor asked me to interview two Norwegian child psychologists, and they were off this morning so I had to catch them at their hotel at first light. You can check it out at al-Rashid.

— It's OK, Takhlef mutters. — But you can't continue like this — you'll be straight out. I've lost a lot of money the days you didn't turn up.

Takhlef is in control. One word from him and it will be over. But I hold the trump card; the wherewithal.

— I apologise for making you wait, and I'll pay double for the days I've been away.

The next day I slip him hundreds of dollars in a white envelope. He then tells me that the German TV channel ZDF has offered him a job.

That suits me perfectly and I throw him willingly to the Germans.

— Television! I exclaim. — What a chance! And d'you know what? I lower my voice. When the Germans say nine they mean nine. Not half past ten!

Having said goodbye to Takhlef I feel free as a bird. But the happiness is short-lived. How can I work without a minder and interpreter?

Frustrated I sit down by my laptop, which I have placed

on the corner of a dirty plastic table outside the Ministry of Information, behind the fence by the pavement. Those of us who cannot afford office space inside are left to this dusty strip between the house and the road. Fortunately it rains little in Baghdad but it can get cold. In the desert the temperature sinks drastically when the sun sets.

I shiver in my winter coat. The satellite telephone is rigged up by the road, the aerial facing southeast to catch the best signal. I send a few emails home and sit around moping about the working conditions. No interpreter, no visa, nothing to write about.

Beside me stands a buxom young lady reading a newspaper. She looks like one of the employees, with down-at-heel shoes, fuzzy woollen skirt and a huge sweater. I try English.

– What do the papers say?

– The same as usual, she answers and laughs. – Do you want me to translate?

She reads, shortens, simplifies and explains. Compared to Takhlef, who stumbled through complicated Arabic news-speak word by word, it is a pleasure listening to her. The woman is called Aliya and she is employed by INA. It is her job to translate Saddam's decrees and INA's press releases into English.

By the next day I have employed Aliya. She inquired about the possibility of working with foreigners and our bosses agreed. As more and more journalists stream into Iraq the need for minders and interpreters increases and Aliya is accepted as being safe enough.

– Everyone who sees me thinks they know me. And do you know why? Because I look like everyone else, was one of the first things Aliya said to me when we met.

She's right. She looks like the woman next door, a typical

Middle Eastern woman. Big, curly hair, rounded hips, broad lips. Beautiful brown eyes, framed by thick, long eyelashes.

Aliya confides in me that her goal in life is to travel. She would like to go to Dubai; get a job as a translator in a foreign firm and earn pots of money. Her travel fantasies are never accompanied by critical remarks about life in Iraq. She is a child of Saddam. She has been brought up with him.

It is not much easier to work with Aliya than it was with Takhlef. Like him she stalls. One of my editors wants a piece about the Baath Party. Simple, I think. The Baath Party owns Iraq, it is omnipresent. But I never manage to get a Baath Party member to talk. One has no time, the other no inclination, the third is away, the fourth does not answer. Aliya herself is not a member, a rarity in the Ministry of Information.

— That's not necessary. All Iraqis are collective members, she says roguishly, without a touch of irony. It is difficult to understand what Aliya really means. Even if she is a lot nicer than Takhlef, and adopts me as her sister from the first day, I am careful with what I say. It is her job to report, on where we have been, with whom we have spoken and what we have spoken about. We never discuss politics. But unlike Takhlef, Aliya treats people naturally and not as if in a police interrogation.

Aliya and I eat chicken kebab in a Baghdad café. I speculate on what to write. It is already three and the deadline is only a few hours away.

This same day Blix's inspection report has been submitted to the UN in New York. Maybe I could ask people what they think of it. Exciting. Really exciting, especially in a dictatorship. Saddam Hussein will take the right decision anyway. That's what he has done in the past, that's what he does now and it's what he will do in the future.

Some teenage girls are sitting at the table next door. A well-dressed crowd who would not look out of place in any Western café. I ask Aliya if we can talk to them.

– Of course. Now, at once?

I jump out of my chair. This would have been impossible with Takhlef. The young, cool bunch in the corner invite us to join them. It turns out that the group of friends are holding a farewell lunch. Noor is leaving next morning. Her parents fear the war will break out any moment.

– We're going to Jordan. We'll just close the house and leave, Noor says. Her family are among those who, now at the end of January, have decided to leave the country. That option is open to few. Not many countries welcome Iraqis. But Noor has relatives in Jordan.

– Maybe we'll meet in paradise, Noor sighs.

– Don't talk like that, says Hadil. – I'll start crying.

Hadil cannot leave. – My father is an Army major. He must defend our country if we're attacked. If he doesn't, who will? So if we die, we'll all die together.

– Nobody wants this war, says Noor. – Only the Americans. They want our oil. Everyone is terrified. How strange that the Americans don't understand that; they should know what fear is after September 11th.

The five friends round the table are all second-year medical students in Baghdad. None of them wears a headscarf and they obviously belong to Iraq's upper middle class. They are the ones with more opportunity to leave because they often have relatives abroad, money and connections. Noor's brother lives in London. – That's where I bought these clothes, she says, showing off her cord trouser suit.

– At H&M, she smiles proudly, before being reminded of the day's leave-taking.

– They've started digging wells at the University; I saw it this morning, Isra recounts. – We've dug one in the garden at home, her friend Mina continues. The girls think that the water supply and electricity will be the first casualties. Anyone unable to dig their own well is collecting water in tanks and cans. In addition people are buying gas stoves, lamps, torches and batteries.

While many in Baghdad show apathy and resignation when questioned about their fear of war, the young girls are more indignant.

– I know that most of Europe's inhabitants are against the war. Even almost all the British. I have watched them on telly demonstrating in the streets of London. Doesn't it help? Can't they do something to influence Blair? Hadil asks. She has both knelt in a mosque and lit a candle in a church. To pray to God in both His ears.

– I wonder if I'll ever see my house again, Noor says gloomily. – I'm taking my jewellery, photographs, schoolbooks and diaries. I can't leave my diaries, they are my life.

Before the girls leave I ask for their phone numbers, so I can contact them later.

A boy sits alone at the end of the table. He belongs to the girls' circle of friends, and stays behind when they leave. While Aliya is away for a moment, he murmurs – They don't say what they really mean. No one can say what they really think.

Then he leaves.

Shortly afterwards Hadil returns accompanied by a furious man. He is incandescent with rage.

– You must never contact us, he hisses.

It is Hadil's father. The Army major whose task it is to

defend Iraq from bombs. Iraqi military personnel receive strict instructions not to have any contact with foreigners.

– Where did you write down the number? Where? Give it to me, he says, and tears the page from the notebook where Hadil has scribbled her number. The father crumples up the paper, thrusts it into his pocket and turns on his heel. He marches out of the café, followed by a trembling Hadil.

We sit down again. Aliya is upset and frightened. Absurd. Hadil's father fears Aliya and Aliya fears Hadil's father.

When I write my small piece about the farewell lunch I wonder whether or not to include the boy's comments. I add them, then cross them out. Someone might find him. Someone might have seen him. But I store the two sentences in my head; the first critical utterances in Baghdad.

I have long been pestering Aliya about visiting a newspaper or a TV station.

– Of course, Aliya says, and nothing happens.

I insist. Nothing happens. More insisting. Nothing happens. Yelling and insisting. Nothing, apart from Aliya sulking. No one has answered her request, she says breezily. I try another brazen tack.

– If we don't visit a TV station, a newspaper or a radio station today, I have nothing to write about. Consequently you have nothing to translate and therefore I won't pay you. Regardless of how many hours we spend waiting at the Ministry, there'll be no salary.

Aliya glares at me. She purses her lips; the corners of her mouth tighten and her eyes narrow. Finally she gets up from the chair and walks towards the press centre. In a little while she comes back. Point blank refusal, no Iraqi TV visit.

– Strictly prohibited; broadcasting is a strategic and sensitive target, Aliya says.

I perch on the plastic table outside the press centre, legs dangling, and look defiantly at Aliya. – Don't give up at the first hurdle.

Aliya slinks back to Mohsen. She returns after a while and says he will let us know in one hour.

– Shall I translate the newspaper in the meantime? she offers. The only thing she really enjoys is translating, preferably from newspapers and preferably from Saddam Hussein, which is really one and the same thing.

– Please do.

– War preparations must be stepped up, Aliya reads.

That is the headline in *al-Qadissiya*, the Iraqi army's mouthpiece. 'War preparations must be stepped up', is also the headline in *al-Thawra*, and in the Government-run newspaper editorial. Uday Hussein's newspaper *Babel* has the same headline. The man who has been talking about war preparations is Saddam Hussein.

When Aliya is halfway through the speech about the approaching war, I stop her. I have heard it all before.

– Maybe we should check the newspaper permission, I say and look meaningfully at the clock which is moving towards afternoon.

Aliya protests that she has not yet finished.

– We can do that in the car, en route, can't we? I smile.

Aliya saunters slightly faster than normal when she returns. Instead of her normal downcast expression, she looks me straight in the eye. The permission is in her hand.

In the *al-Iraq* reception area hang no fewer than thirteen portraits of Saddam Hussein. I feel like commenting on the pictures, but hold my tongue – as usual. Aliya and I do not share a sense of humour. A man arrives to show us around. He asks what we want to see. – Everything, I say. – And I would like to interview the editor.

In the first room two men sit staring into the air. They are proofreaders and wait for the day's text. Above them hangs a fourteenth portrait.

Mohan al-Daher receives us in his office where the fifteenth, sixteenth, seventeenth and eighteenth portraits hang. In one long yawn he enlightens us about Iraqi strength, American cowardice and the enemy which is about to be crushed. When the yawn is drawing to a close I slip in a question.

– Bush gave Congress a strident speech yesterday. What will be *al-Iraq*'s reaction?

– I am waiting for the text, says the editor.

– The text?

– Yes, the text from INA.

– So the news agency writes the paper, I say; I should of course have realised that.

– Yes, says the editor, as though it were the most obvious thing in the world.

– But what do you think the newspaper will contain today?

– I have no opinion about that. The decision will be taken by those most fitted to take it.

Regardless of the text *al-Iraq* can safely begin choosing the front page picture. The motive never changes.

– Only the president is worthy of front-page exposure, the editor explains.

Nineteen, twenty, twenty-one, twenty-two. I count down the wall. Twenty-three. In the basement the text ticks in on a large reel. The letters are imprinted in red ink. The sound of the keys is like that of an old-fashioned typewriter. When the text is transmitted a scribe tears the paper off the reel, hangs it up in front of his computer and imports it into the paper's processing system. Ten men or so sit behind computers and copy in various parts from the reel.

One of the men shows me the paper's picture archive – an ordinary Word programme. The man in charge of photos clicks and opens, enlarges and reduces. Twenty-four, twenty-five, twenty-six, twenty-seven. Forty-four. My head is reeling. Sixty-two. I am guessing. One hundred and eighteen. Roughly speaking, seven hundred and ninety-four. The portraits chase each other across the screen. I forget to ask whether they can choose themselves.

A broad-shouldered man enters carrying some hand-written sheets of paper and tosses them to one of the scribes. Wow, I think. A real journalist. I walk over and ask if he has written those crumpled pieces of paper himself. He confirms that he has.

– What have you written?
– Page eleven.
– Page eleven?
– The sports pages, the broad shouldered one explains before disappearing back up the stairs. The only pages the paper entrusts to its own people.

As I am about to leave I notice him. One of the scribes behind the computers is staring intently at me. His dark eyes follow my movements. The man is skinny and his cheeks hollow. He has lost most of his hair but he is not old. When I walk past he stubs his cigarette out in a dirty ashtray.

I can barely hear his voice.
– But you cannot read my thoughts.

I stop and pretend I'm searching for something in my bag. My back is turned half towards him as a signal that I want to hear more, without looking at him.

– We want freedom, he whispers. The picture on the wall looks down at him. Almighty.

My editor wants a longer article for the weekend. They are keeping a whole page for me. Doubting that I know enough, am not able, have not met enough people, makes me decline. – I've got nothing to write about, I say. But to no avail.

– We've already set aside a page.

On the page they want something from Iraq. 'Something from Iraq'?

I have only disparate pieces and try to string them together. I turn them over in my mind, playing the voices over again.

'Once upon a time', Iraqis relate nostalgically, 'when we were the first civilisation in history, the Assyrians, the Sumerians, Babylon . . .' 'Once upon a time . . .' they go on, 'when we could feed the whole Middle East, and the schools were not lit by candlelight.' Before the war against Iran, before Kuwait, before the bombs. But the memories of a golden past do not light up the dismal reality. A reality where hangers-on and petty black-market kings grow increasingly fat while the remaining inhabitants are kept in fear and poverty.

Seven fat fish from the Tigris swim leisurely around the brick-built swimming pool. Their tales swish quietly. Now and again one or other bobs to the surface and the reddish skin flickers in the sunlight. Small palms wave in the wind over the pool and the manicured lawn. Ali stands by the barbecue waiting for someone to order grilled fish.

The restaurant is starting to fill up. Winter is still in the air. The real heat usually arrives in March. But the restaurant has open fireplaces. Braziers are placed underneath the tables; no one is cold who has warm feet. Two dozen waiters or so in freshly laundered suits react to the smallest signal.

— Before it was always packed here, with ordinary people, Ali says while dousing the flames with some water. There is not much money around now. People eat at home.

Ali makes about £50 a month. That's enough for him and his family and is a reasonable salary by Iraqi standards. The waiters make around £20. — Not enough, not enough, one of them whispers hastily while laying the table. It is safest not to talk to foreigners. The restaurant walls have ears. They who complain are not patriotic.

Mahmoud is one who can afford to eat grilled fish. A one-time owner of a furniture factory, he had to sell owing to sanctions. Now the middle-aged businessman fixes things for other people, he says, without elaborating further.

— The system, he whispers. — The system. Many are poorer, only a few have grown richer. They are here now, he says, and nods almost imperceptibly towards the other guests: four men at a nearby table, gold chains, black bags and walkie-talkies, a benefit strictly controlled by the authorities and a luxury awarded very few.

Suddenly all the tables fill up. Approximately fifty men in suits arrive and as a matter of course take over half the restaurant.

— Ministry of Trade, Mahmoud whispers. — They are important, they have money. Those who hitch on get rich.

He is alluding to those who support Saddam Hussein. — Businessmen, heads of ministries. But the sword is ever-present. Anyone who murmurs or tries to jump ship risks being murdered. I'm part of it myself, he continues. — I have eleven children. The eldest are at university. I have no choice. But I live in fear of the sword.

Mahmoud is not voicing platitudes. The regime of Saddam Hussein has clung to power with the aid of a complex system of informers, violence and brutality in order to crush every attempt at divergence or disagreement. The system is based on a combination of fear and a sophisticated network of informing, and also on the ability to manoeuvre economically through the closed Iraqi market.

Although sanctions have weakened most Iraqis' purchasing power, an increased traffic in contraband has enriched a few. Sanctions were aimed at enfeebling the regime but have actually made people more dependent on it. Sanctions have isolated the country from the outside world and have made it easier to reward loyalty and punish deviation. It is virtually impossible to operate on any large scale without the regime keeping track.

Saddam Hussein makes sure that people are moderately well fed by rationing staple foodstuffs. At the same time, the monopolies caused by the sanctions render it easy for him to favour hangers-on. But woe betide them if they become too mighty or too independent. The regime constantly sends people to their death for corruption or economic activity.

Al-Arasat is Baghdad's Champs Elysées. Here exclusive Armani suits are for sale, soft velvet sofas, all brands of cigars, perfume and luxury articles. Here are up-to-date computers, shops full of exclusive TVs, stereos, videos and other electronic hardware. In spite of the sanctions, in spite of import embargos.

But Al-Arasat too suffers from any comparison to former days. In several places the pavements have been replaced by gravel walks and rubbish is everywhere; but the neon lights keep on shining. Here is the nightclub and restaurant 'Black and White' with a large swimming pool in the garden. Here the well-to-do celebrate weddings and birthdays. Here can be seen videos never shown on state-owned TV channels, and here alcohol is served, if the liquid is discreetly poured into the glass and the bottle hidden under the table. Once upon a time Iraq was one of the most liberal countries in the Arab world, but a few years ago Saddam realised that Islam could help him. Alcohol disappeared from the restaurants and an increasing number of women took to wearing the headscarf. Even Saddam himself, before usually portrayed holding a gun, is now shown at prayer.

The country's social hierarchy has been fundamentally changed by the hyper inflation of the 1990s. Iraq's middle classes were once highly educated and well to do and the country's literacy and writing proficiency among the highest in the Arab world. The salaried classes are the losers. Many have sunk into poverty.

A quarter of an hour's drive away, in a poor part of Baghdad, Wahida and her sons await the month's rations. Here the roads have not been paved for many years, there are potholes everywhere, and the doors to the shops and homes hang crookedly. As no one knows what conditions will be like next month, the UN, for the first time, are handing out two months' rations in one go. During the last seven years Wahida's staple food requirements have been provided for by the Oil for Food programme. The programme means that Iraq can export oil as long as the income is earmarked for 'humanitarian aid'. To this end approximately two million barrels are exported every day.

The agent, as she is called, measures up on scales with large iron weights. Every Iraqi gets 9 kilos of wheat, 3 kilos of rice, 2 kilos of sugar, 200 grams of tea, half a kilo of washing powder, and a quarter kilo of soap. In addition they receive a small portion of beans, peas, food oil, salt and powdered milk.

Since the Oil for Food programme started, the number of under-nourished and malnourished people has decreased. Sanctions had then been in place since 1991, originally introduced to force Saddam Hussein out of Kuwait. But in spite of Oil for Food alleviating the situation somewhat, a quarter of Iraqi children suffer from chronic malnutrition. That and diarrhoea are the most common causes of death amongst the youngest children.

The agent in this part of town is called Karima. She runs a little general store which she took over when her husband died. — Once upon a time we had ten brands of tea, all sorts of cakes, soap in all colours and smells. Today I have one type of tea, one of soap, no cakes. When people get tea through the rations they don't buy any other brand except for a very special occasion. The tea they get in the rations is a mediocre tea, like everything else we get, not bad, not good. Just like the flour, not the best, not the coarsest. Everything is in the middle, mediocre.

Wahida nods while her sons carry out large sacks, the rations for the whole family. The food is heavily subsidised by the regime. Everyone pays 250 dinar, around 10 pence. But when the average monthly wage is £4, the remainder disappears fast. All extras are expensive and the majority have had to cut down on everything: food, clothes, house.

— Life is harder, Wahida admits. — Before I was just an ordinary housewife, looking after my family. Now I get up every morning at five, make cheese and yoghurt, which I sell on the street, from a table by our house. I only return home in the afternoon to attend to my own family, she sighs. Like most Iraqis her husband has to hold down two jobs.

The little woman dressed in black slips out of the door. Turkish delight, sunflower seeds and the mixture of nuts lie untouched. So does Karima's small assortment of shampoo and toothpaste. People are using increasingly less. The quarter kilo of rationed soap is used for most things — face, hair and hands. If one can afford to keep the entire ration, that is. Some are reduced to selling part of it at the market.

Wahida and her sons load the goods onto a rusty car someone has lent them. One can sense the nostalgia in her face when the older woman remembers the times when Iraqis could enjoy the riches the oil brought.

'Once upon a time' children were given books at school, four

million people had not yet fled the country and no one had to sell
their jewels for a piece of meat or some antibiotics.

She waves wearily from the car as they bump off. 'Once upon a
time', when there was life . . .

One day a notice is pinned up on the board outside Uday's
office. Military parade in Mosul. At last we are permitted
to leave Baghdad, with our guides of course, and in a
group, and only as far as Mosul. The town lies in the north
of the country, on the border of the autonomous Kurdish
region. It is one of Iraq's most important and oldest towns
and is where muslin comes from I seem to remember
having read somewhere. We skip about the Ministry of
Information like little children, happy to be allowed out, to
breathe some fresh air, see the country. I proudly tell
Abdullah on reception that I won't be back that night, I'm
off to Mosul.

We dash up the motorway at 120km an hour, the radio
on full blast, Aliya and the driver in the front, Janine and I
in the back.

Janine is the prima donna of the Press Centre. She holds
court in her tiny office, in Prada shoes and Ralph Lauren
shirts. She is the most up to date concerning rumours and
latest news. Something is always going on around her; she is
quick-witted and generous with her ideas. She has covered
conflicts and wars for fifteen years and won several awards
in Great Britain for her reporting from the Middle East,
Chechnya, Bosnia and Afghanistan. She is one of the funniest of our lot and writes for *The Times*, *Vanity Fair* and
National Geographic. When she's not covering wars or writing books she moves in the elite circles of London and Paris.

Suddenly we spot a sign indicating that the road to Tikrit
bears left ahead.

– Can't we drop in and have a cup of tea. We need a break, we ask.

– Are you mad! Aliya shouts. – Our permission is for Mosul!

She frantically waves the stamped permission under our noses. She looks almost desperate, as though we might mutiny, take over and drive into Tikrit with her as hostage. But she need not fear; Heyad puts his foot down and whizzes past the exit. We in the back seat know who is in charge. Saddam can keep his hometown to himself.

The greater part of the road between Baghdad and Mosul passes through desert. Where are the fertile plains I had been reading about? The lush fields, watered by the Euphrates and the Tigris, have throughout the centuries been celebrated for their succulent fruit – apples, pears, grapes and pomegranates. Now all that remains is barren sand.

But the desert also yields a different kind of harvest. From this area originates the very first descriptions of what was later to become both Iraq's wealth and its curse: oil. People believed the brown liquid could heal and bathed in it when they were sick. The traveller Ibn Jubair wrote about the black gold in the 1100s:

To the right of the road to Mosul there is a depression in the ground. It is black, as though it lies under a cloud. From there God lets issue forth wells, both big and small, that throw up tar. From time to time one of them will throw out a large piece, as though it were boiling. Basins have been constructed to gather the pieces. Round about these wells is a black pool. The surface is covered by a thin layer of black foam, which floats to the edge and coagulates. It might be mistaken for mud; it is very sticky, smooth, shiny and has a strong smell. Thus we have, with our own eyes, witnessed a miracle. They tell us that they set light to the mud to extract tar.

The flames devour the liquid and thereafter the tar is cut into suitable pieces and transported away. Allah creates what He wants. Praise be His name.

Scattered lights from Mosul twinkle at us. We are ravenous. But what we would really like is to have a beer, and are about to go looking for one. Heyad asks us not to, it is futile he says. And you girls on your own, it's not safe. He refuses to leave his car, a dark green Chevrolet Caprice, with soft, beige interior. He wants to buy a new car, but we ask him to wait until after the war. He nods. That makes sense. – I might need my money for more useful things then, he says.

We wander from restaurant to restaurant and end up somewhere with blue fluorescent lighting and Formica tables.

The world's press has made its way to the muslin town this evening, for the sole reason that we were given permission to come. Now we are gathered in the restaurants along Mosul's night strip; our ladies' team in one corner, a gentlemen's team from *Le Figaro* and *Liberation* in the other. The neighbouring tables are all occupied by men. As in most Arab countries women are rarely seen out at night, unless there is an important occasion such as a wedding or a birthday. We are given a plastic saucer with chopped onion, another with tomato and parsley. Then we get a chicken each. The rumour about beer was exaggerated. Beverages are tea, lemonade and Pepsi.

Stuffed and dead tired we arrive at the hotel by midnight. The check-in procedure almost exceeds what the Ministry of Information could come up with. Endless questionnaires must be completed and an infinite number of enquiries answered before we can ascend the massive concrete steps to our rooms.

Only next morning do I look out of the window. The Tigris has followed me all the way from Baghdad. The view is like from al-Fanar, only here the river is wider and the landscape seems even flatter. The morning haze lies heavily over the river, thinning as it rises. The air is cooler than I have become used to. I shiver as I stand and hear the march participants streaming towards the main street. This parade has been arranged for volunteers to show that every single Iraqi will fight for Saddam Hussein. What more fitting a town than Mosul, a one-time remote outpost of the Assyrian empire, an 8,000-year-old urban community? The town is also the most ethnically mixed in Iraq; here Arabs, Armenians, Kurds, Syrians, Turcoman, Assyrians, Jews, Muslims and Christians live cheek by jowl. Mosques and churches rub shoulders.

It is the reserve forces who are flexing their muscles – the day before Colin Powell submits his 'conclusive proof' against Iraq. The reserve forces go under the name al-Quds – Arabic for 'Jerusalem' – and were formed by Saddam Hussein during the spring of 2001 to 'recapture and liberate Jerusalem from the Israelis'. Around one third of all Iraqis belong to al-Quds, through their work or local districts, but primarily through the Baath Party. A well-trained paramilitary unit can also be found within al-Quds. Saddam's real army is not present however – it has been called up long ago, supposedly to the borders in the north and south, into the desert and to various lines of defence around Baghdad.

A group of black-clad women have taken up position waiting for the parade to begin. They wear long veils over their faces and have covered hair. Only their eyes can be seen but it is obvious they cannot conceal their curiosity when we approach them. They giggle behind the shawls, but, like everyone else, respond according to the party line.

— We will eat the Americans as if they were rabbits, one woman threatens. Her name is Muntaha. — We will defend ourselves with sticks and stones and we would rather drink our oil than let the Americans have it.

Muntaha has attended training courses with al-Quds three times during the last two years, in periods of two months. — We learn weapons handling, how to use communications equipment and write military reports. Last time we also used heavy artillery. Besides, we have been through survival courses and learnt how to subsist in the desert, says the mother of three. Several women crowd around us, inciting each other with ever more fiery descriptions of how they will kill the Americans.

It is not long before a gruff officer walks over and talks to Aliya. She nods and says we must leave. Before Janine or I have time to even murmur, she is on her way over the road.

— Stop, I cry, and call her back. — What did he say?

— We need permission to interview people.

— Where do we get that?

— We have to go and see the mayor.

I visualise a never-ending swirl from office to office, ending only when the parade is over and there is no one left to talk to, so I try to pull a fast one.

— Listen, why do you think we are here? Do you think we have arrived under our own steam? I say to the muscular officer. — Not at all, we have been sent here by the Ministry of Information. We have permission from the minister himself. Show him the permission, Aliya. The permission implies that we can talk to people. How could we otherwise do our job? Actually, we haven't only got permission to be here, we have in fact been ordered to come. If you prevent us from carrying out this order, which actually consists of visiting and writing about the parade in Mosul, then you are really pitting yourself against Iraq's Information Minister, who has been hand-picked for the job by Saddam Hussein. What is your name, by the way?

I look straight at the officer, who has been listening to my speech via Aliya's translation. He breathes heavily, snorts a few Arab expletives and walks off. I say proudly to Aliya: That's how to do it.

Aliya has pursed her lips and asks me to behave.

– Now you follow me, she says.

The parade begins. The noise is ear-splitting; now it isn't possible to interview anyone anyway.

The female units march at the front. Many wear their own clothes. Billowing lace blouses and home knitted sweaters, flowing skirts with or without splits, pleated skirts, tight skirts, all long. The colour is unique to each unit, but most of the women wear white tops and black skirts.

In spite of the alleged tough training, they would not have got far with the sort of footwear revealed – high-heeled pumps, sandals with golden buckles, slippers that keep on slipping.

– This is a celebration, an occasion, we're not going out to fight today, one of the girls told me when I commented on her plastic shoes. I spot her now in one of the front rows. But she's not wiggling her hips, she is stomping through the streets of Mosul, crying with the others: '*Na'm, na'm Saddam!*' 'Yes, yes, Saddam!'

After the women's brigade come the men. One man catches my attention. Like the others in his unit he marches with knees pulled up high and in the traditional Kurdish costume: wide trousers and shirt, a flower-painted belt round his waist. What separates him from the others are the seven plastic roses he has stuck down into his turban. Behind the roses, anchored in the folds of the turban, is a picture of Saddam Hussein. On the front of the turban is another portrait of the president, a third is pinned on his chest.

The Kurd salutes to the right where Iraq's power elite are seated in a stand, and to the left where ordinary Iraqis are sitting. Some of them have been given placards which they hold in their laps. When the call *'Na'm, na'm Saddam'* is heard, they turn the placards and a huge portrait of the president appears in mosaic. The Kurdish hero Saladin has also been allocated space on the portrait. He was the warrior who forced the crusaders out of Jerusalem in 1187. Saddam and Saladin are fellow townsmen of Tikrit.

Workers and peasants, teachers and old-age pensioners march together in one large group, some in uniform others in work clothes. Many sport a banner across the chest on which are painted two flags, the Iraqi and the Palestinian. On other banners is the slogan: 'Hold your head high, you are an Iraqi!'

Right at the end, on their own, the suicide bombers march. They are in white floor-length hooded robes, with dynamite wound around their waists and grenades in their hands. – We are ready to die a martyr's death, is the message on the banners they carry.

A mother and her son stand quietly watching the parade. – I am a soldier's widow, she says. – From the Gulf War. She clutches a dirty plastic bag in her hand. It is filled with coloured bits of paper which she and her son shower over the marchers. The widow also belongs to the reserve forces but is off sick. Her twelve-year-old son says he is proud of his mother being a member of al-Quds.

– He'll be starting to train soon too, she says. – We'll show the Americans, our children are made of fire and steel.

One boy is spellbound by it all, fascinated by the soldiers, the uniforms and the vehicles. On the back of his jacket is the word 'Titanic'.

– That just about says it all, looking at this lot, a person to my right whispers. – Shipwreck at the first American attack.

When I return from Mosul there's something about my room. It smells different.

A small palm is smiling at me by the mirror. I haven't had time to close the door before Said is there, beaming. He looks at me and can barely contain his laughter. Have I seen it or not?

He points to the palm tree. I thank him, we both laugh. A small sand fly escapes from the pot. Well, I'll never sleep alone.

The day after the parade we are invited up to one of the assembly rooms on the Ministry's second floor. A large TV screen has been erected. On a sofa by the window the Minister of Information is sitting with Uday and a few other serious-looking men. In addition to us journalists the room is full of representatives from various peace organisations. The 'Women in Pink' are the most noticeable. They are dressed in various shades of pink and are gathered around a pink banner in the middle of the room asking for peace. I have seen them everywhere the last couple of days; they usually position themselves in front of the press centre or by the hotel roundabouts where they know they'll be caught on camera. They spent one whole day under pink parasols in Paradise Square outside Hotel Palestine, doling out shocking pink plastic trifles to children. And the protests work. At least enough to appear on TV. They are especially popular with the Arab TV stations. Inside the conference hall it appears that the pink clad are being interviewed constantly, while eagerly scouting the hall for further interrogators.

– The world should be ruled by a pink attitude to life, I hear a lady say in a broad Californian accent.

Close to them are the Spanish 'Mujeres por la Paz'. 'No pasaran' says their banner. But the Spanish ladies are no match for the Californian candyfloss, and eventually sit down on the available chairs waiting for the show to start.

'Voices in the Wilderness', 'Priests for Peace', they are all there. A vicar stands up and declares war a sin. Some Greeks from 'Doctors of the World', all wearing white pullovers, sit in one corner. A large EU parliament delegation, in Iraq to beg the country's parliamentarians to cooperate better with the weapons inspectors, wander about. They don't feel quite at home, either with Iraqi Baath Party activists or pink plastic necklaces.

The TV is turned on. We have seated ourselves with notebooks poised. The room is stiff with smoke. BBC and CNN show the same pictures and after a while, and some to-ing and fro-ing, the Iraqi in charge of the remote control chooses the BBC. Joschka Fisher is greeting his French colleague Dominique de Villepin. The UN inspectors Hans Blix and Muhammed el-Baradei arrive, followed by porters carrying suitcases. A bandy-legged, smiling Colin Powell saunters through the corridors and into the chamber of the Security Council, a briefcase tucked under his arm: the proof.

Minister of Information Muhammed Said al-Sahhaf leans back in his armchair. He watches the screen as if he is able to uncover some of the contents by scrutinising Powell's body language. Uday has one eye on the TV screen and one eye on his superior. The séance takes ninety minutes. With the use of charts and sketches Powell demonstrates that Iraq ostensibly transports weapons of mass destruction around the country. He shows pictures of what he calls mobile laboratories and reveals that Iraq has close connections to al-Qaida.

I steal a glance at al-Sahhaf and Uday as Powell presents his proof. They sit and watch, poker faced, without exchanging a word until Powell has finished. The British Foreign Minister Jack Straw appears, applauding. Fischer demands more time for the Iraqis. Villepin says there must be better cooperation. Blix says time is running out.

As the broadcast finishes the group in the corner get up and leave the room, stiff, without staggering, looking straight ahead. We stay behind and analyse the speech. What kind of proof was this?

Two Spanish peace activists start crying and the Spaniards gather round for communal comfort. The pink ladies roll up their banners. The TV reporters rush up onto the roof to report the Iraqi reaction. But there is no reaction to broadcast. The stony faces left the room without saying a word.

A Swedish parliamentarian shuffles around the premises. – This looks bad, he says. – They don't appear to have understood the seriousness of it all.

I marvel at every day I am allowed to stay. Each day lists with names of those who must leave are hung up outside

Uday's office. One day about fifty journalists are expelled, another day twenty. They are given forty-eight hours' notice. Those who disappear are the unimportant ones, people who work for small countries. My category.

After three weeks in Iraq it is my turn. The extra days of grace from Uday have expired; I am unable to extend my visa and must go. I fantasise about hiding away and reappearing only when the regime has fallen, the Ministry of Information been levelled to the ground and Uday has fled. But it is difficult to go underground in a thoroughly monitored Iraq. The hotels constantly check that residence permits are up to date, and hiding away in a private house is out of the question. It would be impossible to be kept away from neighbours and relatives in a country where everyone is spying on each other and every street or building has an informer. Anyhow, I don't know any Iraqis I could ask. What about the Bedouins in the desert? Like Gertrude Bell? I imagine the sequel: *Desert Queen II*.

The fanciful flight remains fantasy and I pack my bags, book a ticket to Amman and wonder what to do now. Go to Oslo? Wait in Jordan? I know it is virtually impossible to return once one has left. Hundreds of journalists are tripping impatiently in the Jordanian capital, several having waited for weeks. Iraq's destiny is at stake and I am on my way out. Damn.

The last day before departure I go to the Ministry of Information to settle my bill. All journalists must pay $225 per day for the privilege of staying in the country. I owe several thousand dollars. As I am counting the money, Kadim, number two after Uday and a milder type than his boss, whispers:

— Do you want to stay?

– Of course, but you are throwing me out!

– I can help you.

Kadim indicates that the help must be kept secret and asks me to meet him an hour later at the end of a little-used corridor.

– You have to understand. He clears his throat and looks coy. – This agreement must be to our mutual benefit.

Kadim looks penetratingly at me. Until this moment he has appeared likeable. He often jokes with Aliya and me. I have difficulty in reconciling his mild manner with the cut-throat intelligence service he belongs to.

– Mutual benefit. What does that mean?

– You have to pay.

– How much?

– That's up to you. I don't know how much money you have. Bring as much as you can in an envelope tomorrow and the matter will be settled, for now, Kadim says, and disappears light-footed down the corridor.

It is a risky business he has started. Corruption permeates Iraq, but bribery can be severely punished. But I quite understand that Kadim wants to lay his hands on as much as possible before it all unravels.

What is a suitable sum? Not so much that he will think I am a bottomless money bag, not so little that it will irritate him. And I don't know whether this is only for the next ten days. Eventually I put five hundred dollars in an envelope and hope for the best.

Kadim cannot decide alone. He must submit my case to the committee on the eighth floor, whoever they are. At every meeting he has the possibility to promote candidates who will be allowed to evade the ten-day rule. Primarily it concerns large TV companies and newspapers, who pay millions to be allowed to stay. It might complicate matters for Kadim that I come from an insignificant country. He asks me to make a list of who I work for.

Luck is with me this time, but at any moment my name might be staring down at me from the list. One journalist after another leaves the country after their allotted ten days. Did my five hundred dollars really make that much difference?

It is not only Iraq's inhabitants who fear the regime's heavy fist; the journalists too are frightened of its knuckles. To call Saddam Hussein a dictator is banned, to mention the torture and ethnic cleansing is equal to issuing one's own return ticket. Thus the most critical articles are written by colleagues at home. A visa is too valuable to sacrifice for the sake of one crushing report. We walk with open eyes into this self-imposed censorship.

Janine rewrites and changes like the true pro she is in order not to be turned out. Nevertheless, she is constantly being chastised by Uday for leaders and commentaries in *The Times*, a paper which has taken a clear stand for the war. Melinda from *Newsweek* often writes snatches of articles which are later reworked by others and printed under a pseudonym.

One day Remy from *Le Monde* is ordered to catch the first plane out of the country. The Iraqi embassy in Paris has faxed some articles to Uday. In one of them Remy refers to the remarks of a man in the street: 'Let the bombs drop, then at last we'll be rid of the dictator.'

— It is impossible anyone would have said this! Uday shouts. — You've made it up.

— I'm no novelist, Remy says.

— Your interpreter will be punished for having translated this. Where is he?

– He wasn't there. I was alone.

– You have no right to be out alone. You have broken all the rules. Get out! Your interpreter will be punished for not having looked after you better.

– I sneaked out, Remy says, to protect his interpreter.

– I choose to believe you have invented it all yourself.

– No, I did not.

– If anyone said this to you, why did you need to write it? Why?

– I . . .

– *Vous n'existez plus pour moi!* You no longer exist to me. Out!

Remy refuses to leave the office. Then it will all be over. He tries to argue. But Uday is no longer listening.

At that moment Giovanna, a gorgeous Italian TV star from RAI, sweeps in through the door. Uday is receptive to the charms of the blonde beauty, and Giovanna likes Remy. She grasps the situation immediately.

– But Uday, why Remy? What can Remy have done? He is the kindest man in the world. He's part of the family. Give him another chance and I'll make sure he behaves in the future. I guarantee . . .

The expression on Uday's face changes as he looks from Remy to Giovanna.

Remy is allowed to stay, for the moment. But he will never again write critically about the regime. There is no way he will risk missing the war.

Iraq has no embassy in Norway. I fear the embassy in Sweden, until I am told that hardly anyone speaks English there, let alone Swedish. After a few cautious tests I realise no one is checking up on me. I am at liberty to write what I hear and see.

But it is all so tame and bland. I search everywhere for

something to write about. I cannot write the garbage issued by the regime, nor read the thoughts of the man in the street.

One day we are after all allowed to travel to one of Iraq's most oppositional towns – Karbala, a Shia Muslim holy place. It is *eid*, when hundreds of thousands of pilgrims will be on their way. To look after us we have been allocated Janine's minder Hassan; Aliya alone is not enough. So far we have split the two minders. Aliya comes into town with us; Hassan attends press conferences and applies for permissions. At the press centre he pursues all the rumours, power-shifts, intrigues and political games among the bureaucrats. He guards his own position and hopes soon to be promoted from the minister's man with *The Times*, to something on the eighth floor.

When he is out with us he keeps mostly in the background and does not condescend to translate our questions. That is Aliya's job. With his small well-trimmed moustache, eyes that never miss a thing and scheming-like posture, Hassan reminds one of an Iraqi version of Inspector Clouseau.

We set off before dawn. The permission is valid for one day only. After a couple of hours driving, the car comes to a standstill. Pilgrims are everywhere: on foot, mounted, in cars, buses and on the backs of lorries. Then the car splutters on at a snail's pace and at last the town rises out of the desert, like a mirage.

Karbala is a beautiful town, teeming with palm trees, gardens, sacred monuments and over one hundred mosques. Imam Hussein was killed here during the battle of 680. The mausoleum was built on the spot where his blood mingled with the soil.

Pilgrims come here throughout the year and especially during *eid*, the conclusion to the holy month of Ramadan. Karbala is almost entirely inhabited by Shia Muslims and therefore strictly watched over by the regime. Shia Muslims constitute the largest religious group, accounting for around sixty percent of the population, and have been exposed to brutal suppression.

Not only Imam Hussein was slain in Karbala. After the first Gulf War the Shia Muslims rose in protest against the regime. For a few days in March 1991 virtually all Shia Muslim areas in Southern Iraq rose up. They expected help from the Americans; after all, their goal was the same, they thought, to topple Saddam Hussein. The help failed to materialise. On the contrary, George Bush Sr allowed his arch enemy to fly helicopters over American forces to quell the revolt. The republican guard's elite troops made massive use of its arsenal, including chemical weapons.

The holy towns were the last to give in. In Karbala fighting continued from house to house and 30,000 people lost their lives in the first two days; twice as many in the surrounding areas. The mausoleum itself was the scene of battle. Several thousand people took refuge there and missiles were sent towards the sacred place. The town changed its appearance after this Shia *intifada*. While as before the Gulf War there was an overflowing bazaar, narrow streets with small teahouses, shops and work places next door to the mausoleum, today a large square surrounds it. Nothing bears witness to the fighting. The golden spires tower proudly over the town, the newly cleaned blue and green mosaic gleams in the sun.

We walk inside the walls where the bloodbath took place. Dawn has just arrived. Many of the pilgrims still lie asleep on black woollen blankets. Three women sit in a circle on the shining stones, just waking up. One woman slowly inhales smoke from her cigarette. She shivers. This is her third night on the flagstones outside the mosque, where she has come to praise God and ask for help.

— I am sixty and will die soon. My prayers are that I will go to Paradise, she says between leisurely puffs. — I pray for a peaceful death, that I won't be burnt alive during a bomb attack, or torn to pieces by a missile. My husband died last year of a heart attack, peacefully in bed. I hope my death will be like his. If we are lucky we'll meet in Paradise.

Around us people are starting to assemble. Some sit down on carpets and cushions surrounded by their family and read pieces from the Koran to each other. Others murmur to themselves or wait in the long queue leading to the mosque. The buzzing voices are thought to reach Imam Hussein's tomb. After a lot of persuasion Aliya agrees to ask people about the 1991 uprisings. But they just shake their heads evasively.

A man stands alone and reads from a book, loud and chanting. Said has lived in Karbala all his life. He lives close by and visited the mosque every day during the Gulf War. He says he never saw any sign of an uprising.

— But I have heard about it, he admits eventually.

— What did you hear?

— That unpatriotic and evil forces stood behind it.

He fastens his eyes on me and won't let go.

— And the destruction around the mosque?

— The American bombs, Said says. Beside him Hassan nods his head.

Hassan, who is himself a Shia Muslim, wants to go into the mosque to pray. He commands me to wait until he returns. — Don't move, otherwise I'll never find you.

A man who has been following the conversation from behind a prayer book, staring intently at the worn pages, suddenly addresses me in English, in a low voice.

– No one is telling the truth. You might as well not ask.

I stand quietly and watch him.

– We don't even talk to each other about it. We don't trust anyone. Not even our friends, he says, before disappearing into the throng.

The interpreter returns. It is as though I have momentarily visited another reality. For a few seconds the truth flickered. Just as suddenly I am thrown back into the sticky lie.

Hassan wants to find another family for me to talk to. I follow him like a sheep without a goal or any sense. But I've got what I wanted. Someone who talked! Hassan stops by a family sitting on a rug and reading aloud from the Koran. The little boy is playing with a plastic car.

– We pray that Allah might guide George Bush and lead him to the true way, the father says.

– Right.

– But he is fighting Satan.

The man closes the book.

– And what does Satan want? I ask.

– You know him better than me.

One day a cardinal arrives in Baghdad with a message from the Pope. No one knows what it is about but there are rumours that he wants to offer Saddam Hussein asylum in the Vatican.

Aliya comes with us to Mass in St Joseph's, where the cardinal is preaching. She has never been inside a church. Beforehand we take a stroll round the Christian suburb of Karada. In a bar called 'Fruity' we find Joseph. The blender hisses, the seeds crackle and a pomegranate is turned into red juice. Joseph pours it into a glass, adds straws and serves it to us.

– The cardinal is making a peace proposal. The Pope whispered it into his ear and no one will know what he whispered until he tells our President, Joseph explains, who ordinarily is a student at Baghdad technical high school.

– *Insh'Allah*, God willing, it will help, Joseph's boss Hussein says. He is a Muslim but is of the opinion that it can do no harm that the Pope has sent a man to Baghdad.

– It depends on how mighty the Pope is. Is he very mighty? Hussein asks.

– Very, says Joseph.

– But can he stop Bush?

Joseph is at a loss for an answer. – I'll listen to what he has to say. But it would have been better if he had gone to Washington to talk to Bush. He's the one who wants war.

Like most Iraqi Christians Joseph is a Chaldean – an entity within the Catholic Church. Of Baghdad's fifty churches, thirty are Chaldean, and in many of the churches Mass is conducted in Chaldean, or even in Aramaic, the language that Jesus spoke. The liturgy is the oldest in the world and Iraqi Christians try to maintain their culture and rites. The number of Christians in Iraq has nearly halved over the last fifteen years. Now they account for barely three percent of the population or three quarters of a million people. Every year thousands of them try to leave the country, to the USA or Europe. The Islamisation of Iraq and the increasing influence of the imams worry them. In spite of their low numbers, Christians have enjoyed a privileged position in Iraqi society. They have been well represented in the Baath Party and in Saddam Hussein's elite forces. One of the President's most important men, Tariq Aziz, is a Chaldean. – With Saddam Hussein at least we know what we have got. A new regime might be influenced by religious fanatics, goes the refrain.

– There is no antagonism between Christians and Muslims in Iraq, Joseph and Hussein assure me. – We are brothers and worship the same God.

Joseph has been given a few hours off to listen to the cardinal; he takes off his apron and leaves while Hussein waits for the call to prayer from the mosque. We lose sight of Joseph in the crowd by the church. Aliya stays outside. That's OK by me, I would rather be alone.

In the garden behind the church a short, stout priest leaps about. Can he spare a few moments to talk? He can, and in fluent French.

Father Albert does not agree with Joseph that there is no animosity between Christians and Muslims. – The average Christian will get this high, he says, but no higher and points to a spot in the middle of his stomach. – The best jobs, the best pay are reserved for Muslims. But the worst is yet to come – the advance of the fanatics. It's seething and bubbling, he says with a concerned expression.

Father Albert is curious about the Pope's message. – God moves in mysterious ways. But here in Iraq neither popes nor cardinals count. It depends upon the good will of one man. There is now only one way left to avoid war, that our good man leaves the country, he says. – Just write it. I'm an old man and must be allowed to say what I want. Saddam Hussein must leave the country. But that he'll never do.

Father Albert is just as critical of the American president. – He pretends to have good reasons for going to war. But he does not. He just wants control.

The priest belongs to the same church as Deputy Prime Minister Tariq Aziz and knows him well. – He is actually a good man, an intellectual who wants the best. But he is boxed in and cannot do anything differently. He can't tell the President to go to blazes!

If it comes to war Father Albert fears complete revolt. – People have a lot to revenge. Two days ago Tariq Aziz's wife visited me. She cried and wanted a miserable hut to live in rather than the palace she has now. She is terrified of the people's verdict, now that the regime might topple, and asked for sanctuary for herself and her husband in the monastery where I live. But I said no. If churches and monasteries hide the hated it will harm all Christians and fan the flames of the fanatics. Anyhow, he adds, – those people have a lot to answer for.

Father Albert stands on the church square in Baghdad and sets his face against Saddam Hussein. I am suffering from shock and ask him repeatedly whether I really might write down what he has said, which he confirms. He feels safe, he says, and points to heaven.

I include most of it in my article that afternoon, but I call the priest something else and do not mention Tariq Aziz by name. I describe him as 'one of Saddam Hussein's closest collaborators'. That the wife of the Deputy Prime Minister is busy preparing a hideaway for the aftermath of the war could be dangerous if it were known. When Tariq Aziz is away travelling, the family are placed under a sort of house arrest. If he were to abandon ship they would be targeted. Thus it is impossible for anyone in the bosom of Saddam's regime to get out. But like Father Albert said about his erstwhile friend: He walked into it knowingly. He closed his eyes to the Baath Party's torture and oppression. By means of unadulterated opportunism he fought his way up the power-ladder. *These people have a lot to answer for.*

The Ministry of Information has been turned into a building site. From early morning until dark there is hammering, banging, sawing and welding. We circumnavigate wet cement, cutting machinery and blue welding flames. A layer of white dust settles everywhere. When I try to concentrate on the day's article the sounds cut into my thoughts.

One day a workman cuts the satellite telephone cables by mistake. All the reporters and their interpreters rush off to Baghdad's markets to buy new cables or something that can repair the old ones. On another occasion the path between the house and the fence against the pavement is flooded. A pipe has burst. Planks are put out and we jump from one to another.

Dust and mud are everywhere. I fear for my telephone and computer. The rows between the keys are slowly filling with sand. How much more can it take before it breaks down?

The workers try to turn the Ministry into a fortress, and the area facing the boulevard, where we have our communications equipment, grows increasingly smaller. The original walls on the first floor, constructed of glass and steel, are bricked up. The new façade does not touch the glass walls, but adds small rooms outside the glass. The workers spend hours shaping arches over the windows and rounding off corners. In spite of about fifty men being employed the work proceeds slowly.

— So the Minister of Construction is hedging his bets, I joke with Takhlef.

— Hedging his bets?

— Yes, against the war.

– Which war? Takhlef asks. – What do you mean?

– The bombs that will blow the windows in, of course.

Takhlef looks at me, shakes his head and says as he walks away: – They're building offices for you – can't you see. They're building offices.

But even if Takhlef does not fear an attack, most of Baghdad's inhabitants are busy preparing for one.

I return to one of the families I had visited with the child psychologists – the lawyer family Dhafer – to see how they are coping with preparations. Only the sons are at home. Outside the house lies a pile of planks.

– To nail over the windows in case of war, Ahmed explains. He is studying law at Baghdad University. – It depends on where the bombs fall, but it might help to stop the windows from shattering, he says.

Ahmed and his brothers walk to the back of the house, stride over the kitchen garden, past the tethered sheep, past the little well, down some steep steps into a tiny, smelly room. Bottles of water, blankets and mattresses are piled high. – We are safe here, no bombs can reach us.

The bomb shelter was built in the 1980s during the war against Iran. It was used in 1991, 1993 and 1998.

The law student makes it plain to us that the Americans will be breaking all known international rules if they go to war. – We are a peaceful people.

– But there will be war, his little brother Ali says resignedly. He has been taught at school how to defend himself. – If there are explosions you must throw yourself down on the floor. If there are chemical weapons you must hold something in front of your nose and mouth.

– And you must walk into the wind, the third brother Amar adds. – Not with the wind, but into it. Or maybe it was with it? he wonders.

— It depends on where the chemical explosion is, Ahmed says.

— Yes, and which direction the wind is blowing, Amar says.

— No one can overcome the wind, says Ali. — That's an Iraqi expression, think about that.

It's hard to work. It's hard to find stories. As the limits are so strict, good ideas, ideas that could be carried through, are few and far between. It feels as though I am living in a bubble; the world I live in and the one I write about are totally separate. Only now and again do I find a tiny connection to the other world, to the Iraqis.

One day the calendar tells me that it is Valentine's Day, and I remember Nabil's invitation. My company consists of five Frenchmen. As we arrive, the bubble we are living in becomes even more impenetrable. The distance between 'us' and 'them' is total. The entire pink restaurant is covered in red balloons with the words 'I love you'. Garlands in gold and silver stream from the roof. A dance band is engaged for the evening and plays everything from melting Arab *Habibi*-music to 'Lady in Red'. The tables in the middle of the room are moved to the side, and Nabil has got an elegant dancefloor.

When we go in a rose is pushed into our hands, and we are shown to our table. The bubble moves across the room, leaving dirty footprints on the floor. We are incorrectly dressed: creased shirts, jeans, muddy trainers, no elaborate hairstyles.

The Iraqis are dressed to kill in shimmering creations and sparkling jewellery; all in gold, red gold. The women's crowning glory has been sprayed stiff to last the night. We are at two different parties.

Sumptuous dishes are brought to the table to celebrate an American tradition. Neither I nor the French have any special relationship to the day, it is the same for the ordinary Iraqi, I imagine. But Nabil seems to have made a point of making it one of the country's festivals. One of the Frenchmen outlines his project for the evening: to chat up one of the beautiful Iraqi women. But the dazzling ladies are well guarded by brothers and spouses.

– Unfortunately there is no champagne, he sighs. – That might have helped me on the way.

Suddenly I realise I have not danced for ages and I lure the lustful Frenchman onto the floor. The Arab-style pop resounds from the loud-speakers; I copy the ladies I have seen on the music videos and wriggle over the floor. Another couple joins us, then another. At the end of the first number the dancefloor is heaving.

The bubble has burst, at least for the moment. We dance together – square dances, belly dances, folk dances or to old Elvis numbers. Sweat pours off everybody, trainers gyrate among spangle-covered pumps. I feel accepted for the first time. People smile at me. But I know it is an illusion. In any other Arab country people would talk to us, maybe invite us home, advise us on which sights to visit. But in Iraq the foreigner represents danger. The situation's absurdity hits me. It is 14 February. This very evening Hans Blix has presented his report to the UN Security Council, a report which left little doubt of the outcome.

On his side, Saddam Hussein is calling for holy war. In the mosques, during Friday prayer, a martyr's death was upgraded. During his TV transmitted speech and clutching Ali's sword, the mightiest Imam in Baghdad encouraged people to fight against and resist the invader. – I have never before heard the Imam in such a belligerent mood, one man said as he left the mosque.

We of the trainers, jeans, unkempt hair and notebook-in-back-pocket have come to Nabil's to pass the time – waiting for war to start. The well-groomed and bejewelled tables next door wait too. For something to happen.

Nabil interrupts my thoughts. He presents his beautiful wife to me and presses her hand in mine. It is her and the baby twins that Nabil wants to get out in time. When is that? In time?

Close to one of the children's hospitals, it is said that there is a children's graveyard. No one knows exactly where, not Aliya, not the driver, nor any of our colleagues. After a month in Baghdad we have learnt that it does not pay to ask the Ministry of Information. The less they see of us the better. In spite of the strict rules preventing us from travelling anywhere without permission, the system is far from watertight. They quite simply do not have the resources to spy on everyone all the time.

We look in district after district. After several failed attempts, we finally walk in through the graveyard gate, there we find a man dressed in a worn blue overall, a Palestinian scarf rolled into a turban on his head.

The man carries the tiny bundle in one hand. He strides over the graves and mounds of earth. The bundle of white cloth is two-day-old Haidar.

The little boy had died that morning. – Blood poisoning, says the gravedigger. – His face is blue, his body is covered with lumps, he explains, folding the white cloth back for us to see. He covers it up quickly and lays the boy on a stone.

Haidar was delivered by his father to the gravedigger at the gate. — He had no money for either grave or ceremony and asked if we could take him anyway. We accept everyone here, we'll be paid up there, he says and points. — We washed him and wrapped him in this cloth. But there'll be no gravestone or plaque, Kadim says.

It is early morning. Seven children have already been buried today. — One was seven months old, another nine months. The others were a few years old, Kadim tells us. One of the children has a gravestone; a quotation from the Koran and a newly painted name in red and green stands out against the white stone.

— What did they die of?

— Not enough food, no medicine, then they get blood poisoning, Kadim says. That is what he calls the illnesses he can't explain.

The digger prepares a hole in the ground for Haidar, between two other children.

The very smallest are buried here. — Every day we get between twenty and thirty children. A few years ago it was under ten a day, Kadim tells us. A handful are just delivered at the gate. The parents cannot afford a proper burial. The graves are never looked after, never visited.

Haidar's father told the gravedigger that his wife was in a critical condition following the birth, and that he must hurry back to the hospital. Haidar was born two months early.

There has been a large increase in premature births in Iraq. Between 1990 and 1999 the number of children born with a below average weight has increased fivefold, which might imply that the mothers are also undernourished or malnourished. In the same period, the number of deaths during labour has doubled.

Primarily children have been affected by the decline in standards of living following the implementation of sanctions. The mortality rate among the smallest children has doubled in the last decade.

Most children die of what would be run-of-the-mill illnesses in the West; two thirds die of diarrhoea or infections. An average Iraqi child suffers from diarrhoea fourteen days every month, as opposed to three days every month in 1990.

Following the UN Oil-for-Food programme which was put into effect in 1996, the statistics have levelled off and even show a slight improvement in children's health. This is due to the monthly rations received by all Iraqis. But rations sometimes make matters worse. Mothers of very young children get free milk substitutes as part of their monthly package. Because of this, fewer women breast-feed, and others give up breastfeeding earlier than usual. The contaminated water supplies mean that this practice leads to more sick children.

Many fatal illnesses are caused by impure water. Before the Gulf War, Iraq had a modern water system, but lately the water quality has deteriorated drastically. Bad maintenance of water-works and purification plants, power cuts, lack of reserve parts and even chlorine have put many of them out of action. The generators at two of the three plants have stopped functioning owing to a shortfall of batteries and spare parts. There is fear of a cata-strophic breakdown in water supply should the power plants be bombed. Many of the sewerage plants are not working. Half the purification plants in Baghdad, a city of five million inhabitants, are out of service. Half a million tons of raw sewage are emptied into the Tigris every day.

The gravedigger has finished. Haidar is laid down in the grave accompanied by a short prayer. Three bricks are put on top of him and the man throws earth over and treads it down. All that bears witness to the small child in the ground is the freshly dug, darker earth.

Kadim does not believe that Haidar's father will return.

— Those who don't have a burial place don't usually return. After all, they don't know where the children are buried. I'll

remember Haidar for a few days, but then new ones will be brought in and I'll forget.

A little way off a man sits by a grave polishing the marble headstone. It is dominated by a large painting of purple lilies on one side and a quotation from the Koran on the other. Shehad: 1.7.95–3.2.99

– Leukaemia, says the father, who has put the rag aside and stopped polishing. Not a speck of dust remains on the shining white marble. – It is as if life stopped when she died. Our only child, and it doesn't look as though we'll have any more, he says sadly.

– She had blue marks all over her body, but the doctor said it was nothing. Then she became very ill, and we took her to hospital. There they gave her injections but she died after four days. Four days. They didn't have the right medicines. My wife has been sick ever since, she only comes here on Fridays.

– Honey, he says. – Her name means honey. And she had honey-coloured hair and white skin. She was beautiful like a flower.

He leans back on the gravestone and lights a cigarette. He comes here every day and shares a few moments with his daughter.

A wind picks up. Further down the hill the packed earth whirls around. But Haidar is safe under three bricks.

For a long time I have wanted to visit Baghdad's forbidden quarter – Saddam City; a place one should not talk about, not visit, and preferably forget the existence of. Each time we mention the place to the Ministry of Information they look at us and say: What do you want to do there? It's just like every other place. No, keep to the centre of town.

When I ask Aliya she gives a start.

– Don't ask me again, she says. – I do not want to go to Saddam City.

– Why not?

– We won't get permission.

– We can ask.

– We won't get permission.

– If we don't ask we'll never get permission.

– But I don't want to.

What Aliya does not want she does not want. She denies that it has anything to do with it being a Shia area.

–There is no difference between Shia and Sunni. We are all the same.

There are fears that the whole area will rise up against the regime when the American attacks start, as they did during the Gulf War. Then the republican guard tried in vain to calm the inhabitants down. When the uprisings spread, Saddam's son Qusay gave orders that unless the riots ceased in two hours, the entire neighbourhood would be attacked by missiles. The head of the Baath Party in Saddam City asked for twenty-four hours and got them. The riots were stopped.

– There is no difference, Aliya says sanctimoniously. And when I insist she hisses. – Must not talk about Sunni and Shia.

One evening when Amir, my regular driver, brings me home, he advises me against visiting Saddam City.

– They are dirty. Lazy. Not like us. They are uncivilised, look how they whip and beat themselves, he says, alluding to their religious rites. – They cause nothing but trouble.

I am surprised. It is forbidden to criticise the Shias openly. The oppression is supposed to occur in secret, preferably under cover of darkness, under the command of the *mukhabarat*, the dreaded intelligence service. Tens of thousands of Shias have disappeared, just for belonging to a mosque which the regime insists is plotting revolt.

On the surface everything is supposed to be quiet. That is a cardinal rule in Saddam Hussein's kingdom.

— You can't trust them; they smile in your face, but thrust the knife into your back when you turn around, Amir continues.

Amir is a large, huggable bear of a man. He is built like a boxer and has a liking for jeans and leather jackets. In spite of his tough appearance he isn't a bully — his round face gives him away — he is a kind and conscientious driver. When he picks me up in the morning he always brings with him the *Iraqi Times* and the English version of *Babel*, the paper owned by Saddam's son Uday. On trips out of town he brings a thermos with tea or coffee and cakes baked by his mother. Amir is thirty-five years old but still lives at home. His father is dead and Amir provides for the family. Normally he never speaks about politics so I am most surprised when he tells me the Shia Muslims are dirty. I let it lie. There isn't much we can talk about anyway — his vocabulary is limited. But he improves every day. When he sits and waits for me in the car he learns new English words or tries to pick his way through the *Iraqi Times*. When he drives me through the deserted streets at night, on my way home from the Ministry of Information, he plays classical music before dropping me off and returning to his mother.

One day, however, I get the chance to visit Saddam City, not with Aliya but with Janine's interpreter Hassan, himself a Shia. — But he never talks about it, Janine whispers.

Having crossed the river to Saddam City our first rendezvous is at the Baath Party offices. Foreigners need a special permit in order to visit the area, and two minders

— one from the Ministry of Information and one from the local party office. Hassan and the local guide sit squeezed into the passenger seat in front, Janine and I spread ourselves over the back seat. There is no way the local guide wants to share the back seat with us.

A dried out canal-bed separates one world from the other. On one side Baghdad's broad avenues, high-rise buildings and monuments. On the other a slum metropolis. Stinking sewage seeps between the market stalls. Children run barefoot over vegetable refuse and decaying fish-tails. The canal dried up many years ago. Now it serves a different purpose — as a military site, it is rumoured. The canal will act as a trench — several defence posts have already been erected in the dry mud. Not to protect people from the Americans, but in order to protect one district from another.

Saddam City was built after the overthrow of King Faisal in 1958. Two years later the houses were ready, and the poorest citizens moved in. Out of Baghdad's five million inhabitants, one and a half million live here. The palms are dead and the grass scorched. The ostracised of this world live in a slum that was named after Saddam following his visit here ten years ago.

We stop by the market. The first thing that strikes me is the number of flies everywhere.

Led by the two guides we start the first interview. The situation is unbearably meaningless.

— The Party has given me a Kalashnikov, says a green-grocer. — To fight the Americans, he assures us, arms flailing in the air. The insects alight and settle on the tomatoes, cauliflowers and lettuce. Janine and I look at each other in despair. What's the point of interviewing people when we already know their answers?

Flies aren't the only plague in Saddam City. Disease thrives too. We set off for the local clinic. A family is standing outside, crying. A young woman is carrying a child in her arms. It is ashen-faced.

— His blood is damaged, she says. — There is no red in the blood, only white. The doctor says he needs a blood transfusion or he'll die. But I'm too frightened. What if they give him bad blood?

— Talasemi, explains Samir Saleh, a young doctor from Southern Iraq. — It is hereditary and prevents the bones from growing. He needs a bone marrow transplant, but that's impossible. There has only ever been one such transplant in Iraq. Only one. There are so many sick children here. Contaminated water, sewage everywhere, chemical discharge, radioactivity, no food, reduced immunity. I tell the mothers to boil the water, but when have they got time to do that? They spend all day looking for food as it is.

The hospital director arrives and asks to see our permission. We show him the piece of paper. — That doesn't apply to the hospital. You must seek permission via the Health Ministry.

We leave the misery and go to meet one of the area's leaders. In Saddam City the sheiks are the most important people. They dispense advice and act as mediators — instalments on loans, marriage agreements, rows amongst neighbours, Sheik Namah abd al-Alawi explains. The sheiks are heads of tribes or clans ranging in number from a few hundred to several thousand.

— We are preparing for war, the sheik says, and asks one of his sons to fetch his Kalashnikov. It is brand new.

— We'll defeat the enemy, he says, echoing Saddam's propaganda. He hardly draws breath before prolonging the echo, without empathy, without enthusiasm: *May the desert be the graveyard of the aggressors.*

The sheik is a retired Army officer and lives off his state pension and support from clan members. He has also bought a car and set up as a taxi driver, alternating work with his sons.

– Alas, everything has got worse: embargos, sanctions. One time we could live off our salaries, he complains.

On our way out of the district, over the dried-up watercourse, we stop in Saddam Square to buy some nuts. Yasser is sitting on a concrete block. – It was beautiful here once, he says. – Grass grew by the roadside, the streets were swept, no sewage flowing everywhere like now. Look, the centre strip there, it's a desert. All the green has gone.

Nevertheless, there is one flash of colour looming over the roundabout: an enormous painting of the president surrounded by scenes from Iraqi history, from martyrs on white horses and a full-bodied Scheherazade from the *Thousand and One Nights* to state-of-the-art military vehicles.

– That's the best thing we have in this town, Yasser says, pointing to the huge placard. – And we are very proud of our neighbourhood's name, he adds, to the great satisfaction of our two guides.

At the end of the book market there is a steamy teahouse called Shahbendar, a meeting place for authors, painters, sculptors and directors. I bump into a literary critic called Isam.

– Iraq is a theatre, he whispers. – Everyone plays their role. *We all love our president, and are prepared to die for him.* It would be madness to throw off the mask. To speak the truth is to be mad, he mutters between gulps of tea, all the time looking around casually. All Baghdad's teahouses have regular informers.

Isam's family moved from Palestine to Iraq in 1948. Being a Palestinian he is as vulnerable as all Iraqis. So it surprises me when he agrees to meet me at my hotel the next day.

We sit at the farthest end of the room. I ask why he wanted to meet me.

— Because I'm mad. Iraq is the kingdom of fear. No one will tell the truth when you are with your minder or other Iraqis they do not know. Few will even talk to you alone. For one single disastrous word you can go to prison for twenty years, for a disastrous word spoken to a foreigner you can disappear altogether. This country is one great shit-hole. Nothing moves on the surface, it just stinks. We need help to throw a large stone into the hole. That's what we're all waiting for; for something to happen.

Isam believes that most Iraqis are for the war. — It's not that we are pro-America. I'm a Palestinian and I hate Israel and America, and in spite of that I welcome Washington's army, to free us from the tyranny. Then they must leave Iraq to the Iraqis. Nevertheless, Isam fears that an American invasion will lead to civil war.

— The Shias and the Kurds know that it would be best to cooperate with the Sunnis and let bygones be bygones. I just hope the Americans will beg them not to indulge in acts of revenge. It all depends on the length of the war. Very few will take up arms if the regime falls quickly. Then they'll hide in their houses and later dance in the streets. But if the fighting is drawn out anything could happen.

Isam stirs sugar into his tea. – It's all over, he says, and glances around carefully. – The regime is finished. The secret police is less active than before. They don't 'hear' certain conversations. In January we started very carefully, just between friends, to discuss the situation. In our own homes, quietly. In February the conversations continued in the teahouses, still quietly, still carefully. That would have been impossible only a few months ago. It was very confidential and I saw the informers watching, but instead of denouncing us they closed their ears. To avoid problems when it all falls apart.

The literary critic predicts that the resistance will be small, that the Americans can more or less roll in to Baghdad. Many inhabitants might be armed, but few of them are prepared to fight for Saddam Hussein, he prophesies. – People hate him. Iraq has become a country of schizophrenics and cowards, a country where people fear their friends, their family, their own children. Once upon a time Iraq was the lighthouse of the Middle East, but thirty years of oriental Stalinism and twelve years of embargoes has crushed the country and its people.

Suddenly he grows silent and looks nervously to one side. A man in a pinstripe suit is sipping tea a few tables away. He is staring vaguely into space. The hotel spy! Who else? Isam decides it is time to break up. – Don't phone me again, he says quietly before leaving.

I meet him again at Shahbendar the following Friday. He says that in future we must only meet there. His wife had been beside herself with fear when she found out he had met a foreigner in a hotel. – We'll be killed, all of us, she'd cried. But not loud enough for the neighbours to hear.

Isam was the only Iraqi, apart from Father Albert, who

talked openly to me in the months before Saddam's downfall.

— Don't point, Aliya hisses whenever I point a finger at the portrayed president. — Don't look at him; look down or to the side. Don't talk about him, don't ask about him.

It is as though she believes he possesses some sort of magical power and can see, hear and feel if anyone pours scorn upon him. I wonder whether it is him or Aliya who has introduced the rule not to point at the president.

Aliya herself is allowed to talk about him. Every day she reads and translates his decrees. When I ask questions she cannot answer, she always says that Saddam Hussein will solve all in the best and wisest way.

Aliya was born to a middle class family and grew up in Baghdad in the 1970s. On the first page of every school book was a picture of the president and every lesson began with 'Long Live Saddam Hussein'. To Aliya, and to all Iraqi children, he was the great father. Parents took care not to talk disparagingly about him. If the children were to relay any critical remarks it could cost the family dearly.

Aliya was a good student and eventually secured a place at the prestigious English faculty at the university. From there she was employed as a translator by INA. Translating the president's speeches and decrees felt like meaningful work, surrounded as she was by posters, murals, mosaics, statues, impressions, bronze heads and photographs.

Until she started working for me this was her world. From knowing what to translate, word for word, now she has to be on guard. Assess the information she can give to me. When she is in doubt I can see her fighting herself. She wants to do a good job, as good as possible, but she treads warily and is careful not to betray her country. Not once does she suggest an illegal idea, or establish contact with someone risky or unofficial. Time and again I tell her what issues interest me. She nods but nothing happens.

– I'm working on it, she will say when I ask her to investigate something. On the whole our attempts are unsuccessful and I sometimes suspect her of not even asking. Sometimes she will phone in the evening and tell me enthusiastically that Saddam is on television, do I want her to translate the speech?

I always do; I am duty-bound to accept what is available. The entire spring is one big struggle: to do my job, meet people, discover how Iraqis live and what they really think. However, Aliya's innate meekness contributes to my sometimes escaping. Quite simply she is unable to keep up and lets me wander around on my own. Nevertheless, I seldom get more out of my time without her than with her. After three brutal decades the people have become their own minders.

Every Friday, since the very first one with Jorunn and Ali, I visit the book market. Usually I give Aliya the day off in order that I can go alone. I go to buy books and sit in Shahbendar and maybe find someone to talk to.

The Bohemian café is packed with people. Or rather, with men. It's like stepping into another era. The walls are hung with pictures of old Baghdad, sketches from street corners and markets. A 1950s wireless is attached to the wall, and over it the compulsory portrait. A little man rushes around replenishing the tea glasses.

One day a tall, bearded man approaches while I am chatting to a colleague. He addresses us in immaculate, almost aristocratic French.

Je m'appelle Haidar. Je suis peintre.

We invite the painter to join us for a glass of tea and touch on safe subjects: Iraqi art, Babylon, Paris, spring. I want to ask him all sorts of questions but hold back. He tells us he is not exhibiting at the moment; all his paintings are at home in the studio. That means we are precluded from seeing them as it involves visiting his home.

– They are abstract, in strong colours, yellow, red, green, orange. I paint what there is least of here, he says melancholically.

I see my old acquaintance, the literary critic, talking to a friend. He gets up and greets me courteously when I approach.

– I thought I might buy some books, I say.

– Are you interested in poetry? Mizhar asks. – Here is a collection written by a soldier during the Iranian war. Strong stuff.

The man has got up from the stool. In front of him on the ground lies a collection of books, most of them worn and well-thumbed. Mizhar sighs. – I myself am a poet, but at the moment I'm working as a proofreader and bookseller. One cannot survive as a poet. Would you like this book with epic poetry?

In Iraq all recently published books are politically correct and often deal with good overcoming evil. The hero conquering the enemy, Arabic identity and courage, the harshness of life under sanctions, the war against Iran and the Gulf War.

Two years ago Zabiba and the King *was published. It is about a woman, living in the century before Christ, and her loveless marriage. The king meets Zabiba and they discuss God, loyalty, love and the wishes of the people. In one scene Zabiba is raped, reflecting the American invasion of Iraq. The story ends with Zabiba's death on 17 January 1991, the day the bombs started to drop over Baghdad. The author is, allegedly, Saddam Hussein.*

A well-dressed man squats on the ground, leafing through

Mizhar's books. He is looking for a book by Sartre. — Existentialism is in keeping with our times. I have learnt a lot about myself; about the individual's need for freedom and society's limits, Latif says. He is a computer engineer. — It is difficult to keep abreast of developments. In twelve years Iraq has not imported a single scientific periodical. Look around — all old books. We haven't a clue about what has been written anywhere else since the Gulf War. Of course there are plenty of wonderful old books here, but I long for new ideas, he says. — I have read a bit about structuralism but I would really like to read some more.

One boy is looking for books about cloning. — I have heard that it is possible to clone humans, he says, but, like Latif, finds nothing about the subject.

— Iraqis have always craved books. They are our sustenance. Besides love they are all we need, the bookseller says, and recites one of his own poems, about a man who is dying of love but has not the courage to tell his sweetheart.

Traditionally the Iraqis were always considered the most inquisitive people in the Middle East. 'Egypt writes, Lebanon prints, Iraq reads', goes the adage. Before the war began in the 1980s the Iraqi population was the most educated in the Arab world. Now the educational system has collapsed and five million people have left the country, half of whom were highly educated.

The Kurd Jalal specialises in history. Displayed on a collapsible shelf are books about Mesopotamia — the land between the Euphrates and the Tigris, the Hanging Gardens of Babylon and the mythical Tower of Babel. — I buy cheap from old people and sell dear, Jalal laughs. — It's really rather sad. People sell off what they have been collecting during a lifetime, maybe for generations, for a few meals or some medicine for their grandchild's measles.

— The system, he says quietly — it's crushing us. Do you know our history? Do you know what has happened to this country? It's worse than a dictatorship, a lot, lot worse.

Suddenly Jalal disappears up the street, making a sign for me to stay put. When he returns he stuffs a book into my bag. — Read it, then you'll understand all. The author was . . . Jalal whispers and cuts his throat with a finger. — By the regime. Come back when you've read it, but don't show it to anyone. That could give me twenty years inside.

— Why do you take the risk?

— It is dangerous to live nowadays, no matter what. Go now.

I continue down the street, carrying the burning book. Behind each pile of books sits a bookseller, surrounded by a group of friends. Tea-sellers walk about with steaming pots and pour out glasses for a few dinar. The books lie around in the dust, but only the legal ones. Each book carries a stamp to show it has passed the censorship. It is illegal to sell uncensored books and doing so would result in a severe penalty — from six months to capital punishment, Jalal says. Those kinds of books are not spread out in the sun, but are hidden in back rooms and cellars.

Down some steps, in a tiny cubicle, is Rafik. He specialises in western literature. On his shelves are everything from T. S. Eliot's **The Wasteland** *to Hamsun's* **Mysteries**. *On the counter are Dante's* **Divine Comedy** *and Rafik's reading glasses. — Wonderful book, he says. I've got to 'Purgatory'.*

Rafik set himself up as a bookseller during the Iran–Iraq war. The owner was called up and asked him to mind the shop. After university lectures Rafik sat in the shop and read all day. The shop owner never returned from the war and Rafik took over. Now he's kept shop for fifteen years. — It is my soul. Here I live, here I suffer. As you know, life here is suffering. The books save me.

In another dusty basement, an elderly man sits behind a desk. He has brushed back his few remaining strands of hair. He has long, brown teeth and bags under his eyes.

— Have you got Iraqi literature in English?

The bookseller gets up slowly. He bends down, rummages

amongst the bottom rows and pulls out two books. One is Edwyn Bevan's classic The Land Between the Two Rivers *from 1917. — Here you can read what we once were, he says.*

The other book is called The Long Days. *— You must read it. It's about him, he says.*

— About who?

— About him. *The early years, the struggles, his development as a person.*

— Is it good?

The bookseller fixes his eyes on me. — It is required reading.

— Have you read it?

— No, but I've seen the film. I know what it's about, if you see what I mean.

The Long Days *was published in the 1970s and millions of copies have since been printed. It was given to all members of the Baath Party, and at party meetings it is the starting point for analysing a person's qualities.*

The story starts one afternoon on Rashid Street in Baghdad. A group of friends are waiting for a convoy of cars. 'The most reserved and sincere is Muhammed. He always listens attentively to whoever is speaking and stores the words in his head. There he has collected many secrets since childhood.' The character Muhammed is based on Saddam Hussein. The young men on the street corner are planning an attempt on the prime minister's life, a prime minister who 'oppresses and exploits the people'. The assassination of Prime Minister Abdul Karim Qasim was the start to Muhammed's, alias Saddam Hussein's, political career.

— We who are left are dying slowly, says the bookseller. — We live in an unspeakable nightmare. We need an earthquake. Everything must be uprooted. But it will cost dearly. I am an Arab and I am an Iraqi nationalist, and I hate the US and its world dominion, but I see no other way for Iraq. Let the American devils come and let's get it over with. But it could turn into the most

awful civil war; Arabs against Kurds, Muslims against Christians, Sunni against Shia. It will never, never be the same again.

The two customers nod. They are students, one of literature, the other of philosophy.

— In the 1970s this was a beautiful country. We had the best education system, the best healthcare in the Arab world. Oil gave us riches. In 1990 I had a Mercedes, says the bookseller. — Now I have these two legs.

— Anyhow, people no longer read, they don't study either. Look at these two, he says, and points to the boys. — They have come to look for textbooks, but won't find them. I have copied a few sheets, but look at the bad print. Anyway, they don't have time to read, they have to work.

Mansour has postponed his exams several times. — I must help my family and have started an outlet for spare parts, the literature student says. The philosophy student also has a small shop.

— What do you sell?

— What is it called? he says, and tries to find the right word.

— Scrap, the literature student cuts him off.

— The tragedy is that people no longer read. They have three jobs and no time for books. Anyhow, you need peace and quiet to read, don't you? That's not possible when life's all upside down. I used to read one book a day, now I can hardly manage one a month. People don't have the money either, and the libraries aren't operating. They have been emptied, says the bookseller. — By the employees. Some of the books you'll find here in the market.

The bookseller is starting to get nervous. We have been talking for a long time. — I've never spoken to anyone like this before. Here you are, take the books, go home and read.

When I get home I unpack the forbidden book the Kurd gave me. From Revolution to Dictatorship. Iraq since 1958. *Like tens of thousands of intellectuals, the author was murdered by the regime.*

The other book gives a description of Baghdad in the prosperous 7th century. 'Baghdad was the richest city in the world. The river banks were black with boats. They brought porcelain from China, spices from India, slaves from Turkey, gold-dust from East Africa, weapons from Arabia.'

The golden times are over. Neither pearls nor ivory make it to Baghdad now. Weapons, however, always find their way.

Said's visits become more infrequent, the room is already stuffed with knick-knacks, and besides, he doesn't have the time. The hotel gradually fills up. Word gets round that al-Fanar provides cheap lodgings and is nicknamed 'the peaceniks' hotel'. Here the foreign pacifists hang out, plan their campaigns, paint their posters, write their press releases and party at night. A profusion of organisations have made their way to Baghdad during the winter and spring of 2003. They organise conferences and projects, produce websites and paint banners. *Don't kill Iraqi children for oil.* Few editors are interested in articles about the activities of the peace movement in Iraq – mine is not, anyhow. The activists buzz round the Information Ministry like bees round a honey-pot, but their press releases are usually consigned to the wastepaper basket.

None of the peace activists are successful in attracting attention – until the human shields arrive in town. Now the journalists are doing the buzzing. From a newsworthy point of view they succeed where the others have failed. Owing to the high stakes, maybe? During February they arrive in Baghdad in buses, in cars and by air. The first bus that reaches Baghdad is given front page coverage in the Iraqi papers. Saddam Hussein welcomes them, via a comment to INA.

The new anti-war recruits throw wild parties and talk heatedly. Every morning they go out to inspect the installations they will protect with their own bodies. From time to time they mingle with the regime-organised demonstrations, shouting pro-Saddam and anti-Bush slogans in an inharmonious dance. The Western individuals have landed themselves in a difficult situation – travel and subsistence are paid by the Iraqi regime. I follow them for several days to try and understand what makes them tick.

We roll through the streets of Baghdad in two double-decker London buses. We are preceded by an outrider and two Iraqi policemen on motorbikes. People glance up and see a colourful collection of war opponents hanging out of the bus windows. Some of the passers-by wave back, others looked hurriedly down, as though the bus does not concern them.

– We are here to stop the bombs, stop Bush, says Teijo, a student from a technical high school in southern Finland. – I think we are playing an important role.

The twenty-two-year-old has a large rucksack and a sleeping bag in his lap. He is thin and pale, awkward like an overgrown teenager. Today he has left a soft bed in one of Baghdad's hotels to move in to South Baghdad Electricity Works.

– If the power is cut the purification plants won't work and several hundred thousand people will have to drink contaminated water. The fact that we are here makes it more difficult for the USA to bomb. To them the life of westerners is worth more than that of Iraqis.

The buses continue southwards, towards the outskirts of Baghdad. We pass military barracks hidden behind newly constructed sandbag walls, a bridge, and several buried positions, probably for anti-aircraft missiles.

At the electricity works Teijo and the other activists are confronted by a huge portrait of Saddam Hussein. The local workers greet the pacifists with resounding Saddam slogans. He is 'in their heart and soul'. A few of the pacifists unfurl a long banner: *No to war.* But when the workers with the posters of the president line up beside them, they quickly roll the banner up. – We are here for the Iraqi people, not for Saddam Hussein, is the watchword.

Fifteen human shields are expected to move in at South Baghdad Electricity Works today. Several have started to withdraw from the mission. A French boy, Asdine, was taken by surprise when he visited an Iraqi family. – Stop that nonsense, they told him. – We want war, we want bombs, so we can at last rid ourselves of our dictator.

Unlike Teijo, several of the human shields have informed the Iraqis that they do not want to protect the country's infrastructure, but rather lodge in orphanages and hospitals, which are not direct targets. This the Iraqi authorities try to prevent as the human shields are valueless to the regime if they install themselves in hospitals.

– We have started to feel the pressure. The men from the ministry were angry when they realised that so many had withdrawn, and they reminded us why we were here, one activist says, standing by and watching the fifteen who have found a bed each. – I'm starting to regret the whole thing. Maybe the Iraqis will chain us to the strategic targets, civilian and military, the day before the bombs start dropping. I don't think I want to be here any longer.

A sleeping bag under his head, Teijo has made himself comfortable on one of the camp beds that has been put out for the fifteen shields. He watches the others getting ready. This is where he will spend his days and nights, even when the bombs start to drop. – I am willing to accept what destiny might bring. If I doubt, I think about the Iraqis who have no choice. We Europeans can leave whenever we want, it is just a drive to the Jordanian border. They have to stay. It is bloody unfair. I hope thousands more shields arrive. Then it might be possible to stop Bush, Teijo says seriously. He is sitting up in bed. On the wall above him is a picture of the Iraqi president. I ask him what he thinks of sleeping under his watchful gaze.

– He's only a symbol of the Iraqi people. Beyond that I have no opinion about his politics. In Finland too we have portraits of the president on the wall.

I am silent. Is it my place to inform him about Saddam Hussein's harassment of the Iraqi people? About the dictatorship? That he cannot compare the Finnish president to the Iraqi. I feel like crying. Suddenly everything is so sad. The gangling, rather strange boy who has taken on this huge task touches me.

– What do your parents say? I manage to ask.

– They have asked me to return.

– Go home, I beg him earnestly. – Go while there is still time. You haven't a clue what will happen.

I have far overstepped the role of a reporter. Observe, report, write. Don't get involved, don't get caught up. Like an elder sister I feel responsible for this frail boy. As the only Nordic among the journalists I must look after this Finn.

– I hope I'll get home one day, is all Teijo says.

– The question is whether they have more use for us dead than alive when the bombs start falling. We have no guarantee that the Iraqis won't kill us and show us off. – Look what your bombs have done, says the activist on the bed beside him.

– This is starting to taste bad, he says. – Look around. On one side is a military warehouse, on the other side a bridge. The troops might be moved here. We might become Saddam Hussein's hostages. With all the media attention we have been given in Iraq, people might associate us with the regime, and what if that is toppled and there is civil war? On which side do people think we are?

– So why stay?

– I'm staying against my better judgement. Reason tells me to go, but my body says stay. It is pure Kierkegaardesque, he philosophises. On the stool by his bed the *Thousand and One Nights* lies opened.

I know the risk I am taking, but I am not frightened. If I die my death will be wonderful and if I succeed I will have rendered this country a great service, Scheherazade persuades her father, before she crawls in to the bloodthirsty king and starts the story telling, for a thousand and one nights.

Only time will tell whether the activists are as brave as she was.

As February draws to an end the foreign embassies are busy evacuating non-essential staff. Externally the barricades increase, internally they are emptied. The most absurd part of the evacuations are the sumptuous farewell parties.

The French ambassador has not yet recovered from the loss of the plentiful and laboriously collected wine cellar which disappeared during the first Gulf War. Hence *l'ambassadeur* gives a scrumptious reception overflowing with champagne and vintage wine. He is not going to fall into the same trap and, in anticipation of the war, has long since stopped reordering wine. As he says late that night, smiling: Now I can't give *même une toute petite reception!*

Janine and I have taught Aliya to toughen up and we now go around town without permission. A sunny winter's day, our goal is Baghdad's posh neighbourhood. Here we will try and discover whether they too are leaving the country.

We are admitted to Fatima's house. It is late morning but she is still pottering about in a pink velvet dressing gown embroidered with gold roses. Fatima and the children have packed necessities and are waiting for the husband to decide when the time has come to send them off to safety. Necessities represent an infinitesimal part of their belongings. The family live in a palace covering a thousand square metres. There are five bathrooms, in Italian marble, and the family have five children of school age. The enormous sitting room is empty; they very rarely entertain. The shelves in the library are bare.

— We haven't had time to buy any books yet, Fatima excuses herself.

The villa's sitting room windows are ten metres high, covered in thick brocade. Fatima is one of the few who, despite sanctions, has never wanted for anything.

— If you have money you can get hold of everything. Even scarce medicine; that comes in from Jordan, she explains while the maid serves coffee in tiny oriental cups. But not even the richest can buy freedom from the threat of American bombs. Furniture is being covered up, gates locked, cars driven away.

— To Jordan. We have relatives there. There is still time, but the war is getting close, Bush has made up his mind, she says resignedly, looking around the sitting room.

— This is not a safe place. The house is sound but there are many windows, and anyhow there are several military installations around here, Fatima sighs. A heavy lethargy weighs down the rich man's wife. She rarely leaves the house and her maid sees to most things. Not even the evacuation is decided by her. – Allah decides when our time on earth is up, but my husband will best know when we must leave.

Fatima's husband is a timber merchant and one of those who has earned enormous sums owing to sanctions, enabling him to build a palace in the al-Wasiriya district of town. Several of Saddam's confidantes have their mini castles here.

– That is another reason we don't feel safe here. Many of *his* men live here, Fatima confides in us, mimicking falling bombs with her hands. – Their houses will be attacked first.

At the fashionable restaurant al-Finjan, in Arasat Street, the owner Alaw sits with his wife Ani. We meet them a few hours after our rendezvous with Fatima.

Ani's hair is bleached and styled, her fingers full of rings, she wears an elegant reddish brown tweed coat and skirt. Her days consist of mornings in the beauty parlour, evenings at one of Baghdad's private clubs, and long hours at home.

– Life here is dreary, she wails. – It's so boring, nothing happens.

The upper-class wife is well aware that the boring days might soon be over, replaced by an excitement most people could do without. Now Ani's husband is trying to buy her and their son out of both boredom and the unwelcome excitement.

Last year he visited Germany and returned with the latest Mercedes. This year he brought nothing back. He had gone to apply for a residence permit for his wife and son. He knows that their sumptuous home, complete with DVD player, granite floors and European furniture will give little protection against bombs.

– In order to get a German visa I have to deposit 100,000 dollars in a bank as guarantee, Alaw explains. – And even having done that there is no guarantee that they will get the visa. If they don't get the visa there are two alternatives, a farm outside Baghdad, or Jordan. But I would prefer to get them out of the area altogether, to Europe, where it's safe.

In Shahbendar the three friends are saying their farewells. They smoke hookah and sip the house speciality: spiced citron pressé with sugar and boiling water.

Samir is off to Damascus the following day. Once in Syria he will try and obtain a visa for Europe. Samir is one of Iraq's promising young sculptors; the French centre of culture in Baghdad once exhibited his works. Most of all he wants to get to Paris, and his luggage includes twenty sculptures depicting the same theme: a fragile winged woman tries to take off, but her heavy, solid legs hold her rooted to the ground. The woman is fighting a dragon.

– My family are left behind, my mother, my sisters. It doesn't feel good, he says gloomily. – But I want to achieve so much and when I have a chance to escape the bombs then I'll grab it. What can an artist do in a war? All the galleries are closed, people try to sell their art, no one buys.

The friends too would like to leave, but can't. – I'll have to stay and paint war pictures, Haidar laughs. – When the war is over I will arrange a large exhibition, he dreams aloud, and refuses to let the seriousness of the situation take over. – True life is to make your wife happy, work a bit, dress elegantly, smell good, swan around town, discuss with friends. This is the philosophy of an Iraqi artist. You must not contemplate death, because life is not infinite.

— There is no point ruminating about war before it has even arrived, says the quiet Rafik. — War is in any case routine.

— In Iraq we are ready for war, like you are ready for winter, Haidar smiles.

The café buzzes with hushed conversations. Outside the door a boy is selling caramels. People give him money but leave the caramels. The beggar's brat cannot flee the bombs. He can only hope that someone will take him down into a cellar and hold their hands over his ears so he will not hear them.

The farewell party continues throughout the evening. The three artists have arranged to meet in one of Baghdad's better auction houses, not for the purpose of selling but to meet friends. Grasping a glass of tea and with the auctioneer's voice droning in the background, Samir whispers. — I am frightened for my father, who is an army officer, I am frightened of the bombs, I am afraid of the Shias and the Kurds, and the secret police, I'm frightened of everything. Sometimes even my own shadow scares me.

But in spite of worrying about the family remaining in Baghdad, he wants war. — Of course I would have preferred a velvet revolution. But assuming the war does not deteriorate into a bloodbath we will all be singing when the Americans arrive. — *Allons boire une verre* . . . Let's have another glass.

Samir guffaws. — What a happy day that would be!

His face darkens. — Unless all the glasses are broken.

In the hectic last days of February people try to get rid of non-essentials. If they are forced to flee, cash is better than crystal vases. Anyhow people need money to stock up on essentials: food, oil, petrol and water. At Baghdad's numerous auction markets supply far exceeds demand.

In a large, dusty square, men stand on crates calling out one item after another. A large collection of furniture and household goods lies all around, much of it well-used. Around the piles people gather; they either need something or want to get rid of something.

— You need to iron your shirt, the auctioneer calls. People laugh. In a town with limited recreational facilities, this is entertainment. But in spite of the jokes falling hard and fast, the iron remains unsold.

— Five thousand dinar, the auctioneer calls. — I'm starting at five thousand. A shamefully low price, it's worth a lot more. Any offers? Iraqi steel. Hard, immaculate.

No hands are raised, in spite of the price of around £1. For the moment, irons are an irrelevance. People buy drills and spades to dig wells in backyards, industrial tape to seal windows, sandbags to cover walls, warm blankets for bomb shelters, lanterns and lamps.

Some neighbours have come to see if they can find a second-hand generator. — It might come in useful if the electricity plants are bombed. We'll take turns using it so the whole street can benefit.

The two strapping men are the neighbourhood's representatives. But there are no generators for sale this evening. On the other hand, there is a dinner set in a pale blue pattern, over one hundred pieces, one with yellow roses and gold edges in delicate porcelain, some mirrors, scales, a radio, a TV, pots and pans in all shapes and sizes, stoves, stools, beds.

A woman runs her finger thoughtfully round the gold-edged flower service. Then she pulls her coat tighter around herself and walks on. Some children roar with laughter. They have found a pink swing to play on.

Duraid and his daughter Sera are sitting on a plush green sofa. They are waiting for it to be called up and hope someone will come and have a look. – We decided we didn't need it any longer. Anyhow, it has always been too big, and was in the way too, Duraid explains. He is employed as an engineer at a state-run factory.

The descending spiral began in 1980 when Saddam Hussein decided to attack Iran. The war lasted eight years and the costs were enormous both in the loss of human life and for the economy. The disastrous invasion of Kuwait followed two years after the peace treaty with Iran. UN sanctions seriously hobbled Iraq's economy. Following twelve years of sanctions and embargos the middle classes' purchasing power plummeted. Lawyers, engineers, doctors and teachers fought to make a living by taking on extra jobs, driving taxis in the evenings, or selling up old belongings. Auction houses sprang up like mushrooms. They jostled for place along the banks of the Tigris and in the course of a few years Baghdad's six large auction rooms increased to sixty.

– Everyone's waiting, no one is buying, one auctioneer sighs. – I have been calling out the same things week after week. When the stuff has been here five weeks people have to come and take it back.

Duraid and his daughter's sofa is called up. Total silence. The auctioneer tries in vain to entice people.

– Normally it would have been snapped up, Duraid sighs, having sold many belongings over the years. – But people don't want to replace their furniture now. Who wants to buy something that can be shattered to bits in a week or so, or that they might have to leave behind?

Nine-year-old Sera sits sulkily beside her father. She turns away when I speak to her.

– Be polite to the lady, Sera, her father says.

Sera shakes her head, folds her arms over her chest and looks demonstratively the other way. She mutters something into the ground.

– She is frightened of you, she thinks you are an American, the father explains.

– I am not from America, I say, and smile my warmest smile. But Sera is not susceptible to flattery.

– You look like one and you don't have to tell lies.

The father strokes Sera's head and explains that she dreads bombs and war. She has heard on TV that the bombs will soon start falling and that American soldiers will break into people's houses.

– She has changed recently, the father says. – She cries a lot and cannot sleep at night.

Suddenly Sera looks me in the eye.

– Why do you want to kill us?

– Most people don't want to kill anyone. Including the Americans. But some politicians want war, I try.

Sera looks at me sceptically.

– Come on, Daddy, let's go.

Sera grabs her father's hand without condescending to look at me.

– Are you prepared?

It is Janine. She has made all sorts of preparations; rented rooms in three different hotels, so that she has a bed irrespective of where she is when the bombs start to fall. The rooms are equipped with water bottles, tinned food, blankets, batteries, a generator and a bottle of whisky.

She instructs me to keep a ready packed bag by my bed, in case I have to leave quickly. The gasmask must be ready, the bulletproof jacket, a torch and some good shoes.

– You must buy water, Åsne, she says. Why haven't you

bought water? And you should book beds in several hotels, like me.

Making preparations has always been my weak point. I have however learnt to provide the absolute essentials: two of every cable for the satellite phone and computer, two of all chargers, batteries and torches. The remainder can all be got hold of.

I hadn't thought I would need gasmasks or safety equipment when I travelled to Baghdad at the beginning of January. Back then I had no plans to stay until the war started. Now that war is drawing near I am one of the few without safety gear. But unexpected help is close at hand. The Norwegian Embassy left twenty or so gasmasks, safety clothing, bulletproof vests and helmets when they closed down and went home. The kit was given to the Church Aid, the sole Norwegian aid agency still in Baghdad. I leave their offices with tens of kilos of kit which I throw into the cupboard. At last I can tell Janine that I am 'well prepared'.

— But do you know how to use the mask? she asks.

— No

— Didn't you learnt that on the survival course?

— Eh?

— You have been on a survival course?

I am probably the only journalist in Baghdad who has not attended a survival course. There they learnt how to don a gasmask and slip on safety clothing in a flash, how to measure the air's gas content, how to fall down during a possible attack, how to evaluate dangerous situations. Most editors would not send their journalists into crisis zones without such a course, but no one has sent me; I sent myself. Janine thinks I am playing with life and death, as though staying in Baghdad during the war is not playing with life and death, survival course or not.

Peter, *The Times*' photographer, who has been through every conceivable survival course, intends to teach Janine, Melinda of *Newsweek* and me to put on the gasmasks quicker. I include Tor from the Norwegian Church Aid who has been generous enough to supply both Aliya and Amir with masks from the Embassy. The Norwegian human shields are also given masks by the obliging aid worker.

Janine is loath to hold the session at her hotel, the al-Rashid, as people say there are cameras in all the rooms. If we were seen trotting around in gasmasks and survival suits we might be accused of plotting something. We go to al-Hamra, one of the other hotels in which Janine has rented a room.

We are taught how to drink wearing the mask, talk through the opening, change the filter, go to the loo. The suits are tight and uncomfortable.

If deadly gases are used, what are the chances of me being close to the mask and would I get it on in time? What about everyone else in Baghdad, the ones without masks? How long might it take for a Baath Party member with a gun to shoot me and confiscate my mask if a chemical attack occurred? I will probably never use it.

Days pass without my hoarding water bottles in my room. To book rooms in three hotels seems like a waste of money. I am happy in my little al-Fanar, at twenty dollars a night. There is an abundance of food in the markets and I see no necessity to hoard.

– I'll do it later on, I say to Janine.

– When the bombs start falling you'll have other things to do than to buy water. And then the bottles will cost a fortune.

After all it doesn't matter that I am not prepared, because on the last day of February it is all over.

— I can do nothing more for you, says Kadim.

— But . . .

— You must leave.

— But . . .

— Come back another time.

— The war is about to start, I would never get back in time, I object.

— What war? There won't be a war.

For the first time he does not help me. He wants rid of me. His desk is flooded with paper.

— You promised you would always help me, I try.

— But I cannot protect you any more. You have over-stayed your welcome; the immigration authorities have issued your marching orders.

Kadim pauses for a moment. — OK, fill in a new application, go to Amman and apply for another visa, and I'll help you. You'll be back in a week or two.

I complete the form but I know it's pointless. Kadim just wants me out of his way.

— Maybe Uday can help me, I ask Kadim.

— He can do nothing for you.

I have done my best to keep away from Uday, thinking out of sight out of mind. But I know he is in charge of who can stay and who has to leave. He recently called Janine and Melinda in to his office and asked if they were prepared, whether they had covered wars before, whether their survival gear was in order, whether they were frightened. I was not found worthy of a private audience with Uday. That same evening I enter the lion's den.

— Who do you think you are? Uday roars, when I express my wish to stay.

*

Life is looking gloomy as I leave for the airport in the morning. The question is – how to get back?

At the airport my state of mind is so low that even the most zealous attempts to extract bribes fail. Iraqi border guards will always find that papers are missing and consequently demand enormous sums. From me they do not get a dinar.

Two white overalls advance towards me. – Aids test, they say.

Everyone coming to Iraq must be tested for Aids. The tests are a joke; the blood vials are left unmarked on the shelves. Just another way of inconveniencing foreigners. The test costs a few dollars but the penalty for not having taken it is hundreds of dollars.

– I don't have Aids, I say gruffly.

– This is the rule.

– I . . . do . . . not . . . have . . . Aids.

I muster all the authority I can possibly come up with at seven o'clock in the morning. I couldn't care less about the two overalls. Actually I would *like* them to keep me back. That way I will miss the plane to Amman. They mumble something in Arabic, look at me, while I grunt back at them. Then they wave me on. A tiny triumph in all the misery. So that's how to escape bribes – by not giving a damn.

Someone asks me to come in to his office. This time it's the satellite telephone. I know, however, that my papers are in order. He asks me to sit and I crash down like a petulant teenager. I know people leave these airport offices masses of dollars poorer for fear of not being blacklisted.

– You'll have to pay, he says after a long period of silence.

– Eh?

— To take this telephone out with you.

— I have a right to take it out. Here are my papers.

— But you are missing—

— Are you insinuating that my papers are not in order? That the Ministry of Information has made a mistake? Let me phone and ask. May I borrow your phone?

The man sits there, gaping.

— Just a wee *bakhshish*, he begs. *Bakhshish* is the Arabic for a gift or tip. I give him five dollars and get up, ready to leave.

Half an hour later I am on the over-crowded morning flight to Amman.

I drive through Amman in a daze and check in at the best hotel in town – it is large and luxurious but depressing. I long for the grotty al-Fanar, shrill Mino and Said with his endless interior ideas. Once inside the room I even miss the tiny flies that accompanied Said's palm tree.

All is light and shining in Amman's Intercontinental. The beds have soft white duvets and pillows. A velvety dressing gown hangs in the cupboard, slippers are ready for use. Everything smells clean and pleasant, not a single cockroach in sight. There is a TV with numerous channels, room service, Jacuzzi, massage, fitness room, swimming pool, mini-bar. I am in the wrong place.

I ponder how to return to Baghdad. I can forget about the normal channels. The hotel is jammed with journalists waiting for a visa. Some of them have been waiting for months. Instant visas, however, accompanied by a pat on the back from the Iraqi embassy, are granted to the human shields. Once in Baghdad I am sure to escape the chains at the oil refinery.

After just an hour in Amman I show up at the shields'

enrolment office, on the fourth floor of a shady hotel near the bus station. My hair is dishevelled and my clothes are worn out. It is all important to look like a genuine shield.

I am met by a Jordanian who leads me to Shane. He sits wrapped in a woolly Afghan shawl. I feel like asking whether he had also acted as a human shield for the Taliban but resist the urge. Shane is coughing and pouring hot tea down his throat. His eyes are red-rimmed and his skin pale. Suddenly a wet sneeze erupts. Shane points to a chair and I try hard to look as miserable as him to impart the impression that I am one of them. That is not difficult after the frustrated, sleepless night.

I invent a story that I lay awake because of the Iraqi children who will soon be bombed by the Americans. As a precaution, and in case they see all the Iraqi stamps in my passport, I say I have been in Iraq as a volunteer with a team of Norwegian child psychologists. As I have already written about them I can adopt their story without difficulty.

Shane says I can go on the next bus.

– It will be departing in a few days; we just have to fill it up. We are expecting a few more shields. It might be the last bus to Baghdad before the war. But you'll have to see the boss first, she must give you the OK. That shouldn't be a problem, Shane says encouragingly, before another coughing fit overtakes him.

The boss is a gruff British woman. She informs me about all that might happen in Baghdad. The danger of chemical attacks, the danger of being taken hostage, the danger of being chained to military installations. She also tells me that most of the shields are now on their way out. That I know already.

— The party is over, Lydia says. — The mood has changed. None of the shields live in hotels any longer, but spend all their time, night and day, at the installations they are protecting.

I answer that I am prepared to take the risk. Lydia accepts me as a human shield, takes my passport, and asks me to sign a document saying that I am informed of the dangers of going to Baghdad and that I am acting on my own responsibility.

— What is your room number? she asks. The majority of the shields live in the hotel while waiting for departure. They share rooms at fifty pence a night.

— I'm staying with friends, I stutter. Genuine shields do not stay at the Intercontinental.

She asks me to return the next day, but the next day there is no news, nor the day after. An increasing number of shields return from Baghdad. I am nervous that some of the Norwegians might walk through the door and spot me. But something else nearly gives me away. Because I am depressed and my energy levels are low I indulge myself in the luxury of an hotel driver. I normally ask him to wait some way off during my daily trips to the shield office. One day the driver gets nervous because I have stayed so long in the shady hotel and he comes to look for me. One of the employees knocks on Lydia's door while I am there.

— Your driver is here, he says.

I bundle the uniformed driver down the stairs in a jiffy, hoping no one has noticed him, before returning to Lydia.

— We are having problems with the Iraqis, is all she says. — They are not happy with our discipline. Suddenly many don't want to be at the electricity works, but at orphanages and hospitals, and the Iraqis won't accept that. They aren't actual targets and they feel stitched up.

– Ah, but I really want to be at an electricity plant, so they'll have no problems with me.

I return to their headquarters every evening to await some news. One evening I get into conversation with an older woman who has just left Iraq.

– It's no joke any more, she says. – They'll bomb, no matter what. Don't go, she insists, and asks what I do for a living. I tell her the same made-up story.

– My dear, she says. – Surely you can do something better in life than chain yourself to a bomb target?

The next morning at last Shane takes our passports to the embassy. He has mustered a group together and we are off as soon as the visas are issued. The same afternoon I turn up at his office and realise that something is not right.

– Everyone got a visa, except for you, he says accusingly. – They said you are a journalist. Are you?

– No, not at all. It must be a mistake, I say, and disappear out of the door and down the road to my waiting driver. The game is up. The Iraqi Embassy can't be fooled. I am in their archives.

I pass my days in front of the TV. The Security Council negotiations are like a thriller that keep me glued to the screen. I switch from BBC to CNN or Sky News. In Baghdad they demolish al-Samoud missiles but the Americans say 'too little, too late'.

I try everything to get back – via humanitarian visa, cultural visa, business visa. Soon there is no employee left in the Iraqi Embassy that I have not tried to bribe. Well, not me personally, but Muhammed, the driver who drove Jorunn, Bård and me to Baghdad one January morning long ago. He says he needs five thousand dollars to sort it all out, OK, I say, but to no avail. The Iraqi Embassy is quite simply not issuing visas these nervous March days.

One evening I meet Tim in the hotel bar. His speciality is the Balkans, and we have both written books about Serbia. After September 11 he realised he would have to find new hunting grounds, and some weeks later we met by chance on a plane to Dushanbe. Once in Afghanistan we collected stories together, about the donkey smuggler, the child commandant, the veiled TV star. Like then he is working for *The Economist* and the *New York Review of Books*.

— I wrote a whole article about Afghan donkeys when I got home, he laughs. — That's the article I've received most praise for ever!

He is off to Baghdad, having waited ten months for a visa. We agree to meet in the swimming pool before his departure next morning. What a life!

Tim's travelling companion is none other than Bob. Actually, that is not his real name. We know each other from Afghanistan; I remember him as a persistent reporter, always on the lookout for 'serious fighting' or a scoop. I have not seen him since leaving Kabul. He asks me how the book I was writing got on, where he features in the chapter about Khost. I tell him that I changed his name.

— Bob! Bob! You called me Bob?

— What's wrong with that?

— When I've turned into a chap called Bob, I know exactly how you've described me. Bob, bob. You could have given me another name.

— What? Maximilian? Alexander? Bob suits you.

We all oversleep for the swimming pool meeting and the next time I hear from Tim and Bob I am standing outside the Iraqi Embassy waiting for my bribes to bear fruit. They phone as they cross the border, before the mobile phone signal disappears.

— Dinner at Nabil's tomorrow, they tempt me

— Shut up! I'll be there before you know.

Nearly every day I phone Kadim at the press centre. On the rare occasions when he answers, he says: Patient. You must be patient.

— Then I'll phone again tomorrow, I persist each time.

— No, not tomorrow. Phone in a week.

When I phone a few days later he again asks me to contact him in a week. I realise he is never going to get me a visa.

A French photographer gets a tourist visa. Iraqi Airways is the tour operator. There must be a group of a minimum of five and you have to pay for a week-long trip. During the mornings there is compulsory sightseeing, the afternoons are leisure time. The programme takes in Ur, Babylon, Mosul, and Baghdad.

It is unbelievable. But several journalist colleagues go as tourists. A few of us decide to try the same tactic.

Most people just laugh.

— A week? And when that's over? Can you book a two-week excursion too?

Others think we are mad.

— What happens when they find your cameras? Holiday in Hell. Get serious. The Iraqi regime is not to play with.

Eventually there are enough of us to make up a group. Iraqi Airways makes us fill in some forms, curiously simple by Iraqi standards: name, address, occupation. One of us writes architect, another nurse, a third teacher, a fourth firefighter, ballet dancer, model, factory owner – the choice is yours. Strangely enough, we are not required to sign papers saying we enter Iraq at our own risk. I venture to ask who issues the visas.

– The Ministry for Culture, the man behind the counter answers.

– So it is not handled by the Foreign Ministry?

– No, that's not necessary. After all, you're only going on holiday.

The situation is absurd. The world's press is kicking its heels, but the tourist visa is issued in a couple of hours. While we sit in the offices of Iraqi Airways, the fax with our permissions clatters in from Baghdad. The next hurdle is the embassy in Amman. Wonders of wonders, the applications are passed. It appears this tourist office operates independently of the war, as if they have not taken in the fact that the attack will most probably start during the tour's first days. While we're shuffling around Ur, for instance. When one of the Americans asks what will happen to us if the war starts, I stamp on his foot and hiss with my eyes: Let's not start making problems.

The mild one behind the counter just says: – If it gets that bad, why not just leave.

The bus departs the following evening. The kind man even makes a list of our hotels so the driver can pick everyone up individually. He gives us some brochures on sights to visit. At the bottom of the brochures are the words 'Have a Nice Trip!' 'Trap' might be better.

As I leave Iraqi Airways Muhammed phones.

– Your visa is here!

A real journalist's visa, with the right to work, write, transmit and photograph. The group is large enough to go without me.

– Five thousand dollars, Muhammed says when I meet him.

— Five thousand!

— Wasn't that the sum we agreed on?

— Yes, but that was two weeks ago. Now I've spent half of that on hotel bills.

— You don't want to pay?

— That was the sum we agreed on when you said you could get a visa the same day. Two weeks ago! Now you're only getting half.

Muhammed looks at me sadly, as if I have cheated him.

— If you don't pay, I'll have to, he says, eyes fixed on the ground. — These men are dangerous.

I pay it all, of course. My travelling funds suddenly shrink. Back at the hotel I wave my visa at all those still waiting.

An email winks at me when I turn the computer on. 'Dear Friend', it says. I shudder as I read:

> don't come asne, this is a death trap and we are all
> prepared down to the last man.
> you won't be prepared for it.
> i would stay put and safe.
> but if you want to come DO IT FAST.
> i can't advise you – it is your life. be careful
> love
> janine
>
> ps – i am in room 1301 or 330 of palestine hotel
> now

It is pitch black when the jeep pulls up in front of the hotel. A bell boy carries my suitcase. Muhammed puts it in the boot. We leave the well-lit streets and turn towards Baghdad. In time.

During

– My uncle lives in Baghdad. If it gets dangerous he'll come and fetch you. He lives in one of the safest areas of town, just phone him if you're frightened.

Muhammed is staring fixedly at the road ahead. Dawn is approaching. The desert is rushing past us, its colours changing from greyish black to shimmering brown, from blue to violet, until it crackles into golden as the sun sends its first rays over the sand. The hard-won visa burns in my pocket.

– He has a large family.

– Good.

– He has stored food and water for months.

I lose the thread of Muhammed's conversation. Exhausted after sleepless nights, I try to sort out my thoughts but they are all tangled up. If I had been able to draw them I might have got them into some sort of perspective: straight thoughts, crooked thoughts, crumpled thoughts, stuttering thoughts, stabbing thoughts, hurtful thoughts, raw thoughts, fearful thoughts. But if I had scribbled them down one by one they would have ended up one black lump. They lie on top of each other, with no air in between. It is impossible to pry them apart and think of them individually, in spite of the simple question: Is it right to go back to Baghdad now?

Until I got the visa, I didn't think about the danger of returning. I had never really considered whether I actually had the guts; I just wanted it so badly.

My visa had been delivered by the embassy's afternoon shift. That same night Muhammed was driving an empty car to Baghdad to fetch some of the Reuters team. He would leave Amman at three in the morning to be at the border by daybreak. Then he would get to Baghdad by noon and be back at the border before dark.

— I'll pick you up at three, Muhammed said when I got the visa.

— I don't know, I said.

— You don't know?

— No. Maybe I don't want to go to Baghdad.

— But you've just paid five thousand dollars for a visa!

— But I'm not sure I've got the guts.

— You should have thought of that before.

I took a walk around the hotel to find someone to talk to. Someone who could make up my mind. Of all people, I bumped into Bob.

— I thought you'd gone! I exclaimed.

— Yes, but they pulled me out. Security reasons. Damn. They are thinking of pulling out Melinda too. Do you care for a drink in my room?

— I have to pack.

— Where are you going?

— I got a visa.

— When are you going?

— I don't know if I am.

— Come and have a drink when you've made up your mind.

A few hours later I was sitting in his suite. The table was covered with glasses of gin, ice cubes and a small bottle of tonic. The television was showing pictures from the Azores, where Bush, Blair and Aznar were holding their last meeting. It was clear that war was unavoidable.

Three frustrated people sat watching: Bob, who once again was missing out on 'some serious fighting', the Magnum agency photographer, Alex, and me. One of the world's most famous war photographers, Alex was depressed because he had no visa. Every hour that passed his grief increased as he thought about the photos he would never take. Myself, I was not only frustrated but falling apart with doubt. I knew that if I went to Iraq now, I would not be able to get out until the war was over.

My two colleagues on the sofa were of no help. In my situation they would not have hesitated. I needed to talk to a rational being, not someone sitting beside me drinking gin and tonic.

I couldn't phone my parents, if I spoke to them I could never go. I couldn't phone my sister, brother, friends. They had already asked me not to go.

It was around midnight. Bob replenished the glasses and zapped the remote control. All the channels showed the same: the run-up to war.

Suddenly I thought of someone I could phone. I dialled the number and heard shouting and the clatter of glasses through the receiver.

— I'm at the London Book Fair.

— Do you have two minutes?

I outlined the pros and cons as succinctly as possible.

— I just don't know if I dare risk it, I said finally.

There was a long pause.

— The question is: Do you dare risk not going?

The sun is beating down. It hurts my eyes and burns its way into my head. I rummage around for my sunglasses, roll down the window and watch the desert hurtling towards me, pale brown sand everywhere. I sit half asleep behind the dark glasses. Muhammed too has strayed into his own meditation, and tears along the straight road at 100 miles per hour.

— Iraq, he suddenly says, and points towards a building on the horizon. I force myself to wake up, straighten the seat back. Ready.

On the border we meet the first journalists. On their way out.

— Nothing in the world could make me stay in Baghdad now, a colleague says, clearly relieved to have reached the Jordanian border. — The attack might start at any moment. Three thousand cruise missiles day and night. Saddam could retaliate with chemical weapons — he might take us hostage, bring us down with him.

Impatiently, he waits for the exit papers, as if he cannot leave Iraqi soil soon enough. I have handed over my entry visa to be stamped. I feel stupid, like a complete idiot who does not understand what danger is; so dense that I cannot see death when it comes. My papers are stamped first.

The customs officers search the jeep then give it the OK. Muhammed jumps in, describes an elegant turn on the gravel, stops in front of me, leans over the seat and opens the door with a click. I jump in and wave to my colleagues at the border station. Have a nice trip to Amman!

From the bench by the sunny wall they wave back lazily, shake their heads and continue their conversation.

I glance up at the familiar portrait that welcomes us to Iraq. There are not many to greet this Monday morning. Muhammed and I are driving almost alone against the tide. Not only journalists are leaving the country. Cars laden with carpets, bags, pots, clothes and people flee Baghdad.

In the middle of the desert there is a petrol station and a crossroad. This is where the motorway from Baghdad splits in two. One road continues to Jordan, the other to Syria. There is a huge queue for petrol. Three Persian carpets are tightly rolled up on the roof of the car in front. On top of them several cardboard boxes have been tied down. Inside the car five people sit squeezed together between suitcases, crates and boxes. A suit hangs from the window and a bag of lemons lies squashed under the seat. I ask Muhammed to translate.

– We're going to Syria to stay with some relatives until this is all over. My wife is about to give birth so Baghdad is no place for us, Jasir says.

The mother, an older woman, draws heavily on a cigarette, all the while fingering the packet. – Whatever happens, Allah decides our destiny, but sometimes we have to give him a hand, she sighs.

The queue moves slowly, the cars several rows deep. Some have come to hoard, others to fill up and get away.

– The petrol price is the only thing that hasn't changed in the last days, says Muhammed. It still stands at under ten pence a litre but it is harder to get hold of.

– I have four hundred litres in my garden, in a large tank. I dare not hoard more – what if it explodes?

Muhammed is chuffed that his driver service has increased in value. – Now it costs seven hundred dollars per person to get to Amman from Baghdad, he says. – Tomorrow it will go up again, and during the war the price will rocket up.

He laughs and gives a convincing impersonation of someone shooting into the air. – Fighting, he says. – Big fighting.

I turn away. A couple of buses carrying Jordanian youths with Iraqi scholarships are on their way out. Like other countries, the Jordanian authorities have asked their citizens to leave Iraq.

In yet another crammed car is a family that has come the same way as us – from the Jordanian border. The family was denied entry. – We are without visa, but I have papers showing that I have business in Akaba, in Jordan, look, here they are, the father tells us. – They wouldn't accept them and turned us back. Now we're going to try Syria.

The majority who flee Baghdad go there. It is the only one of Iraq's neighbours which will allow entry without a visa. The borders to Saudi Arabia, Kuwait and Iran are closed. In the border areas, the no-man's-land between Iraq and Jordan, refugee camps are being planned. The Iraqis might come here but no further. When Muhammed and I passed by in the early morning hours, the desert was still naked. All we saw were a couple of men measuring the ground.

– The majority have decided to stay. But many will panic when the bombs start falling, and then it might be too late, a lady on her way to Damascus says. – Yesterday I said good-bye to my relatives. We just sat and cried. No one has a clue what will happen. Do you know, on the way out of Baghdad I saw two collisions. People can't even concentrate on driving. That's how it is to live under the threat of bombs, she sighs, still a hundred or so cars away from the pumps.

The afternoon is drowsy and hot when we finally arrive in Baghdad. The familiar cacophony of horns, bells and car engines wakes me up. At the Ministry of Information total chaos reigns. A long queue of journalists try to settle their accounts. If their bills haven't been signed they get no exit stamp. Mister Jamal, a thin, toothless man, who always walks around with a suitcase full of money, is stressed. He counts and lisps and bickers and counts. The queue moves at a snail's pace. No one knows Jamal's background, but we are certain he guards a secret. He has no fingernails. He counts notes with soft fingertips. Has he been tortured? Has he spoken against the regime? Or been punished for pilfering the funds?

This is not the day for speculation. Correspondents from leading British and American newspapers are about to leave the country.

— You should go too, they tell me.

— But I've just arrived.

We queue for the same bureaucrats. They to leave, I to stay. People rush past each other, wait side by side, dodge the queue, push and plead. Once again my details are recorded, once again the telephone is registered, again the seal is broken, again I promise to use it only at the Ministry. This time, however, no one asks for a list of places I want to see or people I want to meet. And no one bothers to give me a minder.

The ministry seethes with panic, from the rulers on the eighth floor to us lowly subjects on the first. From the floors above us furniture is pulled, pushed and carried down the stairs and out onto the backs of lorries. Archives, computers, shelves and boxes, everything goes – God only knows where. The Ministry of Information is high on the American list of targets.

— Åsne, you must leave, Peter, *The Times*' photographer, mumbles in my ear. – Please, leave!

Panic is starting to overtake me. I am given the opportunity to leave with some colleagues the next morning. But I have to write an article first, just one. I couldn't have come all this way in vain. It takes hours to complete the registration. In reality that means I can't leave the next day, the departure procedure would take just as long. I am fooling myself. Then I see him – and he me. Kadim. Who wouldn't give me a visa.

– How did you get back in? he asks, grabbing my arm and looking at me darkly.

I don't answer. – Everyone's leaving, I say instead.

– You bought a visa, he snorts.

– Well, what was I to do?

– I tried to phone your hotel room in Amman all day yesterday and all day today, to tell you that the visa was ready. How much did you pay?

I shrug my shoulders. – A lot.

– You were stupid, mine would have been free. Why didn't you trust me? I said I'd send you a visa.

– But it dragged on for so long, I excuse myself, as if I've been naughty. – Anyhow, I will probably leave tomorrow. I don't want to be the only one left here.

– Hardly anyone is leaving. It'll be all right, Kadim says. His voice softens. – Are you frightened? Do the bombs scare you? Think of all the Iraqi children who aren't afraid. We Iraqis are never afraid. Look, here's my phone number. If you're frightened, come and live with me. I have a wife and five children who can look after you, he says, and hands me a slip of paper.

Bomb-filled nights at home with Kadim. I feel a story coming on. – *The Bureaucrat of Baghdad*. I feel a bit safer. Or would he hand me over to bandits when the time comes?

From round a corner, Janine comes walking towards me.

— So you came, she says. — Welcome.

Janine is awaiting the decision of *The Times*' editor-in-chief. Just this morning the MOD in London had summoned representatives from leading British newspapers and TV stations and urged them to withdraw all personnel from Baghdad. They had to expect chemical weapons, hostage-taking, or worse, being chained to military installations as human shields. Besides, the bombing campaign — *Shock and Awe* — would be harder, faster and more awesome than anything ever before.

The majority of those leaving today have been ordered out by their employers. It is hardly encouraging to see the large TV companies pack up crates and cables and go. Like being abandoned.

First I need a place to stay. My beloved al-Fanar is out of the question. There is a choice of three hotels: al-Rashid, al-Mansour and Palestine. Most journalists have until recently lived in the enormous al-Rashid, but now this has an air of danger about it. At the entrance a sign proclaims '*More than a hotel*' and rumour has it that it really is more than a hotel. Under the enormous structure there are, allegedly, secret tunnels, passages and surveillance systems. The hotel is an obvious target.

The second best hotel, the concrete colossus al-Mansour, is situated between the Ministry of Information and the Sinak Bridge. The very fact that the Ministry and the bridge are targets prompts the remaining journalists to leave al-Mansour and crowd into Palestine, a high-rise opposite the Presidential palace, and the least unsafe, according to rumours. Everything is based on rumour these days. They begin as small whisperings, a light tinkle in the corridors, then turn into a gentle breeze which flaps around receptive heads, until the flood of words blows up to a hurricane, raging in people's ears. – Have you heard? Is it true? Will we die?

Hotel Palestine looks impressive and proud from a distance, surrounded by palm trees and gardens. A large swimming pool is placed under the shade of the trees, but the water is muddy, a sort of greenish brown slime. The bottom is covered by earth and sand and the pool walls are marbled with green algae. A rotten stench hits the nostrils of any passer-by. In the garden weeds flourish among the flagstones, the lawns are brown and the beds flowerless. Under a faded canopy there is a large outdoor grill, but a lot of time must have passed since lambs and oxen were barbecued here.

– No room, a receptionist informs me.

– So where should I stay?

– No room.

I know he is lying. There are hardly any guests left. He wants money. I am about to produce a couple of hundred dollars when Jean Paul from *Le Nouvel Observateur* comes to check in. He makes a big fuss when he hears about the extra money and – hey presto – there are no rooms at all.

Over the stone floor Janine approaches like a whirlwind, photographer, driver, porter and interpreter in tow.

– They have ordered me to leave, she bursts out, clearly exasperated. – We cannot tell you all we know, they whispered down the receiver. The war will be awful, the editor told me. I have never heard him so serious, so determined.

She looks me straight in the eye.

– Think twice.

– Yes, I will . . . I stammer.

– Take care, she says, and hugs me. – I'm actually quite

relieved. Now I don't have to make the decision. You know, I'm getting married in August. Take my room, she offers, and slips me her key. The receptionist seems like he wants to protest; there will be no extra money for him now.

My room has blue walls, a red carpet and a pervading smell: unwashed, smoke-saturated, sewers, decay. The wall to wall carpet seems to have a life of its own. The bathroom tiles are cracked and, like 707 al-Fanar, the loo leaks constantly. Like its predecessor, 734 Palestine has one advantage, a balcony. High enough to command a view, but not too hellish in case of power cuts, when stairs are the only way up and down. The bottom floors are the most popular, it feels safer living close to the ground. But from the seventh floor I can see the whole town, and best of all I have a view over to the Presidential palace on the opposite bank of the Tigris. An area covering several square kilometres, where *he* allegedly keeps lions and tigers, deer and watchdogs. If the place blows up I'll be the first to know. If I'm still conscious, of course.

At last I can sit down and write. Within the blue walls I concoct a missive about the mood in Baghdad, the people fleeing, the ministries emptying. I need to go to the Information Ministry to send it and hitch a ride.

The Ministry is almost empty. The large equipment-laden crates have been driven away, the TV companies' satellites are gone, but no one has bothered to take down the tents. In the darkness of the evening they have been left to face the wind and the bombs. The corridors, once seething with voices and the sound of telephones, are silent and empty. Janine's office is locked. The vociferous Spaniards next door have gone. The beautiful correspondent from CNN Turk, who got the name Turkish Delight, has bolted her door. ABC has gone, NBC has gone, so have CBS and CBC. Even the tea man, Abu Ali, has taken his hot-plate and made himself scarce. There is a padlock on *Newsweek*'s door, but Melinda is still around. Michelle, the Sky reporter, is sniffling outside her door. She has decided to go and cries for the colleagues she leaves behind. She barely sees me through her tears.

— Are you back? she breathes.

— Came this afternoon.

— I'm leaving at dawn — can't bear it any longer.

My steps resound in the corridor and I reach the offices of RTL, where my satellite telephone has been locked up. Antonia had to guarantee that it would remain in her office at all times.

— It won't be for much longer. Every morning I fear that the equipment is gone and the office sealed. They don't ask any more. They'll grab what they can when they see the end coming, Antonia whispers. Walls have ears in the temporary offices of the Information Ministry.

— Are you staying? I ask.

— Of course, she says, and applies a last layer of powder to her cheeks. — I haven't bribed, begged and fawned for the last two months in order to leave when it all starts.

Her brows are oval arcs and her eyelids get the latest Christian Dior treatment. — Remember to lock up, she chirps, while putting brushes, pencils, powder-puff and mirror back into her bag before rushing up to the roof to deliver her live report to Cologne.

My satellite telephone refuses to work. — It's impossible, says an Italian, frantically pressing the repeat button. What's wrong? Have the Americans jammed the sky? Yet another argument to go home. What's the point of covering the war if I can't send anything? The clock ticks towards deadline. No doubt the desk is waiting and wondering what has happened to my article. I phoned from Amman the day before and said I would try and send something. At home no one knows that I actually got in. They'll only know when they see the article in the inbox.

It feels strange to sit by Formica tables outside the Information Ministry again. They are covered with thick layers of dust, the cables are gone. Whereas there used to be a huge competition to bag chairs and tables, and many had to resort to sitting on bricks while writing, now only the Italian and I try to send our messages into the spring evening.

Ah. The whir from the satellite sounds like the most mellifluous bells. There is contact. In a few seconds thousands of words are transmitted to the waiting newsroom.

I sleep like a log after the night drive through the desert. While I rest, America's president appears on TV screens around the world. *Saddam Hussein and his sons must leave Iraq within 48 hours. Their refusal to do so will result in military conflict commenced at a time of our choosing.* Behind him are portraits of his wife and daughters. *For their own safety, all foreign nationals, including journalists and inspectors, should leave Iraq immediately*, he continues.

The speech has an effect, if not on the Iraqi president, then on the stragglers, who leave this Tuesday morning. I give myself one more day. Will just write one more article.

I look for Aliya. No Aliya, they say at the Information Ministry, and give me a new minder, Rawda, who speaks French. Her hair is coloured orange and her eyes are pale. She is distant and cool, and makes me miss Aliya. Rawda uses the correct *vous* form of address and repeats the jaded phrase that I can do what I want, we just have to apply first.

– This is no time for applications, I say curtly. I have learnt that it sometimes pays to be gruff, and haul her out of the Ministry. On the street I hail a taxi before she has a chance to react and ask the driver to take us to the nearest school. There I ask her to inquire of the headmaster whether we can talk to the pupils. Of course we can't. We must have permission.

I know the procedure. Nothing is possible. So I try a bit of common sense.

– In a few days the bombing of Baghdad will most likely start, I say to the headmaster. – Bush is portraying the Iraqis as enemies. By turning you into demons he tries to whip up support for the war. Many people, including many Americans, do not want this war. By letting them know about the individuals, like these schoolgirls, their teachers, people with real faces, it can wake people up and get them thinking: How can we kill these people? But you won't let me. You are missing out in the propaganda war.

I can see that they are thinking hard as my little speech is being translated by Rawda. Her eyes blink nervously, but she goes on. In the end the headmaster says OK.

While I am interviewing the girls the headmaster, three teachers and the school caretaker pay close attention. That's what it's like doing interviews in Iraq. I have got used to it and the interviews are just a source of simple information. How much food have they hoarded? Have their houses been fortified? Will they be coming to school tomorrow?

The schoolgirls have learnt how to defend themselves in case of an attack: In the event of bombs or missiles; throw yourself on the ground.

– First of all you must open the windows, one of them explains. – So they don't shatter.

— But if it is a chemical attack, then we must close the windows, another girl interrupts. Her friends continue: You take a piece of cloth, dip it in water, pour salt on it, lots of salt, and hold it in front of your nose and mouth.

The girls talk animatedly about the safety training they've done: How to clean wounds, bandage fractures, put out fires, secure windows. The seriousness of the matter cannot overshadow their enthusiasm to share their knowledge with a stranger.

The conversation turns out to be less trivial than I had feared. I am even allowed to accompany one of the girls home.

— See you tomorrow, they cry happily to each other at the gate.

— I hope the town won't be completely ruined, Marwa sighs when she has taken her place on the school bus. Through the windows she looks out at heavily laden cars leaving town, empty shops, windows covered in strong plastic sheeting, and not least military positions on the street corners. They look unassuming, the sandbags reaching no further than the soldiers' hips.

— We will continue our schooling irrespective of the bombs. We've been through this before.

Her words exactly match the party propaganda: Iraqis will resist and eventually defeat the enemy.

The fifteen-year-old jumps off in the al-Dourrin district. Here the alleyways are so narrow that cars cannot pass. The roads are not tarmaced and children run barefoot in the gutter. Women in long shawls steal by. Marwa opens the door to a traditional Baghdad house — a covered yard in the centre, surrounded by rooms on one floor and an attic above. The windows are covered in plastic sheeting, string and tape. The attic is packed with sacks of rice, flour and beans. Like other Iraqis the family has been given three months' worth of rations in advance, in case the war lasts.

Marwa lives here with her mother, father, four siblings, uncle, aunt and three cousins. Her mother has recently given birth, the aunt is seven months pregnant. The atmosphere in the house is resigned.

The father delivers his required speech of support for Saddam Hussein. Then come the worries and the questions. – Why the Spaniards, he suddenly asks. – I wonder what in the world we have done to them? We have always been on excellent terms with Spain. I understand that the Americans and British are against us, but the Spaniards? he wonders, and alludes to Jose Maria Aznar's backing of the coalition forces.

To supplement her daughter's first-aid wisdom the mother has a few simple remedies that she used during previous attacks.

– Cotton wool in the children's ears, says Rana. – When the bombs fall the explosions that accompany them can drive you crazy. I'll stop the children's ears with cotton wool so they won't be frightened. And I've bought sleeping pills and calming extracts so they can get lost in dreams, away from the awful events, she says while breast-feeding the youngest child.

– We're not thinking of fleeing, says the father. – We'll stay at home and take care of each other. Our relatives' houses outside Baghdad are already overflowing and we don't want to be a burden to them. So where could we go? To a refugee camp in the desert? No, we'll stay here and see it out.

Najih has a little clothes shop. Trade has been slow lately. – People don't buy dresses any more. I can understand that.

Who on earth is thinking of dressing up? People need their money for food, water and heat.

Marwa listens to her father as he talks. She sits quietly on the floor, a black-and-white-patterned shawl tied under her chin. From time to time her eyes wander. Her school-bag is still on the floor beside her.

When we are about to leave she pulls her books out. She starts her physics homework for next day. 'Movement, vibrations and oscillations' is the heading of the new chapter. It could be her last homework for some time. But in the months to come there might be an abundance of movement, vibrations and oscillations.

In the parking lot I meet Amir. He freezes when he sees me. – Miss Hosna! What are you doing here? Why have you come back?

The huge driver's eyes are panicky.

– It'll be all right. Relax, it'll be over soon, I say.

When I return to the hotel the majority of those who had considered leaving Iraq have left. Only the fearless remain. Those in contempt of death. Or the idiots? A handful of American journalists have boycotted their editors' demand to leave and have stayed on, with the excuse that they had not paid their bills and would consequently be arrested at the border. To be cooped up in jail when the bombing starts would be the worst scenario, so it is better to stay on.

These are among the most experienced war correspondents, people who defied danger during the last Gulf War, and in Chechnya, Bosnia and Afghanistan. Leave Baghdad now, before the drama has even started? The editors cannot come and haul them away either and the desk will take their articles, when the bombs start falling.

Fredrik and Aage from Norway's TV2 have decided to stay. We agreed with the Norwegian consul to hide in the empty embassy building should the Iraqis want to take us hostage. The preparations are half-hearted; I cannot imagine sprinting to the Norwegian Embassy, scaling the fence, pursued by armed men.

Remy from *Le Monde*, who always has the best contacts and knows the secret routes, whispers his plan to me. – The French Embassy is not empty, like everyone thinks, he says quietly in the back seat of Amir's car. – The Ambassador has gone, the wine cellar is empty, but ten French Special Service soldiers are hiding there. They are armed to the teeth, and the ambassador told me before leaving that should the situation turn threatening all French citizens would be let in. You can come with me, he promises. That sounds like a better idea. I dare say I could hide behind ten French fighting soldiers.

Janine's advice keeps ringing in my ears. *You must be prepared.* She herself had enough bottled water and food to last a small eternity in the three different hotel rooms in town. But her driver collected it all when she left. The time has come to take some precautions, and I meet up with Rawda to go looking for what I need, or think I need. On the way out I bump into Tim, who joins us as he has nothing better to do. If Woody Allen ever were to play the role of a war correspondent he would look like Tim; absent-minded, intellectual, funny, sometimes unintentionally funny. In addition to that Tim is fearless. He seems to experience all that happens from a distance, not sensing the incident first hand, but filtering it all quick as lightning in his mind so that he actually experiences it as it will later appear in the *New York Review of Books*.

With Tim tagging along I buy tinned food in every

variety – maize, sardines, baked beans and olives. I even get hold of some cheese in a box. I pick up large bags of nuts, tea and coffee. There is still electricity and I pin my faith on my water-boiler working a bit longer. I hoard matches, batteries, soap, loo paper and napkins. In one booth I find wonderful candles – fat logs in various colours and patterns. Some are coated in gold, others moulded in the shape of roses, vines or fairytale figures. Tim wonders on which cloud I live when I agonise over patterns for teaspoons, cups and saucers.

– How long are you intending to stay, he laughs.

Knives, spoons, forks, scissors, nutcracker, nail file, dishes, plates, light bulbs, bottle opener, cut glass in various shapes – they all disappear into the shopping bag. When I arrive at the saucepans Tim calls a halt. – And where are you going to cook? In the hotel kitchen?

I realise he is right and put the saucepans back, but grab a cushion instead. Might come in useful in the bomb shelter.

– Some survival strategy, Tim laughs in the car. – Now at least you have a dowry should the need arise.

– I'll never invite you for tea, I threaten. – It's important to be prepared.

– With twelve assorted types of teaspoon, and porcelain cups in oriental patterns. In eight varieties. All the while American forces aim missiles at Baghdad!

Tim crunches on nuts. A kilo of almonds, nuts and raisins is all he carries away from the market.

Loaded like a donkey I break my self-imposed ban against using the lift. To be stranded in the lift during bombing raids and a subsequent power cut is a nightmarish thought. It could happen any time. But I am weighed down and decide to live dangerously.

Amir phones from reception and says he has bought me some water. He arrives with a whole trolley and it is the good stuff; not all Iraqi mineral water tastes fresh. In addition he has carrier bags full of food – his mother's homemade cakes, dates stuffed with walnuts, bananas, tomatoes, bread and a large drum of popcorn. I thank him, hoping he cannot see my own hoarded supply. There is really no risk of that. Whenever Amir brings me something he phones from reception to make sure I am prepared and dressed. Having knocked on the door he takes two steps back and one to the side so that he cannot see into the room when I open up. There he remains, several paces away, to guarantee my privacy.

This morning I have booked him a room in the hotel. He lives on the outskirts of town and I envisage the distance between us eventually proving insurmountable. I am lucky to have him as a driver and want him close by. Now he asks me whether I need him. Do I want to go out and eat? When I say I will remain in my room he requests permission to go home to his mother and sleep there.

That's OK by me, although what is the point of renting a room when he wants to sleep at home? But I cannot say no. Amir is the kindest person in the world; he always anticipates what I want, even without me knowing it myself, like the drum of popcorn – and that's in spite of him not wanting me to be here.

The next morning Melinda gives me a ride to the Information Ministry. Her teeth are clenched and she looks cross. Melinda has been ordered to return home but is one of those who have delayed payment to the Iraqi bureaucracy and consequently cannot leave without incurring reprisals. It is Wednesday 19 March, the last opportunity to leave the country before George Bush's ultimatum expires. The previous day several journalists and aid workers were arrested at the border. My Norwegian colleagues Line and Tor from *Dagbladet* were dispossessed of 14,000 dollars. Others lost even more. Some had to stay overnight at the police station in Ramadi, a few hours' drive south of the border, and Tor Valla, from the Norwegian Church Aid, was despatched to Baghdad to get bank guarantees authorising him to take the large sums of money out of the country.

Melinda has had the order from her boss to settle her bill and get out that same morning, but the nail-less Jamal doesn't give a toss for the decisions of *Newsweek* and has vanished into thin air when we arrive at the press centre. Melinda gives herself a midday deadline; if the book-keeper has not turned up by noon she will have to stay. By then it will be too late to get out before dark.

This morning, mail has arrived from my editors, my mother, father, brother and sister. They all implore me to leave.

Reason tells me to leave the country. No one can foresee what will happen, or if we will ever get out. But reason doesn't get its message across; I push it to the side, I don't want to think about it, I'm not able to think about it.

In the end I say to myself that if Melinda goes I will think about going too. Melinda is engaged in one desperate phone call to New York after another. At the age of fifty, she is one of the most experienced *Newsweek* contributors. Like all media establishments *Newsweek* had encountered big problems obtaining visas for their staff. All correspondents had been encouraged to seek entry permits. The Iraqi Embassy in Beijing was the most flexible and the fastest, and Melinda was transferred from her position as bureau chief at *Newsweek*'s Beijing office to cover the war preparations in Iraq. Like all of us she had struggled to keep her visa, fought with the minders, tried to circumvent the censorship. Her whole being now rebelled against leaving.

Noon comes and goes.

– OK, I am staying, she says when the hands of the clock are vertical.

OK, so I'm staying too, I think. As usual I have allowed circumstances to decide for me. I leave Melinda's office and walk out of the building.

There, right outside, I meet Aliya. Good old Aliya.

– I knew you would come back, she cries when she sees me. We hug each other and laugh.

– Let's work, she exclaims. I dismiss Rawda, and Aliya and I set out into town to see how people are coping.

We go to Khadimiya, one of the poorest and most densely populated areas. Rubbish and filth litter the streets; they are solidified mud. A jittery atmosphere caused by hoarding crowds is evident around the market booths. Several shops are already closed, others are in the process of closing.

We stop by a tailor's outlet. On the floor is a distorted female body. Two arms have been flung to one side. Part of the torso totters on a stand. The naked display dummies are being unscrewed and stowed away. Round about are large stacks of *abayas* – the black, loose-fitting coat that women in Baghdad wear.

– I have been wanting to close for many days, but only today did I realise there was no other solution, the owner says. – The ultimatum expires today. I can't risk losing my stock so I'm packing it all up and taking it home.

Karim specialises in *abayas*. To an outsider they all look

exactly the same, but the nuances of lace trimmings, borders and ruffles are important to the women who buy them. Karim is known as a good tailor and he normally does a roaring trade. The majority of Khadimiya's inhabitants are Shia Muslims; amongst them the use of the *abaya* is more widespread.

– I'll lose a lot of money through this war. What will my family live on if it lasts? I'm angry with this Bush, he's a criminal. He should stop his plans, at least for the children's sake.

The tailor points to his son, third-grader Abdul, who has returned from his last day at school – for some time. – We'll keep him at home now that the attacks might start, the father says, folding together the displayed *abayas* and stuffing them into large black sacks.

A friend arrives from afternoon prayer. The mosque was overcrowded. – Now we'll have to leave our fate in the hands of God, he says. All day he has been trying to avert the war, in his own way, by complying with the will of God.

– I have fasted, given alms, kept the hours of prayer. If anyone owes me money I have cancelled the debt; I want to go into this war with a clean conscience. When you look death in the eye it is important not to have anything outstanding, he explains.

Both Karim and Niyaz say that if Allah cannot stop the war they are determined to fight. Karim is a member of the Baath Party and has been issued with a weapon. He is attached to a volunteer unit in the neighbourhood and has been told where to meet and what to do when the war starts. Niyaz too has a gun at home and promises to shoot every American who gets in his way. – I will be a martyr, he assures me.

The mood is changing in these last hours before the deadline. While the Iraqis have hitherto met the threat of war with resignation, frustration is now turning to anger.

– Let Bush come and he'll get this shoe in his face, a woman cries outside the tailor's booth. She kicks off her shoe and brandishes it in the air, her tears flowing. – Bush has no conscience, he's a tyrant! I lost my son because of the Americans. He was an electrician, and was repairing a power plant that had been wrecked during the last war. It short-circuited and he was killed. Bush and the Americans must take responsibility for his death. They are the ones who destroyed the power plant.

The woman hops away on one foot before putting her shoe back on and continuing in a low voice.

– Now I'm responsible for his two children, she says. – I'm buying a large bag of sweets, so at least they have something before they go to sleep this evening. Who knows what the night might bring, she sighs.

Dusk has fallen and the tailor's tiny shop is soon empty. Only the mirrors are left hanging. – I'm leaving them behind, they'll break wherever they are, Karim says resignedly.

People hurry home, carrying bags full of food, candles and blankets. Today's purchases might be the last for a long time. Before closing the premises, Karim takes one last look at himself in the two mirrors.

– God willing, they'll be hanging there when I open again – once it's all over, he says. – *Insh' Allah*.

In the evening I go to the press centre to send my article and attend the news broadcast. NRK, the Norwegian public service TV channel, phoned the previous day to ask if I would report for them; actually they had already agreed time with Reuters, as had the associated channels SVT in Sweden and DR in Denmark. So it was just to show up.

The press centre is empty. I imagine people have spirited their satellite telephones over to their hotel rooms. I erect mine and am about to connect when Josh from Sky News comes rushing.

— Get the hell out of here, they'll start bombing any minute.

— But I'm not connected yet, I say, frantically pressing the keyboard.

— We're carrying our things down from the roof now, the car goes in three minutes.

— But I'm live on Norwegian, Swedish and Danish TV in half an hour.

— Fuck the lives, there's no one left here. Everyone's gone, no one's doing lives from here this evening.

Wonders of wonders, I get through on the third try, the article is sent, then I pack the equipment up in great haste and squeeze myself in between the Sky News packing cases. The driver puts his foot down and we tear off over the bridge, as if the bombs are hard on our heels. No one speaks. We stumble from the car outside Hotel Palestine. I'll have to phone my editors and explain why there won't be any live transmission this evening.

I send a telephone report from my room instead. Immediately before the news starts Josh phones from the sixteenth floor.

— There'll be an attack very soon. This evening, tonight, at any minute. The MOD has warned us, he says, and tells me to don my flak jacket.

— Inside? I ask.

— Yes, there might be shrapnel from the windows. Have you taped them?

– I couldn't lay my hands on any, I say, whereupon Josh orders me up to the sixteenth floor to fetch some.

First I must finish the report, and I view the fragile windows nervously and stay as far away as possible from the glass while I talk about the latest developments. Afterwards I run up nine flights of stairs and Josh hands me the roll and rushes back to the phone. I criss-cross the windows and the door to the balcony with tape until I can hardly see out of them. A colleague who comes visiting later tells me to take half of it off. – It's too much, now you risk the whole window rushing in on you in one piece and exploding in the room, he says.

I laboriously pick off half the tape and the beautiful view of the Tigris returns.

– Always keep the balcony door open. That's the best guarantee that it won't get blown in by the air pressure, he says before leaving.

I remember what Josh said about wearing the flak jacket. I try it on, but quickly take it off and lay it by the bed together with the helmet, the gasmask, the torch and my shoes. The evening and the night remain dark and quiet.

At four in the morning Bush's ultimatum expires. At five-thirty the first bang is heard. I am wide awake, my heart thumping. I sneak out onto the balcony, first crouching in case of missiles, then standing up. Powerful impacts, aircraft noise and vigorous shooting from Iraqi anti-aircraft missiles can be heard. From the balconies above I hear a Babelesque confusion of voices – Spanish, Arabic, English, French. We all stand staring out into the half-light and see the dim outline of the Presidential palace on the opposite side of the Tigris. Even the river appears dark and ominous. While the attacks are going on somewhere on the outskirts of

Baghdad, we start to work. The telephones ring. Muffled voices report. It is forbidden to use the telephones in the rooms and I set up the satellite antenna as discreetly as possible. No one screams, no one shouts: 'The war has started!' Everyone murmurs quietly into their receivers. It feels almost soothing, the constant buzzing of voices between the explosions. It is also reassuring to know that the phones work, that no e-bomb has landed.

We have been told that the Americans have developed a bomb which destroys electronic equipment, including Iraqi defence systems, without human life being lost. The weapon works like a pent-up lightning strike. In the twinkling of an eye two billion watts would be let loose. The electric shock would reach deep into bunkers via ventilation ducts, water pipes and aerials. Circuit boards, chips, telephones and hard-disks would be destroyed. I had asked Amir to buy me a large lead case; that would apparently protect against the rays. There I would keep my equipment when it was not in use. Amir returned with an aluminium case, and I persuaded myself that it would serve the same purpose. In any case, the telephone still works and is ringing non-stop.

The minders outside the hotel turn their heads upwards. First towards the explosions, then towards us. It is not possible to completely hide the satellite antenna. I fear there will be a knock on my door and they will come and take the telephone away. What to do then? But I have to take the risk, for why am I here if not to report?

While I am connected to Marienlyst, NRK's headquarters, I peer nervously down on the guards who are walking around with Kalashnikovs and pistols, before turning to focus on the horizon and describe what I see.

– Have you any information as to whether Saddam Hussein might have been killed, the radio host asks. How the hell would I know? I think. But choose to say: So far we have no information as to whether the Iraqi president has been hit in the attack.

— How could they start the attack during the hour of prayer.

Aliya is incensed. She had just woken up when the first explosions were heard and the anti-aircraft missiles flashed in the sky. She bundled up her rug and went down to the cellar. Her house, in one of Baghdad's most densely populated areas, was full to bursting point. Relatives, who lived close to obvious targets like ministries, military buildings and communications centres, had moved in with her family.

— We don't think they'll bomb residential areas, so now we're living on carpets and mattresses all over the floor. Anyhow, we like to keep together when something threatens, Aliya reports on the phone. She tries to keep her spirits up and hopes no civilians lost their lives in the attack, which was directed at a suburb to the south of the town.

— However smart these bombs are they can go wrong. We're just waiting, as if tasting life and death one after the other.

Aliya is in no way gripped by panic.

— I fell asleep after the attack. This was nothing. The explosions were never so loud that we could not hear the neighbourhood dogs bay like crazy at the sky, she says and laughs a touch.

— When do you need me?

— Come as quick as you can.

While I wait I write a hasty report for *Aftenposten*'s afternoon edition.

In reception the guards are sitting down, chain smoking, as if nothing has happened. The breakfast room is seething. The waiters pour out mugs of steaming hot tea. The hard-boiled eggs share tin plates with greasy scrambled eggs. The bread is dry, as usual, the tomatoes watery, the olives too salty. In other words, it's business as usual.

When the danger-over siren sounds over Baghdad, the streets fill up quickly. A few cars pass by, followed by ambulances. But there is no information about what has happened. Iraqi TV and radio plays military music and songs of homage to Saddam Hussein. Late in the morning the president appears on TV and thus the world knows that the Americans missed.

The morning's bombing raid was aimed directly at him. American intelligence had been tipped off that the president and his closest cronies were in a building in the southern outskirts of Baghdad. Missiles reduced the place to smithereens. Triumphant, Saddam opens his speech in the same indignant manner as Aliya: The Americans initiated the attack during the hours of prayer. In addition he encourages everyone to fight against 'Little Bush', as he calls George Bush Junior. He concludes the speech by reciting classical Arab poetry; fighting horsemen, sword in hand.

Aliya is hardly fighting fit when she turns up. – It is not the bombs that I fear the most, but what might evolve afterwards. Civil war. If chaos follows and there is a power vacuum someone might take advantage of the situation and avenge themselves on the regime. Shias might attack Sunnis, and the bandits will do as they like.

This is the first time Aliya has expressed any doubts about Iraq's ability to defend itself and control its population. The mere mention of the possibility of civil war is forbidden. Happiness and harmony is the distinguishing feature of the relationship between the various ethnic groups. When I ask more she stays quiet. She coughs and looks away. As if to emphasise that the conversation is over she starts to tell me what has been broadcast on the news.

— The Minister of the Interior has called on people to open their shops. To demonstrate that we are unbeatable, that we can withstand even extreme challenges, Aliya trots out. — Are you afraid? she suddenly asks. — You mustn't be afraid. Whatever happens, I am here with you. I'll look after you.

Aliya grabs my hand. — You are my sister. If anyone attacks you I will protect you with my body. We can hide in my house if it gets dangerous. And anyhow, our destiny is in God's hands. Everything will happen according to His will. You are my fair sister and I am your dark one. Shakra and Samra. The fair and the dark. OK? We'll look after each other. Won't we?

— Like sisters, I say.

— Like sisters, Aliya repeats.

Having drunk several glasses of tea and forged the chains of sisterhood, we seek permission to inspect the damage from the night's bombing. That is denied us so instead we go for a stroll round the centre of town.

In spite of the minister's appeal, nine out of ten shops are closed. It seems that people fear that the next attack might come at any moment, particularly as the Americans did not even respect the hour of prayer. Only a few people scuttle along the pavements by the river. In Abu Nuwas Street a handful of cigarette vendors' stalls are open. The greater part of Baghdad has gone underground. The city's many mosques are the only places that people flock to. The moment the muezzin calls people to prayer, they come to a halt, go down on their knees, on the pavements and in parks. An unusual sight in Baghdad.

– Goal!

Eleven players cheer. They are leading 3–2.

– We usually come here every afternoon. Why shouldn't we be here today? seventeen-year-old Hamdi says. He is watching from the touchline. – But we go home when it gets dark. Tomorrow we'll meet again, whether they bomb or not.

Nevertheless, the football team has dwindled over the last few days.

– Some have left town with their families. The countryside is safer for the moment, but most of us have stayed behind. Someone has to defend the city.

The football ground is not the safest place, surrounded as it is by strategic targets: the television and communications centre, where a huge portrait of Saddam Hussein on the phone adorns the wall, two further government buildings and the Sinak bridge which leads to the Information Ministry on the opposite bank of the river, the state-run TV channel and the Congress Palace.

The match's only onlookers are a bunch of soldiers in green uniforms. They lounge about, each with a Kalashnikov over the shoulder, under orders to defend the buildings surrounding the pitch.

– We are defending our president and our country, say the young lads in threadbare uniforms and worn-out shoes.

I cannot resist asking the obvious.

– How can you defend Baghdad with Kalashnikovs?

– We'll take the Americans, we'll show them that Iraqis are strong, is the only answer, like a broken record. They point to some stairs in the brick building. – We live down there; we have all we need.

I need to change money, and after a long search I find an exchange in Sadoun Street, behind the Hotel Palestine. The premises are empty bar three cashiers staring at us from behind the counter.

On the wall is a dollar bill. The face of George Washington has been superimposed with that of Osama bin Laden.

– This is our way of demonstrating against the bombs, the money changer says. – If Bush continues this criminal assault we'll send him Osama bin Laden in return. The world cannot accept this injustice. America thinks it can go ahead and behave just as it likes, even breaking international law, like now.

The man talks and counts simultaneously. Gradually stacks of dinars pile up on the counter. He gives me a plastic bag full of money. The exchange rate has nose-dived and even for small purchases you need a bunch of notes. – I don't have anything against the Americans in general, the money changer says. – We just don't want them to occupy our country. If they come and visit we are only too pleased to exchange their money and do business with them. We'll do business with anyone. But Bush should keep away from Baghdad.

On a central reserve in Abu Nuwas Street I suddenly spy Teijo. Together with two others he has chained himself to a tree. 'No to War' is the message on the placard he is holding up. I ask Amir to stop the car and walk over to the young

Finn. So he has stayed, despite most of the human shields having left long ago. I ask him how he got through the night.

– I was woken by someone screaming: 'The war has started.' Most of us went down to the bomb shelter but I went down to the river. I wanted to see the bombs drop. I felt very upset and disappointed; this meant that our protest had not worked. But still, it is my moral obligation to stay, Teijo says. – In between my heart twinged when I thought the bombs might have hit my power plant.

South Baghdad power station is a so-called *legitimate target*, adjacent to a military establishment and the bridge to Basra.

– I hope I'll survive. But if I don't, that's my fate, Teijo continues.

– Have you been in contact with your parents recently?

– They're still asking me to come home. But when I tell them that this is very important to me, that it's something I really want to do, they understand. I know I'm not a coward, but I would *feel* like one if I went home. If I go home it will be like letting my dreams die.

His eyes shine. Teijo is adamant. Standing beside him, a civil servant follows the interview closely. When night starts to fall Teijo untangles himself from the chains and goes back to South Baghdad power station – to yet another night on the camp bed, accompanied by yet another bombing symphony.

It is soon nine o'clock in Baghdad. Norway's *News Night* theme tune plays on the other end of the phone line. While I wait to join the live broadcast I hear and see it. An enormous explosion, one more, then several, not as last time like crashing thunderclaps on the horizon, but close by.

The sky is lit up – from its colour it looks as if Baghdad must be burning. The darkness erupts in a sea of orange flames. One missile after another strikes on the other side of the Tigris. Iraqi anti-aircraft guns crackle. In spite of the noise from the laser-guided missiles, I hear the whine of the fighter planes. I lie down on the floor, as far away from the window as possible, but close enough to see out. Another explosion follows. I crawl over to the balcony to get a better view. The spectacle is overwhelming, and there is no doubt of the night's target: the Presidential palace on the opposite bank, a few hundred yards away. The palace is in flames, and continual explosions, probably from the stores of ammunition held there, can be heard and seen through the bars of the balcony.

I report what I see. The bangs are audible in the studio via the telephone receiver. Some of them cause the enormous concrete hotel to shake and the windows to vibrate. A crash, I speak, another crash, I continue to speak, and then we say goodbye to Åsne Seierstad in Baghdad. The studio hangs up. The attack intensifies. Metal hitting concrete, metal striking marble, metal colliding with iron. I remain on the floor. So this is what being bombed feels like. My fists are clenched, arms tense, eyes staring into space but seeing nothing. Now it's for real.

There is a knock on the door. Remy and Pascal wonder how I'm getting on.

– Shall we go down to the air-raid shelter? I ask.

No response.

– Isn't it safer down there? I ask again.

– You are just as safe here, Remy says.

– Or rather, unsafe, Pascal laughs sarcastically and walks past me into the room. He puts a bottle of wine on the table.

Very few journalists spend time in the air-raid shelter during the bombing. The few of us who are left are too curious to allow the drama to unfold without watching it. Isolated in the cellar, you can't hear the planes or see the flames. The air-raid shelter is anyhow full of Iraqi women and children. The Information Ministry bureaucrats and hotel employees have brought their families here, reasoning that the Americans will not bomb a hotel full of western journalists, as if that would constitute an invisible safety net. At night they sleep in the shelter, during the day they return home. Children run around, getting in the way of anyone still brave enough to use the lift; they play in it, up and down, up and down.

My two French friends' visit is not purely altruistic; my balcony has the best view of town and faces the Presidential palace. We watch the final act of the bombing drama. My fear-filled time on the floor has toughened me up. It makes no odds where you are, on the balcony or on the floor under the bed. If you are hit, you are hit.

After an hour the violent attack is over; now the ambulance and fire-engine sirens cut through the air. Below, on Abu Nuwas Street, cars rush by, possibly carrying the wounded to hospital. During the attack our guards remained on the square below, trying to gauge where the missiles hit. Now, once again, they turn their eyes to us. I sneak the telephone inside, hide it behind the cupboard, empty my glass and fall asleep.

According to the Information Minister Muhammed Said al-Sahhaf, thirty-seven people were wounded during the night.

The following morning people are woken by the sound of the mullahs' call to prayer, as opposed to the bombs of the previous morning. It acts as a cue. People swarm out of their hiding places. Shortly after sunrise Baghdad's usual morning symphony is once again audible – drivers sound their horns, buses snail along, people ride creaky bicycles and wear clip-clopping shoes. Although the traffic jams aren't quite as bad as usual, nevertheless it is a near normal spring morning in Baghdad, sunny and buzzing.

However, something indicates that this is only a temporary respite from the war: the selection of goods for sale. Vendors stand behind little tables, by cars or on stools. One man has three items for sale: batteries, torches and candles. Another sells oil lamps, rechargeable lamps and primus lamps. A third man has just one item for sale: thick, brown window tape. Business is brisk. The price of batteries has tripled in the last few days, as have lamp and torch prices.

One man is flogging *Bazooka* lamps. 'Your weapon in the dark', the Chinese lamp advertises. – Usually I sell a couple every month, now I've sold one hundred and twenty in three days, Sami says, selling from a table in front of his closed electricity shop. He has taken the necessary precautions. – I have removed most of the stock to prevent it being destroyed by bombs, but also in case the shop is looted. Of course I'm delighted to be making money now, but I don't like the bombs, the street seller assures us while demonstrating the lamp to a customer.

I buy a *Bazooka*. Tim makes do with candles, which is just as well because I never get the lamp to work.

– Bush says he's going to liberate us, says an indignant man. He says he wants to occupy the country for humanitarian reasons. So why does he send bombs which kill and maim and make our days so difficult. Without power, without water?

– He won't bomb today, another man assures him. – It

is impossible to bomb on a Friday, he establishes. – That would mean Bush doesn't respect Muslims, and that means he doesn't respect Christians either. After all, we have the same God, and He has asked us to keep the day of rest holy, so there'll be no bombs on Friday or Sunday, he says confidently.

– Bush couldn't care less, a third interrupts. – He's an atheist. Otherwise he couldn't have planned all the ghastly things he's doing to us.

We leave the discussion about Bush's faith and cross the road to gauge the mood in the bird market. Doves, falcons, parrots and rare birds twitter and chirp at the sun. But it has been a bad night. One vendor is mourning two birds killed. – Because I had to close my shop I was forced to put several birds in one cage. The strongest won, these were pecked to bits, Taha says, and pulls the dead birds out of a box. – They're worth one hundred dollars each. Alive. Now they're worth nothing.

– My doves were nervous during yesterday's bombing, another bird vendor tells us. – But I gave them some extra food and then they settled down.

However, both men are pleased with sales. – There's nothing else to do but wait, so there's plenty of time to buy doves and parrots, Taha says. He sells birds in the daytime and guards the streets at night. – I wear a uniform, get out my rifle and go where I'm told. I'm a Baath Party volunteer. I'm at it again tonight.

In the middle of the square the bird cages give way to shiny water containers – the fish market. Like the windows, the containers are secured with tape.

– This is a risky business. Hardan is worried. – In the event of a major attack, the containers will crack and all my fish will die.

On the way back to the car we pass the local fire station. A firefighter tells us he helped put out a fire at the Ministry of Planning. – I have never seen such enormous flames, he says. The burly chap fits exactly the American idea of a heroic firefighter.

Before we have time to ask more we are hassled out of the area. A gruff man waves us away and we make ourselves scarce. This is not the time to irritate Iraqi officials. Close to the fire station is the headquarters of one of Baghdad's electricity works. Large mounds of sand are piled up outside the building. Two men are shovelling it into bags and positioning them by the entrance. The final preparations before the next onslaught.

Restaurant al-Maida is situated at a crossroad. Chicken and kebabs are being served at white Perspex tables. The queue by the grill is long.

– I have bought in several hundred kilos of chicken, says the owner, Latif, a grey-haired, weather-beaten type. – I intend to stay open come what may. Last night I was open until midnight. I was standing outside and watching the bombs fall. I refuse to give up. But then, I'm raking it in, because most people are closed. I'm too old to take part, so my challenge is to keep this joint open whatever happens. I despise the Americans; they're cretins, just like their films. There's no truth in them, it's all crap.

He sits down heavily at our table. – I think tonight's the night for the big one. I feel it. When night falls the bombs will return. And I'll be here grilling my chicken, he grins.

– They call it *Shock and Awe*, Tim jokes, mimicking the politicians' loud, sometimes pious description of the war. – The problem is: *It doesn't shock the Iraqis!*

*

Latif was right. The bombing this night is considerably stronger than the night before. This time buildings on our side of the river are blown up. We try to guess where the blasts strike. The Ministries of Planning, Education, Communications, Commando HQ. We have no maps detailing the location of buildings, and either Aliya is not prepared to tell us or she does not know. And anyway it is forbidden to report what has been hit. BBC, CNN and Sky News, the only remaining English language TV channels, are closely monitored. When the journalists are reporting, a minder stands nearby listening to what is being said. It is prohibited to use words such as 'dictator', 'tyrant' or 'brutal' to characterise Saddam Hussein, or to pinpoint targets that have been hit. They can be no more specific than 'a large building, close by'.

During the attack I imagine Uday standing on the balcony below me, or Mohsen lurking on the side. I wonder what to do with the telephone. The night before thirty telephones were confiscated from the balconies. CNN and the BBC both lost some of theirs; hardest hit was the French news agency AFP who lost seven telephones.

We all devise means of hiding, covering up or sneaking off with our phones. Andrew Gilligan of the BBC, who will later attain notoriety by accusing the British Government of having 'sexed up' the dossier detailing Iraq's weapons' arsenal, has a secret code. Anyone wanting to enter his room must use a symphony of knocks and pauses, composed by Andrew and shared with very few. It is said he never opens the door to anyone who is ignorant of the code; he stays quiet and waits for them to leave.

I adopt a different strategy. When talking on the phone I turn the shower on full, undress and wind a towel around me. If anyone knocks on the door I call out: Who is it?

If it is the guards I pour some water over myself, open the door a crack and ask them to wait while I get dressed. That gives me time to hide the satellite telephone and the antenna.

There's no point pretending one is not there. After all, the guards all have keys.

The night is alive with flashes of light and flames. I jump up at every boom, trying to determine where it came from. It is like a massive, everlasting firework display. Planes roar over the skies, dropping their deadly cargo to resounding thunder.

Interspersed with the droning of the planes and the crash of missiles are shouts from the Paradise Square mosque. For every crash, every explosion and every fire in the area, the call to prayer starts up. I try to sleep but give up. I try ear-plugs but it doesn't help. Only when the attacks die away in the early hours of the morning do I fall asleep, exhausted.

If the night glows with light and flames, the day reveals the real terror. The fires have been put out and the sunlight exposes the targets: craters, ruins, collapsed buildings. Every night hundreds of wounded Iraqis are brought to Baghdad's hospitals.

— This is my mother, this is my father, a low voice whispers. Lying on a blue sheet, under a blanket, with an orange towel for a pillow, two brown eyes, a little nose and a long pigtail peep out at me. The pigtail, tied up with a pink elastic band, meanders off the pillow and drops down towards the floor. The weak voice starts to talk.

— My name is Russul.

By her side a woman stands crying — her mother. A man watches the mother helplessly — her father. He pulls the blanket away. Russul's slender chest and one of her arms are heavily bandaged; in several places the blood has seeped through the dressing.

— We had been visiting some relatives, the father says. — I had just unlocked the gate. My wife and two of my children were on their way into the house. Russul was lingering behind. I opened the door for her, she was in a good mood and made a few dance steps, when suddenly, a bang, the father continues. Russul's big brother adds: — It was like a red ball flying through the air. It landed on the ground and then it exploded. I felt something fall behind me. When I turned round I saw it was Russul.

Russul herself remembers nothing of what happened after they walked through the gate, but her mother does. — She was lying in a pool of blood. I thought she was dead. I threw myself on top of her and noticed that her heart was still beating. We tried to find a car, but it took ages. No one in our street has a car and at that time no one else was about, everyone feared the bombs. We shouldn't have been out either, but we had only visited our relatives on the other side of the street and we thought it was safe. In the end we found a car which took Russul to the hospital. I still remember how the blood dripped on the ground as they carried her to the car.

Russul lies still, listening; it hurts when she moves. The shrapnel has gouged deep cuts in her body. Now and again low groans escape from her.

— Goodbye, nice to meet you, the ten-year-old says when we leave.

In the street where Russul and her family live is a hole. Some boys show us excitedly where the missile landed. Several of the doors along the street have marks caused by shrapnel, but only Russul was hit. The depression in the ground has a small, round mound in the middle, which might indicate that it was caused by an Iraqi anti-aircraft missile, not an American bomb. During the night's bombing the Iraqi air defence tried, unsuccessfully, to shoot down

American planes. What goes up must come down, and sometimes the Iraqi missiles land in residential areas and explode there. But even if the American bombs are more accurate and are primarily aimed at targets connected to Saddam Hussein's regime, shrapnel could hit where people live. It travels several hundred metres.

Russul is one of the victims after the second night of bombing. At Yarmuk hospital, where she is a patient, they received 101 wounded following the previous night's attack. These are civilian victims; the number of military casualties might be a lot higher. If soldiers are killed or wounded it is not disclosed.

— People are suffering from the same injuries as they did in the last Gulf War, Doctor Abid Hassan says resignedly. — Leg wounds, arms torn off, shrapnel wounds, crushed limbs, burns.

Yarmuk hospital was itself hit. The hospital director shows us several smashed windows. — But we won't give up. We'll hold out until Bush gives in. Or until he goes into exile — I mean Bush of course, the director says, followed by a short, rather forced laugh.

On a bed just beyond Russul a woman sits holding a boy in her arms. The boy has white bandages around his head and hands, and is wearing tattered pyjamas, the ones he was wearing when the attack started. The holes in the material are caused by shrapnel.

— He was playing with his sister, Duha says. — They were both hit, but his sister has already been discharged, she got a small cut behind the ear.

Ahmed has been unconscious since it happened. He is stiff in his aunt's arms.

— We were all gathered in the sitting room, for supper. Just when we called the children in it began. They both fell down and we got them to hospital. That was fifteen hours ago.

Ahmed has not yet gained consciousness. At the back of his head shrapnel is pushing inwards.

While we are standing there the boy suddenly starts to move. Faint sounds emerge from his lips. He wriggles slightly. Duha bends down and whispers something into his ear. Then she puts her head close to his mouth. Is he saying something? The tears well up. — *I want to go home. I want to go home,* he says softly and opens his eyes.

— *Where is my egg?* he mumbles. Duha's tears flow freely.

— He had just been given an egg when the wall opened up and he fell down. A boiled egg.

Turning towards Ahmed she promises him as many eggs as he could possibly wish for.

Loud screams and low moans issue forth from the room next door. Twelve-year-old Warda is the source of the noise. It has taken hours to rid her legs of shrapnel. Now the wounds must be cleaned; it stings and the little girl howls. She squirms and wriggles but the doctors hold her down. Tears of pain flow from her eyes.

Next to Warda is Hanan, her aunt. Her baby is due in one month. Her leg is shattered but she is denied painkillers as they might harm the foetus. She writhes in pain. Her eyes roll around, sweat and tears moisten her face, the flower-patterned nightdress is dripping wet. — *So much pain, so much pain,* she cries.

Her cries are drowned by a noisy crowd outside the room. A group of nurses and ancillary workers enter, fists clenched, screaming slogans for Saddam Hussein.

'Saddam Hussein — your name is honour. Saddam Hussein, a finger of your hand is worth more than all the USA', is the catch-phrase. The women start dancing around, stamping their feet and clapping their hands. The healthiest of the patients shake their fists and join in the chorus. Iraqi state radio is visiting. Someone thrusts out a microphone to catch the battle cry. He interviews people about the war, Saddam Hussein and the USA. The answers are identical, everyone knows what to say. Some patients look the other way when the broadcaster turns away from them.

They stare emptily at each other — the first victims of the war.

*

One day Amir bangs on my door. – I've got a scoop for you, he says excitedly. – An American pilot has been shot down. Right by my house.

– Blast. I never caught that on the news.

– It's just happened, they don't know about it yet. Do you want to come and talk to the guys who shot it down?

We might at least check it out, I think, and invite Remy and Pascal to join our expedition.

– Then you'll get to meet my mother, Amir says, his spirits soaring further.

During his briefings the Minister of Information is constantly reporting downed American helicopters, rarely confirmed by the Americans. The farmer who shot down a helicopter with the aid of a rifle was elevated to national hero. The pictures of him and his neighbours performing a victory dance on the wreck were broadcast continuously. The old peasant was even decorated by Saddam Hussein. So why not something like that in Amir's neighbourhood?

In the car we discuss the latest news from Hotel Palestine: CNN is leaving. CNN, always there whenever anything happens, has been thrown out because it failed to comply with press centre rules. In contrast with the rest of us they moved all equipment, all cameras, all telephones, all satellites, all personnel from the press centre to the hotel. This meant they could no longer transmit al-Sahhaf's press conferences direct, and it made the minister angry. As a result he expelled the entire CNN team and has given them a few hours to pack and clear off.

Knowing that there was at least one American TV station in the hotel had provided us with a feeling of safety, albeit a small one. Now, bar Peter Arnett who works on contract for NBC, and a freelancer from ABC, no American TV networks remain.

– They knew they'd be thrown out if they evaded the minister's orders. This gave them the opportunity to leave with their heads high – without being considered cowards, Pascal suggests.

Amir pulls up in front of his house. His mother is just as I had imagined, large and sunny. Amir shows us proudly round the house, which looks as though it has been cobbled together and patched up over generations. His mother serves coffee, strong as dynamite. His brother Sadik, who was present when the helicopter was brought down, looks like a younger version of Amir.

– It happened this morning, Sadik tells us. – We were by the school, discussing where the night's bombing had struck. Suddenly we heard a shot and saw a helicopter descend. The pilot ejected and landed on the school roof. I was right there, doing the rounds as security guard. From the roof he opened fire in all directions until he realised he was surrounded. Then he threw his weapon down, put his hands on the back of his neck and went down on his knees. The police handcuffed him and took him away.

The youngster looks remarkably calm despite having witnessed such drama – as though catching American pilots was a daily occurrence.

– Could you see the pilot?

– Oh yes, I was standing right there.

– What did he look like?

– His skin was white, no moustache or beard. He was wearing a helmet, and in a pocket on his thigh was a map. He was wearing pilots' fatigues with a long zip in front. On one shoulder was the American flag. He looked petrified. He trembled from side to side, like this, Sadik demonstrates.

A good description of an American soldier, but maybe no more than could be expected from having seen *Top Gun*.

– Can we go and have a look? I ask.

Sadik hesitates. – I don't think so. It's sure to be cordoned off.

– But surely we can get a bit closer. There must be masses of bullet holes there if he was shooting wildly. Is the wreck still there?

– Oh no, they took that away immediately. Anyway, it crashed many kilometres away.

Sadik is a member of the Baath Party. One of their tasks is to raise morale by making people believe that Iraq will win. As there are few triumphs to celebrate, a downed helicopter or a captured soldier is presented as an awesome heroic deed. The TV channels show old clips from military parades and footage of soldiers in training jumping over blazing tanks, practising karate or sprinting up steep mountain sides, as if taking part in a training camp for James Bond stunt men.

– Iraq will win, says the eighteen-year-old. – We will cut off the enemy's hand.

Sadik then reiterates how important it is that we write about the grounded pilot in our papers.

– We cannot write anything unless we see the place for ourselves, we object.

– Not possible, says the young Baathist.

As we leave the house, Amir whispers that he will take us to the school. If we are stopped, however, we must not say why we are there, just that we are on our way home. OK?

Having arrived at al-Kindi school there is no sign of the morning's drama. We ask Amir to stop. He refuses. His big body starts to shake. That's when we see the militia guarding the building. They are carrying weapons and watching us.

– Let's stop and ask, I say, but Amir drives on, staring fixedly ahead. Away from the school, away from the neighbourhood. It was as if he had caught sight of the devil. Amir flaps at the smallest thing. Now he is convinced he will be arrested as a spy if we stop and ask about the American pilot. News about the incident has not yet been released. His brother might be accused of informing the enemy, and he for playing into enemy hands. We sit in silence. No story from the school.

We go to the press centre to see if there is any news. There is. As we drive into the parking lot the whole press centre, like one great bounding monster, is on its way down to the Tigris. Ferocious shooting is audible from afar. We rush after them. Volleys of gunfire strike the water; the river gobbles up the bullets.

Five boats patrol the river bank; they search among the rushes and try to create waves to make it difficult for whoever is hiding. The alarm is sounded: An American helicopter has been hit and the pilot has ejected – into the Tigris. The story of the downed helicopter has moved from al-Kindi secondary school to the river bank.

Several divers are in situ. They reconnoitre, emerge, then search some more. Men in uniform pour oil on the rushes and set them alight. The flames and crackling are greeted with jubilation. From time to time someone calls out: Come here! The river bank is alive with spectators rushing here and there, following the call to come and see.

The bridge spanning the river is black with people. For hours they follow the drama, the only show in town. Isolated bomb blasts occasionally distract their attention away from the spectacle. Once there are seven bangs in a row. A white cloud of smoke rises up on the horizon, followed by loud discussion as to the whereabouts of the blast.

Where is the helicopter? And the parachute? Has anyone actually seen them? A little boy is sure he has seen them fall. An engineer is equally convinced. – They're there in the water somewhere, or on the bottom, he says from his vantage point on the bridge.

The coalition forces deny that a helicopter has been lost: None is missing, the statement runs.

In the restaurants and teahouses of Baghdad the rumours run amok: American captives, downed planes, military victories, swingeing losses. And what about Saddam Hussein? Has he been wounded in the night's attacks or not? Someone is said to have seen him leave one of his palaces in an ambulance.

Everyone has seen something, or knows someone who has seen something, or knows someone who knows someone who has heard of someone who has seen something.

While the town seethes with increasingly wild stories, Baghdad is hit several times. Powerful cracks cause windows to vibrate, but after four nights and days of bombing curiosity has overtaken fear and people want to see where and what has been hit.

In the dusk the last spectators leave the bridge over the Tigris. The river flows on peacefully as before, on its way to the Persian Gulf, as it did when God punished the people with the confusion in Babel, a long, long time and many, many wars ago.

It is not only rumours that haunt Baghdad this first week of war. Speculation and guesswork follow. Speculation about how it is really going. General Tommy Franks maintains that the coalition forces have made 'dramatic advances' and that they have met only 'sporadic resistance'. The troops move on Baghdad at a steady pace, he says. The Iraqis, on the other hand, boast about their victories. Each day at 2pm we are roped in to listen to Information Minister al-Sahhaf. Each day the press briefings are equally soporific, as are the TV broadcasts translated by Aliya.

– The enemy has been weakened, the anchorman says every evening. By now he is wearing the military-green Baath Party uniform. – We are triumphant on every front.

We never find out when or where these battles take place, how many are killed, or how far into the country the Americans have advanced. The broadcasts are coated with a thin skin of information and are otherwise pure propaganda. They are designed to make the man in the street feel that he is part of the struggle against the Americans. The front pages of the papers promise a handsome reward to anyone who strikes down the enemy. One hundred million dinars to anyone who brings down an aircraft, fifty million to anyone who hits a helicopter, the same if the pilot is captured alive. Only half if he is killed.

One day Saddam Hussein appears on TV again. The message is that the Americans are about to fall into a trap.

Many believe his words have come true when a ferocious sandstorm blows up that same afternoon, halting the advance on Baghdad. It turns out to be the worst sandstorm in forty years. The wind howls round street corners, whistles outside people's doors and knocks over everything that is not fastened or bolted down.

– Allah has come to our rescue, the mosques resound. – He stopped the infidel with His power.

*

The desert storm bathes the town in a magical light. The squalls carry with them thin, yellowish sand dust from the south. It blends with the huge pillars of smoke that rise in a circle round the town. The lowering clouds, the smoke, the dust and the sand lie over the city like a lid.

One afternoon while we are waiting for al-Sahhaf, the heavy soup is being whirled around by strong gusts of wind. Through taped windows we see the palm trees swaying menacingly. Suddenly Kadim comes crashing in.

– Go to Shaab market, he calls. – The press conference is cancelled.

We run to the cars, fearing that he might change his mind and nail us to the hard chairs in the press room, and tear off north. The majority of Baghdad's inhabitants have stayed indoors on this grim day and the few who are around huddle into their jackets and coats. A few empty crates bounce along the road.

It is midday but it is difficult to see. Above us the sky looms black with soot from oil fires and desert sand.

We stop by the market.

Charred buildings gape at us. Twisted car wrecks lie abandoned in the middle of the road. People are crying. Pools of blood have percolated through the layer of sand on the ground. With the help of eye-witnesses, neighbours and relatives I try to reconstruct what happened on this stormy Wednesday in March.

It is nearly midday. Zahra will be home soon. She and her family have decided to move back to the house in the Shaab district of Baghdad. In order to escape the bombs they have been living with relatives in a Baghdad suburb for a week. Now that the ground war is drawing near they feel it would be safer to live closer to the town centre.

Zahra sits at the back of the minibus holding the baby in her arms. With her are her husband, sisters, mother and three children. The bus stops and they get out.

A tanker is parked nearby. The driver wants to have his lunch in Restaurant Ristafa, one of the few to stay open. The premises are half-empty. A bunch of children play in the dust that covers the ground after the last days' sandstorms.

Before the driver has made it across the street the bomb goes off. A missile hits the pavement close to the lorry. Flames shoot up. The driver and those standing close by are killed instantly. The air pressure causes Zahra's entire family to fall to the ground.

Out of a house close by Muhammed comes running. He heard the noise and wants to see what happened. A further missile zips past, hits the ground and radiates deadly fragments in every direction. The twenty-two-year-old falls, screaming. One leg is a bloody pulp, the other peppered with metal. Around bodies fall to the ground from the air pressure, the shards, the shock. The tanker is blazing and twenty other cars catch fire. Anyone who was passing by when the missile hit perishes in their burning cars. The market shops lie in ruins and ten or so apartments are a total loss. Ristafa is crushed; those partaking of lunch are killed.

Screams rent the air. Blood runs into the sand on the street and pavements. Those who can, get up.

Zahra and her family lie still; they are all unconscious. Muhammed is on the ground bellowing with pain. By his side lies a man whose artery has been severed; blood pumps from his body. They are both conscious when the ambulance arrives.

About thirty wounded are brought to al-Zahrawi hospital close by. The man with the severed artery dies on the way. Those killed are taken to al-Kindi hospital from where their bodies are collected by their families to be buried the same day.

Torn off body parts are removed from the street. After a few hours only the blood in the sand remains.

Then the rain comes and the puddles are filled with blood. Burning oil wells, desert sand, soot and smoke descend as rain-drops. Cars, houses, windows, faces — all are coated in yellow-brown spots. The rain draws the blood out from the sand and fills the puddles with red, muddy water.

Angry, frightened and soaked to the skin, people remain stand-ing there. Their neighbourhood has been attacked.

— Bush said he would only attack military targets, but what is this? someone screams. — They want to destroy us, someone else calls out. — This is no military target. It is revenge for our advances on the battlefield. He should be ashamed of himself!

Zahra wakes up. She has shards of shrapnel all over her body and four broken ribs. Her daughter Aisha stands by her bed. Aisha's hair is matted with mud but she is unhurt. She pats her mother's shoulder, caresses her arm.

Zahra gives her daughter a faint smile. Her husband lies in the bed next to hers; he has wounds all over his body. Her younger sister is nearby. She has leg and chest wounds. Grandmother lies by the wall. Her ear was ripped off and she wears a bloody bandage round her head.

— Where is Hamudi? Aisha asks.

— Hamudi is at home. He's alright, Zahra says. She has just been told what happened and that ten-year-old Hamudi and the baby escaped injury. Her tears flow.

— Three babies have been seriously wounded; one has deep cuts in its head, the other was hit by shrapnel. A tiny baby whose mother lost hold of it in the blast was thrown against a wall and is seriously wounded, Doctor Sermed al-Gailani says. He is treat-ing the first patients following the missile attack.

— Awful, the doctor sighs. — These are innocent people and did not deserve this. But such is war. More will be killed, more will be wounded. To believe anything else would be to deceive oneself. This will be far worse than anything we have previously seen, he says quietly.

The sandstorm continues to rage on outside the hospital walls.
Darkness falls; people disappear indoors and only the charred cars
remain. The boom of bombs falling on the outskirts of Baghdad is
audible. The war carries on while the blood in the puddles is
washed away by the rainwater.

It is pitch black when we return to the hotel. We hear
explosions but do not know where the bombs hit. There
are hardly any cars on the road. If I were to imagine the
Day of Judgement this would be it: violent storms, drifting
sand, smoke blotting out the sun, blended with screams,
blood and severed limbs.

Drenched and covered in mud I reach my room.

I turn on the computer to write. An email from the
Politiken's foreign editor appears on the screen. Subject:
Advice.

Dear Åsne,

Hope all is well, appalling about the bombing at the
market today.

I would just like to give you a word of advice in this
time. Make sure your bed and desk are away from the
window so you will not be exposed to broken glass if
your windows blow apart during bombardments
– after all, they happen at night when one is sleeping.

Put a glass of water on the windowsill. When the
water moves it might mean that a plane is
approaching.

Make sure you soften the mental strain by getting

enough sleep and reading about things other than war and Iraq. – I would suggest Barbara Cartland (however, if you make your face up the way she does your TV career is over, so look out). Your thoughts must be clear and precise.

Always carry the protection gear and mask, you might find you need them very suddenly – the danger of being overcome by chemical weapons is more severe when the wind is blowing away from the American positions and in towards Baghdad, but just be careful about everything.

Best wishes,

Michael

The desk is bolted to the wall and cannot be moved; the bed is already some distance from the window. Barbara Cartland is nowhere to be found, nor her make-up box. The advice about enough sleep and minimising mental strain comes from another world. The protection gear and mask are by the bed but I don't have the strength to carry them with me everywhere. I hope I am acting upon the advice about keeping my thoughts clear; in fact I make myself believe that my thoughts are crystal clear. The strain invigorates me, I am super-concentrated. I don't sleep, I don't eat, yet I'm working twenty hours a day. I don't feel myself; I'm writing, reporting, recounting. I am aware of everything, don't trouble yourself, dear editor.

Amir has a friend called Abbas. He looks like a beach bum: sleek brushed-back hair, tight jeans, cap and colourful

T-shirt. Like Amir, Abbas drives for foreign journalists. In contrast to Amir, Abbas is quick and fearless, at least that is what he says. While Amir never utters a word against the regime, Abbas is more outspoken.

— We live in a prison, he will say to someone he trusts. — We are being slowly suffocated.

Abbas looks back with nostalgia to the years when he could travel, had money and lived the good life. — This life is the dregs.

But Abbas is not one to mope. He is full of good humour and his one care in life seems to be how to keep the various girlfriends from each other and not least from his wife. He describes in detail how he gives one presents, invites another to the park, disentangles birthdays, and during missile attacks attempts to render a little extra solicitude to all.

— But not in the western way, he insists, as if it is clear to all what 'the western way' is. — I just give presents and maybe we kiss. They're not really girlfriends, but friends.

I envy Pascal, who is working with Abbas. He does what few drivers do — he supplies Pascal with stories.

One afternoon Pascal knocks excitedly on my door.

— I have come across a deserter, he says when he is well inside.

Abbas had taken him to his relatives' house. They were talking about this and that, food supplies, targets bombed, the weather. A young man entered the room and sat down. Pascal asked him where he was from.

— Hillah, he answered.

— Hillah? What was the fighting like there?

— We had no chance. We had no will. I left.

— Left?

— I ran. No one fired, no one pursued me. Here I am.

— He has deserted, Abbas explained. — Deserted!

Pascal has a scoop. No one else has met a deserter; most of us have hardly met anyone at all. We are limited to controlled interviews with tea vendors and tea drinkers, battery vendors and battery buyers, people in bread queues, people who sell bread. It is all the same — Baghdad on the surface. A surface that keeps its secrets.

One evening Pascal tells me Abbas' story.

— He used to be high up in military intelligence. He worked for the regime, but increasingly had doubts about it. He kept his thoughts to himself, but as he saw through the cruel oppression, he started to talk to his nearest and dearest. One of his girlfriends worked in the same office. After a while he got tired of her and wanted to get out of the relationship. She begged for just one more night. The next morning he was arrested. She had placed a microphone in the bed. The girlfriend had tried to get him to criticise the regime, and in spite of not having said much he was imprisoned for four years. Had he been more talkative that evening he would not be here now. When he got out he had lost his job in intelligence. He started driving. But no one must know this, not until Saddam has gone; not even Amir.

One day Pascal lends me Abbas because Amir is visiting his family. I find him crying in the car. Suspecting the worst, I get in. Has someone in his family been struck by the night's bombs?

— My best friend returned from the front in Najaf yesterday, Abbas sobs. — Dead. We buried him yesterday afternoon. He left a wife and three small children.

Hamid was the commander of a detachment at the Najaf front, 200 kilometres south of Baghdad. Abbas knew nothing about how his friend was killed, just that he had met death in the desert.

– He was like a brother to me. We grew up in the same street, did everything together. We got drafted to the military together, served together. Now he's gone, Abbas cries.

– Hamid is already a martyr, he says bitterly. – I might be the next one.

– You?

– If the Americans come, I'll fight too. I'll never ever let them take Baghdad. Pascal will have to find himself another driver.

The previous day Amir had told me: – If the Americans attack Baghdad I can no longer drive for you.

– OK, I said, thinking he would be hiding in his mother's house.

– If they do I must defend my country. My brother has already enlisted and this afternoon I'm going to the Baath Party to collect a weapon.

– You must do what you have to do, I answered.

– They said their targets would be military. Since when was a pregnant woman a military target?

An increasing number of Iraqis talk about taking up arms should the Americans capture the town. The propaganda is doing its work: it is the duty of every citizen to fight for their fatherland. But is that the reason for Abbas' and Amir's sudden patriotism? Or has the press centre ordered all drivers to tell us they desire martyrdom? Is Kadim behind it all?

Knowing what Pascal told me about Abbas, I find it difficult to picture him fighting for Saddam.

I have never liked the Ministry of Information; now I hate it. I loathe walking into the building, or up onto the roof to send my TV reports. Invariably the recordings are interrupted by planes overhead. Then we rush down the stairs and stand waiting in the car park until the planes disappear. As if that were safer. When I use my phone I keep to the edge of the car park, as far from the buildings as possible, but within the official area, in order not to break the rules. TV transmissions are made in the daytime as no one wants to remain near one of the Americans' main targets in the evening.

Despite my dislike of the Ministry, I am obliged to come. The press briefings take place here; the compulsory bus trips depart from here. One day we are gathered for a briefing on the first floor, we hear the sound of low-flying planes. A huge boom reverberates close by. Broken glass tinkles, followed by a screech and yet another boom. People plunge headlong out of the building, certain that another missile will strike at any moment. As usual I have set up my phone outside and the thought rushes through my head: Do I leave it?

No, I can't leave my phone. As people run past me I hastily pack the cables, the phone and the aerial. The planes whine above us, we can hear the bombs dropping. I close the equipment bag and make a dash for it.

Amir is waiting with the engine running; Aliya is already in the car. I throw the phone into the boot. Amir puts his foot down and we are off, away, away from this awful place where bombs fall one after the other. I decide never to return as long as the war goes on.

That evening the Americans drop a large bomb on the Ministry. The anti-aircraft defences on the roof and the minister's office are both hit. The top floors catch fire. According to rumours, al-Sahhaf himself was in his office when the attacks started. He got out unscathed but fear got hold of him. Next morning a notice proclaims that the press centre has moved — to the Hotel Palestine. From now on we will be able to use our satellite telephones from our own rooms. What a relief! No more rising at the crack of dawn, connecting the phone in the dusty car park, transmitting outdoors. No more playing the hero during live broadcasts, scouting for approaching planes.

Uday, Kadim and Mohsen move into the empty offices of Iraqi Airways. Three gruff men sit outside at a table bearing a piece of cardboard with the words Press Centre, and an image of a hand pointing towards the door at the back. The men fiddle with long lists in Arabic, drink tea and smoke. God knows what is on their lists.

— We'll arouse suspicion, says Amir. — It's not a good idea to drive around the same streets too long.

There is a man I want to find. I have searched all the monasteries but didn't find him. He gave me the name of a monastery but no one knows its whereabouts, or they won't tell me. Having driven round in circles in Karada, Baghdad's Christian district, Amir gets nervous. I insist on continuing the search. We knock on doors and ask but no one has heard of St Anne's. In a church a man gives us directions. A blue gate, he says, but we never find it.

— Someone is following us, Amir gasps suddenly. A black car really is driving behind us through the narrow lanes. We hotfoot it back to the main road. The car follows us right back to the parking lot in front of the hotel, where it passes us slowly.

— Hell, they got my number. As soon as they spotted your blonde hair they'd have been interested. They'll think we're looking for something we shouldn't be looking for. I saw the militia observing us. I wanted to turn round but you were so keen on finding this priest. Sorry, you won't get me back there again.

Baghdad is drenched in fear. Everyone is watching everybody else. The ruling elite are also fearful, of being annihilated by the Americans, imprisoned and humiliated in front of their subjects.

I return to the hotel, disappointed at not having found Father Albert. As I pass through the glass doors Kadim's voice sounds over the loudspeaker: 'Press conference with the Defence Minister. Take your seats immediately.'

It would not hurt to hear what the Defence Minister has to say. Anyway, it's time to show my face to Uday and Kadim. I am an infrequent audience at the daily briefings, and am forever being hauled over the coals by Kadim.

From reception into the auditorium the soldiers stand to attention, in two lines, rifles at the ready. I sit down directly in front of Kadim.

— Did you watch Saddam? Antonia asks. I shake my head, while the well-informed RTL correspondent brings me up to date. Nothing earth shattering. What is sensational is the fact that the man can actually deliver speeches on this, the seventh day of the war. In spite of American efforts to stop Iraqi newscasts, they keep on broadcasting. The Iraqis have several mobile TV transmitters, their whereabouts unknown to the Americans. Every day, whether a new recording or a re-release, the president pops up on screen. He talks of heroic battles and the need to stand together. He charges every Iraqi with the responsibility of defending the country.

— Do not wait for orders, take the initiative yourselves if you are attacked, or whenever the enemy draws near, he says.

— Those sandbags on the street corners, is that what they

should throw at the Americans? Antonia laughs. She is a fascinating woman. Come sandstorm, rain, wind or bomb attacks, she always looks as though she has walked straight out of a shampoo advert. She is one of Germany's most popular TV journalists and is nicknamed 'Correspondent Lionheart' for her quick-witted and engaging reports. Owing to RTL's tight schedule she does not have much time to walk around and engage people in conversation. When we meet in the evenings I relay the mood of the town and she updates me on the news front.

After a forty minute wait the Minister of Defence rolls into the auditorium. He is the fattest Iraqi I have ever seen. The place is teeming with soldiers, some watching the doors, others watching us. The Kalashnikovs are cocked.

The minister's voice booms across the auditorium.

– The enemy tried to surround Najaf yesterday, Sultan Hashim Ahmed starts. – Their lines were broken, however, by our attack, and they retreated to the desert with heavy losses.

I remembered Hamid who fell near Najaf. Would he be remembered? Or his fellow soldiers? No, according to the fat man in the green uniform it was the Americans who suffered heavy losses.

Hamid might get a grave in Baghdad but he will not figure in any death statistics. They do not exist, not now, not during the last Gulf War. The authorities never report military defeats, just victories. 'The Iraqis continue their heroic jihad against the invading powers,' *al-Thawra* had written this morning. The reports of Iraqis pushing American and British troops back are spiced up with details: 'One helicopter, eleven tanks, twelve armoured personnel carriers, two unmanned planes were rendered harmless. We caused the enemy heavy losses, a large number of dead and wounded lay on the battlefield. Their forces are in shock and chaos thanks to our intrepid soldiers.' Not a single line about the thousand soldiers allegedly killed by the Americans in the desert during the battle for Najaf. They, like Hamid, are only remembered and mourned by their relatives and friends.

It is suddenly pitch black. The electricity has gone. Everyone remains in their seats – the best course of action considering the many armed men present. A few torches light up narrow slits in the room while Kadim guides us out. Like a flock of sheep carrying notepads we are herded over to the Sheraton Hotel on the other side of the parking lot.

– I'm bailing out here, Antonia whispers. I have a live just now. Tell me if anything happens.

We settle in the new auditorium and wait yet again for the minister. After a while the man wearing the XXXL uniform mounts the podium in the empty hotel and continues as if nothing has happened. While he talks about Iraqi gains in the war we hear it continuing full strength overhead. There are dull thuds as the bombs strike who knows where. The Defence Minister refuses to admit that the defence lines around Baghdad have been breached. – We Iraqis know the desert. Our trenches might be only sixty centimetres deep and half a metre wide, but they are effective. If a bomb should strike ten metres away from the troops, the soldiers will escape unhurt, says Sultan Hashim Ahmed, and calls the Americans cowards. – They bomb from such heights and cannot be accurate; they dare not fight man to man. The enemy has the capacity to go where it wants, but in the end they must attack this town if they want to win, and it will cost them dearly. The enemy thought this would be a five-day war, or a six-day war, or a seven-day war. I myself wish the war were over, but if it lasts it will only mean heavy losses for the enemy. The Americans might advance on Baghdad, they might be here in five or ten days, but they will never capture it, he says.

I glance at my watch; it is time for a live transmission. I get up and tip-toe towards the door in order not to interrupt. The door is locked. I try another. Also locked. A soldier approaches and shows me back to my place. I point to my watch and then to the door. Kadim comes over.

– I have to go, I say.

– You cannot leave before the minister.

– I have a transmission in ten minutes.

– You cannot leave before the minister.

– But what will my TV station do without me?

– You cannot leave before the minister.

– You cannot stop me from leaving the room, I say; the whole ministry is getting up my nose. I can no longer keep my mouth shut and argue using their own rhetoric.

– The president gave an important speech today. A speech which I have prepared in order to recount to my viewers.

– You cannot leave before the minister.

– Excuse me, Mr Kadim. Is the Minister of Defence more important than Saddam Hussein?

Kadim looks penetratingly at me, turns and walks away. The door remains locked. The guards follow me around. I wait for a small eternity.

Chairs scrape the floor up on the podium and the Minister of Defence waddles out. We are to remain seated until he has left the hotel. To hell with the Defence Minister. To hell with my live broadcast. I will have to phone and tell them I was held hostage at the Sheraton. One–nil to Antonia, who left on time.

I run down to report on the minister's speech. Antonia's minder is sitting on a plastic stool. He is proficient in German and watches over her every word. They are always quarrelling about what she might or might not say. He is stubborn and strict but has met his match in Correspondent Lionheart. The minder does not like her use of the word 'regime'; it is negatively loaded. Instead of 'Saddam's regime' she should use the expression 'The Iraqi Government'. And why not treat him with some respect and call him 'President Saddam Hussein' rather than just 'Saddam Hussein'? After all, you say President George Bush, don't you?

When she has completed the transmission he gets up.

– I think you should talk more about children.

– The theme today was war and politics.

– I still think you need to talk more about children.

– I talk about children all the time. You haven't paid attention! she hisses as only an Austrian can, and turns on her heel. Her lips are narrow slits and her eyes flash.

I wait my turn by the live point. Thank God no one supervises me. I can say what I like; the Baghdad spy-school is not that advanced – Norwegian is not on the curriculum.

The roof and garden below the hotel are humming with cameras and reporters. The assembly line principle is in operation. News agencies like Reuters and AP establish positions with cameras and satellite connections to the rest of the world and hire out time to reporters; ten minutes each, for thousands of pounds, and a scramble for slots. My permanent employers, NRK, SVT and DR, book slots a week in advance.

Over the course of the three weeks of the war, my work-load has increased steadily. I report for Norwegian, Swedish, Danish, Finnish and Dutch TV, as well as several radio stations. Occasionally I work for BBC World and CBC in Canada, although without using my name as I fear Uday and his mob will punish me or throw me out of the country if I say anything contrary.

One evening while reporting for Dutch TV from the roof of Hotel Palestine I become aware of a man sitting on a stool opposite me. In the dark he appears threatening and sinister. I lose my train of thought. Have I really just said that it is difficult to get to grips with what Baghdad citizens say, because this is a dictatorship? I am angry with myself. Will I now be thrown out for being careless? I must cut out the English transmissions. I gather my thoughts, pick up the thread and mumble about heavy civilian losses, wounded, killed. '*Kinder, kinder, verletzte Kinder*' rings in my ears, an echoing of Antonia's minder. I conclude with something about wounded children.

When the transmission ends I quickly sidle past the glaring man. I pray he has not realised who I am. He remains seated in front of the cameras to monitor the next reporter, a petite brunette who ferociously lisps her way through the transmission – in Spanish.

Today is 27 March and Josh has invited us to a birthday party on the sixteenth floor. The blond Scot is the kindest and most helpful in Hotel Palestine. I have to find him a present in bombed-out Baghdad. A few food shops are open but there is not a gift in sight. I think of all the times Josh has invited me for breakfast; he tempts with three kinds of porridge: banana flavoured, with raisins, or plain. In addition he serves coffee and tea. I *have* to find him a present. I ask Amir to drive me to the book market. As we draw near he stops the car – a man passes by carrying a basket of home-made leek bread on his head. The area is windswept and deserted. The streets leading off the book market are empty, the windows shuttered. The wind gets hold of anything lying around: rubbish, magazines, plastic bags whirl around in a sad dance.

A tiny booth is open, selling stationery: A4 paper, paper-clips, staplers. I wrack my brain wondering if any of this could be a gift. I turn and twist a stapler, wondering whether Josh might need it. Gift-wrapped with some spare staples? The man in the shop looks at me quizzically. He must be wondering what I need stationery for now. I myself wonder why the hell he is open.

– I was crawling up the walls at home. Idleness drives me crazy, he answers. – But it's almost worse here. I'm just sitting waiting for customers.

– Have you had any?

– You are my first customer today, he says, and looks out over the dreary street before adding a few phrases of homage to Saddam. Half-heartedly. They still have to be included; after all, who is the dark-haired woman accompanying me?

Then I spot them. Large, bound books with pink, mauve, black and green covers. The pages are lined. A perfect diary. Encouraged, I select a colour. Pink is too feminine, mauve too faded, black too depressing, while hope springs ever-green, or in this case, grass-green. My eye is caught by something on the next shelf – a card with a pink teddy bear and the words 'Happy Birthday'. I open the card and a thin, creaking sound streams out: 'Happy Birthday to you.' I close the card quickly; no good wasting the battery.

There's a whole gang of us celebrating Josh's birthday that evening. Sky reporter David is sprawled over a low armchair and greets me happily with one of his well-aimed remarks. He has a very well-educated Oxford accent and was at university with Tony Blair. His swept-back greying hair and easy manner make him look as if he has just returned from a golf tournament – victorious.

Tim is submerged in the only other available chair, whispering that he misses his five children. Remy is on the bed, absorbed in the map Josh has downloaded from the Internet, a huge document from the University of California's home page.

Veljko and Milan, the two Serbian cameramen yanked in by Sky at the last moment when their own photographers chose to leave, are on the floor, against the wall, drinking 'champagne' brandy out of plastic mugs.

The Red Hot Chili Peppers boom in the background. Josh is standing in the middle of the floor.

– When I got home today the chambermaid's trolley was parked outside my door. I entered and as I passed the bathroom I froze – so did she. She was trying out my electric toothbrush and had a mouth full of toothpaste!

Josh laughs and says he gave her the toothbrush. I hand him my present. A pink light shines from the card when the birthday song is played. I had failed to spot that in the windblown shop. The Chili Peppers are turned down so that everyone might hear 'Happy Birthday'. The thin sound belongs to another life.

There's a crash; the entire hotel is shaking. The building sways from side to side. We rush out onto the balcony. In the west, towards the Tigris, I catch a glimpse of what look like smoke bombs. Beams of light rush across the sky, the crackle and flash of ack-ack guns is everywhere. There is another crash. Several of the buildings near the Ministry of Information are ablaze. Swoosh, a missile and blinding light flies past the hotel. We hear a target being hit on the other side of the river. Swish, one more, then another. The hotel sways again, but we are rooted to the spot; we must see what is going on. If a tomahawk arrives it won't matter where we are. David rushes out to deliver a quick report. The rest of us have no more transmissions and stay up, drinking brandy into the night. The ack-ack flashes continue to decorate the sky, as if to convince Baghdad's inhabitants that the air defences are working; a fragile defence against wave upon wave of cruise missiles and B52s which drop their cargo from thousands of feet up. While we watch the sky, mothers comfort petrified children and tend cradles occupied by premature babies, older children count bombs, and fathers fear that the next strike will bring the house down around them. To some, this horrendous night will stay with them for years to come.

The noise quietens down, and we hear it. Josh chucked the birthday card away when the attack started. Now it lies as if nothing has happened, playing 'Happy Birthday' in the same tinny voice.

— That's certainly some card you got hold of, David crows. Must have the best battery in Baghdad. Not like Josh's quality Swiss watch!

Josh's watch stopped on the second night of the war, when the bomb hit the Presidential palace, on 21 March, 01.05 local time, never to start again.

The birthday guests soon droop. We are exhausted from lack of sleep. It is as if we are ice cold inside, immune to feelings of happiness, to brandy, fear, hunger. We walk the earth in a numb existence, an existence filled with trauma and insomnia.

A warm breeze makes the curtains flap. We sit silently. Now, when it is no longer possible to leave Baghdad, the discussions about fear have evaporated. It would not do to talk about it, it is actually taboo. Never once, after the war started, have I heard anyone utter one word about fear. When the bombing is at its worst we stare fixedly into the air, out of the balcony door, into eternity – but never into fear.

I thank Josh for the brandy, switch on my torch and make my way down the stairs. Another torch is on its way up. It is Lindsay from Channel 4. She stops and scrutinises me. – Is everything OK?

I nod, but suddenly everything is not OK. In the torch-light we talk about the war, about the Americans and the rumours.

– You shouldn't sleep alone, she says. Why don't you come and sleep with us? We can put an extra bed in the office. Timothy is there, so I'm not frightened at night.

The myth about hardened war correspondents is exposed. Many of them are grown women, with a well-developed maternal instinct. But they too have rules: comfort others, protect, but never, ever talk about your own fear.

– Come and have supper whenever you want, says Lindsay, and the torches part, hers up to the thirteenth floor, me down to the seventh.

Supper with Channel 4 is not to be sneezed at. Every evening, round about 10pm, when the last reports have been sent, they settle down with their guests. Lindsay and Timothy's kitchen is well-equipped as far as pots and pans and raw materials are concerned.

They also have four microwave ovens, none of which are used for cooking. They are earthed to the electricity supply and never turned on. Every night, before going to bed, Lindsay and Timothy place all their computers, satellite telephones and sensitive editing equipment in the microwaves. The tenor of Timothy's theory, who had served in Rhodesia under Ian Smith, was that the microwave would protect against the dreaded e-bombs. According to Timothy the electromagnetic rays cannot penetrate the microwave ovens. Channel 4 would be the only channel left transmitting.

On the balcony are generators which supply power to the computers and editing units. They have several satellite telephones, some legal, some hidden. In addition Timothy has three Thuraya telephones. These are forbidden as the Iraqis believe they are capable of guiding missiles from the ground. In addition they are also more difficult to detect than the satellite telephones which are huge and take time to erect. The Thuraya phones are no larger than mobile phones and work almost as well as satellite phones. Timothy had trawled the hotel to find clever hiding places. One phone was hidden in a shaft between the ninth and tenth floors. The shaft was full of plastering and dust and the phone was lying in a plastic bag underneath some rubbish. The second was squeezed under a tile in the bathroom and the third glued to the wall behind a wardrobe.

Every morning a trail of sweat leads from the basement of Hotel Palestine up to the roof. Over seventeen stories the sweat mixes with the smell of sand, dirt and garbage. Walking up the stairs, someone will breathe heavily behind you, or tear past you on his way down: a dripping man in a Puma T-shirt, shorts and sweatband, he will deposit a kiss on each cheek while crying '*Ciao Bella!*' This is Lorenzo, the *Corriere della Sera* correspondent, training for his next Mount Everest expedition. Every morning, for two hours, he runs up and down the Hotel Palestine stairs, bombs or no bombs.

After that he is the happiest man in the world. '*Vuoi un cappuccino?*'

Lorenzo has an enormous stash of cappuccino powder in little sachets, which he serves *caldo* or *freddo*.

This morning he is fretting over having missed a marathon. – I had booked everything, flight, hotel, registration. I never thought this war would drag out so. It should have started in January, which would have suited me better. Now I'm worried the Mount Everest expedition will leave without me. They're off at the beginning of May, so if the war's over by Easter I'll make it, he muses.

– But my basic fitness is not brilliant. Rushing up and down stairs is rather monotonous. Just imagine if the war had been in Afghanistan . . . Then I could have run up and down the mountains. D'you like my cappuccino?

It is difficult to take in every word Lorenzo utters; he speaks as he lives – *allegro*.

We sit in the two easy chairs in his room, our backs to one of the beds Lorenzo has pushed up against the window. There is food everywhere – cans of tomatoes, vegetables, cheese and pasta. People's food preferences are transported into the war. Lorenzo maintains normality by cooking pasta all'Arrabbiata. Stefan's room is packed with boxes of wurst. Remy hoarded red wine and cigarettes, while Janine's cupboard was full of chocolate. Josh disposes of every conceivable type of compo rations – chicken curry, vegetable stew or Christmas pudding. I myself boast a huge selection of dates, pistachio nuts and raisins.

One day I hear something which makes me shudder. Five journalists have disappeared without a trace. Armed men from the security service forced their way into their rooms at five in the morning. With guns at their heads they were ordered to pack up and leave. I am told what happened by a reporter who shared a room with one of them. It gives me a fright when I realise who they are. Three are from the tourist group with which I would have re-entered Iraq had I not been issued with a journalist's visa at the last moment. The two others entered the country on human shield visas. They were all living in Hotel Palestine and worked as journalists.

I ask Kadim where they are.

– They hid under the pretext of journalism, but really they are spies, he says.

– But where are they?

– I have no knowledge of that. They are now in the hands of the security service.

– But you must tell us where they are!

– Do not ask about them again, Kadim hisses. I have no knowledge whatsoever about them.

The journalists at Hotel Palestine decide to refer the matter to the International Red Cross. They still maintain a presence in Baghdad and have a better chance than us of making some headway. I call on the Swiss head of the Red Cross office on several occasions to ask how the investigation is going; he never has any news.

– To be honest, I just don't have a clue, he whispers. – We have no idea of where they might be.

Melinda phones me from the third floor. – No one should sleep alone following these disappearances. And as you know, I'm closer to the ground, she says. Melinda phones at intervals to find out how I am. – Push one of your beds up against the balcony door, she admonishes. – That'll protect you from shrapnel. And remember to keep the bath full of water. Keep money and safety equipment close. Put a stool in front of the door and use the padlock.

Once again, the women excel at looking after each other.

– Go, go! Get a car and go!

Kadim is down in reception directing us. It is already dark.

– But what about an interpreter? And a minder?

– Just go!

Dumbfounded, we stare at the gesticulating Kadim. We had been hanging around in reception to glean the latest news when he suddenly orders us to leave. This is the first time we have been given permission to drive at night. Luckily my notebook is in my pocket; I am prepared. Aliya is spending the night at home, Amir is nowhere to be seen.

– Jump in, Pascal calls.

It is spooky convoy-driving at night. If the Americans spot us from the air they might mistake us for something else. An Iraqi Minister, maybe, with his bodyguards. But where are we going and why?

– To al-Nasser, in the north of Baghdad. A missile has hit the market, Abbas says.

We fall silent while Abbas finds his way in the deserted streets.

Before we get out of the car we hear the screams; heart-rending howls reach our ears. The drivers leave the headlights on to act as floodlights; some of us have flashlights. Torches have been attached to a house. Otherwise it is dark.

We stumble across the market square. Distorted iron bars and smashed crates lie around. The stalls and most of the wares lie spoilt on the ground. Someone is shining a torch into the missile crater.

We are surrounded by residents and stall-holders. Some

beat their chests. Others calm down the chest-beaters.
Many appear to be in shock. I lose Abbas and Pascal in the
melee and latch on to another interpreter.

– A lot of children were sitting over there on the pavement. Now they're all dead, a man moans. A little shoe is
all that remains. The pavement is covered in blood, as is the
wall of the house. Broken glass and bits of metal are everywhere. The children were carried away, dead or dying, a
few hours ago.

– The planes flew low overhead. Suddenly we heard a
whining sound. Then all we saw was smoke and bodies.
Bodies without heads, without arms, without legs, a man
relates. – The wounded lay writhing among the dead.
People started to carry them off, blood everywhere.

– How many were killed?

– I counted fifty, an elderly man says. He cries and turns
away, lowers his head, then makes his way through the crowd.

– Massacre, massacre, a woman intones. – Massacre.

Many of the coffins are already in the mosque. Outside,
the relatives of the dead gather. One talks about a cousin,
another about a nephew, a third about an aunt.

– Where is your democracy? Where is your humanity?
an elderly man cries. He has lost his grandchild.

I spot Abbas and Pascal in the crowd. They are leaving
for the hospital to survey the extent of the damage. Abbas
finds his way through the blacked-out streets.

– I have admitted about sixty, the doctor says. – To many
I can issue death certificates on the spot.

– Go and see for yourselves, he says, and points to a
small greyish building.

Pascal and Abbas enter the hospital, while I walk through
the courtyard, on a narrow path behind the hospital. The
building's door is open. The room is packed. They lie in

three-storey bunkbeds. A boy wearing an Adidas tracksuit and a white T-shirt has had the top part of his body smashed. His face is covered in blood.

Another boy, he might be a teenager, has a crushed skull. He lies on his side. His head is a gaping cavity. Fibres of skin and hair, stiff with blood, cling to him.

Two children share a bed. Their eyes and mouths are wide open and they appear to be grabbing at each other. Their splayed fingers touch each other. The clothes are bloody and ripped to pieces, their bodies full of deep cuts.

A chubby woman wearing an *abaya* and a black shawl lies on her back. Blood from her nose and mouth has coagulated. The wide tunic is open, an arm exposed. Broken bone shafts protrude from the arm.

Another young woman appears to be sleeping; her eyes are closed and her chin raised. One feels like placing a pillow under her head, so she will be more comfortable on the cold bunkbed.

A boy wearing a chequered shirt has got one side of his body cut off. His leg lies beside him on the metal plate, ripped away. He's only fourteen, maybe fifteen. His face is narrow, refined.

I cannot move, I cannot walk away. If I leave, reality will devour me. Then they will all really be dead.

It's as if I have seen them before. The boy in the Adidas tracksuit, the children who must have been killed in the same instant. The woman, who might have been carrying a bag full of fruit away from the stalls.

In this room of death, like the bodies in their beds, I too have stiffened. Why don't I go? Why don't I leave the dead to themselves?

How vulnerable humans are! How easily a skull can be

crushed. So suddenly life can be wrestled from a living soul.

I am woken from my trance by a man and a boy who hurry into the room. Their eyes are wide-open, desperate, searching the bodies in the beds. Their shoulders droop, dispirited, their faces are dark. The man gives a tormented cry. It escapes from deep inside him, as though it is many hundreds of years old. He stiffens, then rushes over to the boy in the chequered shirt. He sinks to his knees and embraces the bloody bundle. The boy with him kneels by the dead body. Both sob.

Two men enter with a coffin. The man and the boy, maybe father and son, get up from the floor. They lift what might be a little brother off the metal bunk and place him in the coffin. Then they put the leg in with him and close the lid. He will be taken to the mosque to be washed. Tomorrow he will be buried. The man and the boy carry the coffin away down the path.

Left on the bunkbed is a pool of dried blood, nearly black. Some drops are redder, fresher; the blood that just ran out of the boy's body.

This is what the reader and the television viewer do not see. Nor the politicians and the generals. It is too gruesome to publish. But those who are in the morgue this evening will carry the pictures with them for ever.

In addition to the dead, around one hundred wounded are brought to Noor hospital this night. Children and adults share beds. Infants wrapped in bandages howl and moan; others are unconscious, have flesh wounds all over the body.

When a missile explodes, shrapnel, at a temperature of many hundred degrees, is ejected. The pieces can be as small as a nail or large as an axe head. Glowing hot and sharp they easily bore their way into a human body – or cut it in two.

A doctor rushes past. – They said they would not kill civilians, he cries.

Hassan stands alone by a bed. In it lies his brother, with shrapnel in his stomach. His face is yellow and he rambles incoherently.

– He must live, he must live, Hassan cries.

Amidst the tears he talks: – We were standing outside our house, Ali, Jamil and I. I wasn't hit but my little brother fell down in a pool of blood. Ali lies here, Jamil was killed on the spot. He had just turned six.

– Where are your parents?

– My father is in the mosque washing Jamil, he sobs. – My mother is at home with my sisters.

I must carry on. Have to go to the mosque. I glance at my watch and see that I have missed my first deadline, my second too. But I can get it into the last edition; I must tell about the massacre.

Abbas stands by the entrance to the hospital, smoking. He gives me an empty look, but says nothing. We set off for the mosque.

I am not wearing a shawl and tie my jacket around my head. The mosque is full of people. Some scowl at us. Should we leave? Are we being intrusive? The atmosphere makes me giddy and I want to go when a man grabs my hand. He looks mad. His eyes are wide open and his mouth distorted. The man is tall, with light brown dishevelled hair and freckles. His jacket is open. He halts by a coffin and talks to me in Italian. He holds my hand tight, stares into my eyes, then he lifts the lid of the coffin. I look down. Inside is a boy wearing shorts and a shirt; a large cut crosses his chest. The boy too has freckles and the same light hair as the man. His knees are grazed, his clothes spotted, the trousers are green. Surely his knees were grazed before the missile struck. Maybe he was playing football, or cycling. He will never get any more scratches.

— *Perché? Perché?* the man says, his voice faltering, his eyes roaming between me and the coffin. — Why?

No answer exists.

I cannot tell him it's because the USA thinks Saddam Hussein has weapons of mass destruction.

That's not what he is asking.

The words stick in my throat. He begs for an answer and I have nothing to give. I look up at him and feel I am falling. But I stand with a jacket over my head; I stand and weep floods of tears onto the little boy with the freckles. The man collapses over his son. Several of the men nearby weep quietly.

The boy is like a petrified sculpture in the little wooden coffin. His eyes are open, fixed on the roof of the mosque — towards heaven — into eternity.

Another man grabs my hand and leads me to the back of the mosque. He pushes me through a door in the end wall. Into the wash room.

Fatima lies on a bench. She is naked and is being washed by three women in black tunics. Fatima has a cut in the knee, in the stomach and in the back. Her face is untouched. She has dark curly hair and might be about ten years old. She looks like a Madonna. Her skin is pale, flawless; it seems so soft, I want to touch it. The brown eyes appear still to be seeing. Through reality.

— Tell the world, the man had said in broken English as

he pushed me through the door. – Take pictures, show the world that our children are dying!

I take out my camera and look questioningly at the three women. They nod.

The women lay a transparent plastic sheet around Fatima, then wrap her in a white cloth. It is rolled around her several times before being knotted at both ends. They cut holes for her eyes and mouth.

On the floor there is a coffin; her mother Hasina is already lying in it. One of the women recounts what happened. – They were on their way to the market and happened to be where the missile hit. Hasina had eleven children; she leaves ten behind.

Fatima is lowered into the coffin beside her mother. Washed clean – on her way to Paradise. Outside the cubicle two of her brothers cry.

Back in room 734 I have twenty minutes to write Fatima's story. I forward a picture of the beautiful young face. *Aftenposten* cannot publish it; actually I already knew that. I sent it so as not to be alone in having seen her.

A week later the *New York Review of Books* wants to print pictures of the last moments before Fatima was lowered into the coffin. But not of her face.

I send the last image. Where she is lying on the bed, rolled in a white cloth knotted at both ends. A dead child's face is too strong an image for the international press. But that is what war is about – people dying.

The next morning we return to the market place. To discover in the light of day what had really happened. Sixty-five bodies had been put into coffins during the course of the night.

*

— My sons! My sons!

Shamsiya sits on the floor, beating her chest with clenched fists. Beside her are her mother, daughter, sisters, aunts, nieces and neighbours. Black-robed women come and go. They do not talk but listen in silence to Shamsiya's lament. Now and again they strike up, clap their hands together rhythmically, then fall silent again. Or cry. All attention is directed towards Shamsiya. The room is heavy with the atmosphere of sympathy and sorrow.

She lost three sons. Shrapnel from the missile which struck the market shot into the backyard, smashed the doorway and flew in through the window.

— The whole house shook, the windows shattered and I heard screams. I rushed out and they were each lying in a pool of blood. I froze, just stood there looking. It was as if I entered the gates of death with them, then I was hurled back, the mother cries.

The youngest son died instantly, from shrapnel in the heart; the two older brothers died in the hospital the same night.

— I had asked them to stay at home because so many bombs had hit the neighbourhood, the mother says between sobs. *— And look, they met their death at home,* she cries, and points out through the door to the backyard, which is full of shrapnel. The blood has not yet been scrubbed away. Flies buzz around, soaking it up. Shamsiya interrupts her tale with wailing: *My sons! My sons!*

She pulls a photograph from her bosom. It shows her five sons. Now only two are alive.

— How beautiful they are, she sobs. *— Muhammed was hit in the heart, Hussein in the forehead, Abbas in the chest. Muhammed was only twelve; he was born during war and died during war. The night he was born was one of the worst bombing nights of the Gulf War,* the mother recalls.

— They were so young. Still at school. I have breast-fed them, washed them, clothed them, taught them to speak, sent them to

school. What shall I do now? Bush has ruined my life. Why does he kill families? Why?

Her lament grows in strength and the other women join in. The wails reach the street and blend with the low hum of voices from the market.

In a room on the other side of the backyard sits Kahlil, the boys' father. The old man is crying. He sits up against a wall, his legs crossed. This is where he was when the missile struck. — *If only my boys had been in this room with me. Then they would have been alive now. How can I go on living, with my sons dead? If only the missile had hit me instead,* he moans.

A man enters the room. His eyes are bloodshot.

— *Jovid is dead,* he says quietly.

Jovid is the boy next door, one of Muhammed's friends. He was out on the street when the missile came and was hit in the stomach by shrapnel. He was taken to hospital and died in the night. His uncle has arrived to impart the news. Khalil nods silently, grabs the uncle's hand and prays.

Out in the backyard is twelve-year-old Muhammed, together with his big brother. Not the Muhammed who was killed by the missile, but his friend and namesake. When he heard that the missile had struck his best friend's house he came running immediately.

— *When I arrived I saw Muhammed lying there,* the boy says. His eyes are empty. — *I ran home and returned with my mother and father. He was our best football player and fastest cyclist. I think of him all the time. Last night I couldn't sleep.*

Out on the street the coffins pass by slowly. They have been secured to the roofs of cars and move in procession through the desolate market place. After the victims had been taken to the mosque to be washed and prayed over, the coffins were returned home for a last night under their own roof, to be buried today.

At the market place people walk around and inspect the damage; the crater made by the missile, the burned-out cars, the *twisted iron bars and ripped canvas. Small missile fragments lie everywhere. When the missile exploded the bits penetrated whatever they reached. The bits that didn't hit anything lie scattered around, hard and cold.*

— Allah will make us forget, forgive, says a man who accompanies his friend to the grave.

No one really knows what it was that exploded at the market. Several who were there immediately before the missile hit said they saw a plane circle above. They say it was the plane that dropped the missile. But it might equally have been Iraqi anti-aircraft guns aiming at the plane. When journalists arrived at the market that same evening Iraqi police had cleared away any large bits of missile, probably to prevent anyone from identifying it. The crater was one metre in diameter, too small to have been made by the bombs used by the Americans.

However, undeniable is the fact that Muhammed lost his best friend and Shamsiya and Khalil lost a twelve-year-old, a fourteen-year old and an eighteen-year old son.

Spring has long turned into summer. The mercury is creeping towards thirty degrees. The everyday life of war has reached us: no electricity or water in the hotel, the fridge is useless and the water-boiler superfluous. I bribe the hotel electrician and he connects a lamp in my room to the generator. Amir buys me some wiring and – hey presto – my computer and phone have electricity.

When there is water in the pipes we let each other know, and anyone with time on their hands can take a shower – in cold water, of course. We fill up the bathtubs to wash ourselves and our clothes. The bell boys have long since disappeared and the hotel slowly fills with rubbish. I can sympathise with them not wanting to come to work. They have enough to do looking after their families, or maybe they are doing the security rounds for the Baath Party, like Amir's brother.

I ask Aliya how her family are coping. – No problem. We have a gas cooker – all Iraqis have one. No one is naïve enough to think there will be electricity every day – not even in peace time. And we have a water tank on the roof and masses of food. No one in Baghdad is suffering because of the war. Well, apart from the ones who are hit by missiles, she adds.

On one of the warmest days we are waiting for al-Sahhaf, as usual. We are expected to be on time, the minister arrives when it suits him. I sit talking to Robert Fisk, one of the most knowledgeable and interesting among us. Always restless, always toying with new ideas. Now he is discussing depleted uranium. It is used in the American missile-heads to penetrate panzers, bunkers and solid surfaces. Following the first Gulf War there was an increase in the incidence of cancer among soldiers who had served in Southern Iraq; the same was the case for the people of Basra.

– Tanks and bunkers which have been hit continue to radiate depleted uranium, Robert says. – And you can be sure that the military vehicles are soon crawling with children playing. They climb on to them, slide down the bonnet, clamber around the burnt-out chassis. Then they go home, with uranium dust in their pockets, in their clothes, hair and little bodies.

Robert is interrupted by the Minister for Information, who strides in. Proudly, al-Sahhaf announces that from now on Iraq will use unconventional weapons against the Americans.

I look at Robert questioningly. Unconventional weapons? Does that mean weapons of mass destruction? Chemical, nuclear?

That same evening Iraq's first suicide bomber strikes. Ali al-Nawani drives his taxi straight into an American road-block outside Najaf and blows it up. Four Americans are killed.

The next day we are told that *this* is Iraq's new unconventional weapon: suicide bombers.

Aliya is sitting in reception engrossed in *The Revolution*. Usually she translates automatically, not always able to stifle a yawn.

— What are you reading about?

— Ali.

— Ali who?

— Ali, the martyr, of course.

Aliya shows me a picture of the twenty-year-old. He looks strong and determined, but the picture was probably taken long before he decided on any terror action.

Aliya looks around, thoughtful. — He must be brave. He's so young and beautiful. It can't have been easy . . .

Then she becomes serious and whispers. — You know, suicide is forbidden in Islam. It's considered *haram* — illegal. But because he gave his life to Allah, *haram* doesn't count.

She breathes a sigh of relief, pleased that she has managed to explain such a complicated theological issue.

— Now he's in Paradise and will get his reward, she assures me, and lightens up; a reward in Paradise compensates many times the loss of one's life. — He'll go straight to the top, you know. In Paradise there are seven levels, and he'll go to *al-firdous* — the top level. Only the Prophet Muhammed and holy men and martyrs are there.

Aliya translates the article, which is on the front page, or rather what is left of the front page beyond the usual portrait of the president.

'President Saddam Hussein hails the martyr' is the headline. 'The president entreats Allah to open the doors of Paradise to Ali'. In addition, Saddam Hussein honours the martyr with two posthumous orders. 'This is Mesopotamia's first martyr. Ali – one of the military forces' most outstanding heroes. By turning his body into a destructive bomb and following the example of his Palestinian brothers, he taught the aggressor a lesson. Now his sacred soul rests with Allah.'

Ali had been an NCO. The newspaper reports that one day he had informed his superiors that he was prepared to sacrifice his life in a suicide attack. According to the paper he chose his own method and place. While the Americans claimed that four soldiers had been killed, the Iraqis claimed the figure was higher: Eleven killed and ten wounded, and in addition two tanks and two armoured cars destroyed.

– Most countries in the world condemn acts of terrorism, I object.

– Well, what are the Americans doing? Killing innocent women and children. Isn't that terror? The Americans might be our superior in arms, but we are morally superior. Anyhow, Allah is on our side, says Aliya.

Increasingly, people resort to religious rhetoric when talking about the war. Paradoxically, as long as Saddam Hussein has been in power, Islamic and fundamentalist religious groups have been brutally persecuted. During his first years in power Saddam Hussein insisted that Iraq should be a secular society. He feared that religious groups

would upset his power base and executed tens of thousands of religiously active Muslims accused of radical
fundamentalism. During the 1990s his strategy changed,
as he believed religious behaviour could help him. In time
he started to employ religious platitudes to increase his
support in the fight against Bush. The Islamic groups,
which had sought refuge in neighbouring countries to
escape persecution, are now welcomed home as heroes
and liberators.

Over the loudspeakers we are ordered to attend a press
conference with Vice President Taha Yassin Ramadan. I
would rather go into town with Aliya and talk to people
about Ali, the martyr. On the way out we are stopped by
Kadim. — Where are you going? The press conference is
starting.

— We thought . . .

Kadim looks at me with his sad eyes.

— Why do you not go on press conferences? Why do you
not go on bus trips? What are you doing here? If you do not
turn up we have duty to show you out.

We go and sit at the back of the auditorium, waiting for
Ramadan, one of Saddam Hussein's closest colleagues.

— They arrive with their B-52s, capable of killing lots of
people. What is our answer? To wait until we Iraqis have
designed the same type of bomb? No, for that we do not
have time. Now all Arabs will turn themselves into bombs.
If one bomb from a B-52 can kill five hundred or more, our
freedom fighters will kill five thousand. Suicide bombers
are enlisting every day. This is just the beginning, Ramadan
says. — You will get more good news in the days to come.
We now have a force of several thousand warriors from different countries. They will martyr themselves for our
cause; they have even said they do not want to be returned

to their home country after their martyrdom. They want to be buried in sacred Iraqi soil. They seek Paradise and the road leads through Iraq.

We are alarmed when we discover that the recruitment office is in Hotel Palestine. Suicide bombers belong under the same department as the human shields – the Ministry for Peace and Friendship – and share their offices. Between the lift and reception is a door I had never noticed until I saw potential suicide bombers disappear inside. Behind the door is a corridor and down some steps the recruitment office.

With every day that passes, more and more sinister types appear in the hotel lobby. It is easy to distinguish them from the close-cropped Iraqi bureaucrats, each sporting a neat moustache, but otherwise beardless. The sinister types have dishevelled hair and wear either the traditional tunic and wide trousers or various military personal effects. They all wear the Palestinian scarf. They are everywhere, in the reception area, on the roof, in the garden from where we broadcast our TV reports, lying around in the grass. I feel their glowering looks but never dare return their stare. It is a relief that the entire Ministry of Information, together with women and children, live with us, the infidels, in the hotel.

Next door to Antonia a 'dozen gloomy types sporting Islamic beards', as she describes them, move in. On the second floor are Tunisians, Syrians and Jordanians.

Lorenzo has been spying on the foreign warriors for several days. He notices that they are marked down on lists before taking their leave and disappearing. None of them stay long at the hotel.

At the beginning of the war they crossed the border

without problems. A journalist who had accompanied one bus said that no one was checked at the border; they had been allowed straight through.

One day an entire busload of warriors is bombed. After the Americans gain control of the roads from Amman and Damascus the border crossing becomes more difficult. Travellers report seeing men sitting by the roadside, arms bound, guarded by Americans.

– They still cross the border, a driver says. – Now that they can no longer use the roads, they come through the desert and go straight to their positions.

In Iraqi news media the hero status of the foreign warriors compares favourably with that of Ali. Front page homage is paid to the first two foreign soldiers killed in battle. *The Revolution* reports: 'Iyad and Fadi killed many infidels before the two Syrians themselves became martyrs. They are now in Paradise, the enemy they killed in hell. To honour the two martyrs a 24-hour raid against enemy positions was initiated. Twenty-three enemy soldiers were killed. Thirty-five tanks, six armoured personnel carriers and one helicopter were destroyed.'

The newspaper's commentary becomes increasingly vindictive and poetic as the war advances. The article about the two foreign suicide bombers ends thus: 'The mothers and wives of the enemy will cry blood, instead of tears, when their men are slaughtered by our hallowed soldiers.'

– They give me the creeps, Lorenzo says one day when a couple of suspicious types trot past us in reception. The TV station transmits interviews with mujahideen warriors. One after the other, Kalashnikovs cocked, they promise the viewers they will liberate them from the occupiers.

— I had a good job in Hamburg as an engineer, says one of them. — But I woke up one day and realised I could not go on living in the same way and so I enlisted.

According to Iraqi TV, two brothers sold their hair-dressing salon in Oran in Morocco to pay for a ticket to Iraq. — When an Arab is in danger we must help, they say.

— Why don't the Americans bomb that TV tower? Lorenzo whispers.

The *Corriere della Sera* correspondent himself lives a shady existence. He is one of those hated by Uday. He was actually expelled a month and a half ago, but refused to leave. On one of his last days in Iraq he interviewed Tariq Aziz, who told him he could stay as long as he wanted. Uday was informed but he had already expelled him and was so angry he ripped Lorenzo's accreditation from him when he next saw him. One of Uday's subordinates picked it up from the wastepaper basket and gave it back to Lorenzo.

Every time they meet Uday snarls. — Get out. No one is protecting you here.

Lorenzo tries to avoid using reception and instead enters and exits the building by the back stairs. The disappearance of the five other unaccredited 'illegal' journalists has given him a serious fright. They too were without the 'protection' of the Ministry of Information.

— *Cossa posso fare?* What can I do? Leave Iraq to you guys? he says despairingly, throwing up his arms and inviting us to his room for a cappuccino.

One morning I am woken by loud noises from the car park. I peep over the balcony and see a busload of warriors, fully armed, rush towards the hotel entrance. Has hell been let loose? In that case, safest to stay put. The telephone rings. It's Tim.

— Thirty suicide bombers from Yemen have arrived, come and have a look.

I shuffle down the stairs to secure an exclusive interview with a Yemeni. I suppose it does not matter where I am if they are going to blow the hotel to smithereens. In the reception area they are performing a war dance, Kalashnikovs raised over their heads. They too have learnt Saddam slogans.

> The victory is yours, oh Saddam
> We sacrifice our blood, our soul
> For you, oh Saddam
>
> You are the perfume of Iraq, oh Saddam
> The water of two rivers, oh Saddam
> The sword and the shield, oh Saddam

After a while I spot Kadim in the background. Naturally, the show's producer is the press centre's number two. The suited bureaucrat lets the Yemenis holler for a bit, then ushers them determinedly into the auditorium. They are followed by a handful of journalists clutching notebooks. Kadim claps his hands and nods to one of the dancers.

— We are from Saana in Yemen and are here to fight side by side with our Iraqi brothers. Together we will defeat the enemy of mankind — USA! the leader of the crowd cries.

— Attack! Fight them! Kill them! is the refrain.

— We will attack from all sides. They won't even draw breath, another chimes in.

— The time has come to introduce jihad to the world.

We will defeat Zionists and Christians, the leader cries. The group dance and clap their hands a little more, then march in step out of the hotel and into the waiting buses.

Thirty-year-old Salah Rahman is sitting on the front seat of the bus. He arrived in Iraq the previous week and says he is prepared to fight with Iraqi troops to defend Baghdad.

– The USA thinks it can decide everything. Bush is a terrorist. He cares more about his dog than he does about the rest of the world. He is the agent of the Jews and wants to control all Arabs. The USA is a snake, the fangs are Israel. But this time he's mistaken; Allah is with us and therefore we are stronger, is all he has time to say before the doors close on him. The bus leaves the car park, heading towards the desert in the south.

Tim has a problem – his surname is Judah. To be a Jew in Saddam's Iraq is dangerous. He could be accused of spying for the Zionists, the ultimate enemy.

Before World War II nearly a quarter of Baghdad's inhabitants were Jewish. Following a Nazi-inspired coup in 1941 many hundreds were killed and many more decided to leave. When Israel was created seven years later, 150,000 Jews were still living in Baghdad, but most of them left over the course of the following years. To leave was tantamount to losing everything – Jews were not allowed to sell their property.

Now only a handful remain, thirty-four to be precise. The synagogue lies hidden behind a stone wall but few have the courage to visit it. Along the east bank of the Tigris the walls and houses were once decorated with the Star of David; now the stars have been hacked away and deep wounds left behind.

Tim's ancestors left Baghdad and the emasculated

Ottoman Empire in the nineteenth century. They made for the prosperous British Empire: Bombay, Calcutta, Singapore and Shanghai. When Tim's father was four years old the family moved to London.

Tim has always known that he originally came from Baghdad. – We came to Iraq in the year 596 BC, his father had told him. – Once upon a time we lived in Babylon.

When Tim applied for an Iraqi visa the first time, a process which took him ten months, he omitted to mention that he was Jewish. In the space on the form for religion he wrote 'Christian'. Thus the first Judah in over a hundred years arrived back in Baghdad.

But then there is the surname, which in Persian actually means Jew.

– Judah? What sort of name is that? people in Jordan asked him.

– It's just a name. It doesn't really mean anything, Tim answered. In Arabic a surname exists which is pronounced in virtually the same way.

Every day, before and even after the war started, our ears are pumped full of anti-Jewish propaganda. Officialdom in Iraq never uses the word Israel as the regime does not acknowledge the formation of the state of Israel; they call the country 'The Zionist State'.

One day, when we are stuck in traffic, Aliya suddenly says that all people are of equal value. – Well, apart from the Jews, of course.

Tim doesn't say a word.

Aliya thinks for a moment and then adds generously: – But I do think, even among Jews, there are some decent people.

Tim nods. He has by the way one more problem to deal with: his nationality. To be British is not always an advantage when stopped by Baath Party officials. One day, while shopping at an electrician's, they approach us.

– Norwegian, I say.

– French, Tim says, and waves his French passport. As his mother is French he has two passports. The French are popular in Iraq owing to their uncompromising attitude to the USA's warmongering.

– Why does it say British on your accreditation? the officer asks. – British? Tim says. – That must be a mistake.

The officer looks doubtfully at us before entering into a long conversation with Aliya, who eventually manages to extricate us from the mess. Tim was unaware that the Arabic on his yellow accreditation card, which we have to wear round our necks, classifies him as British.

– You must be honest about your background, Tim, and not boast that you are French when you are really British, Aliya scolds.

In the end I find Father Albert. The monastery is hidden behind pale blue doors, as I had been told, in a lush and beautiful garden. A lean nun lets us in. Having spent seven years in the Vatican, she speaks Italian like a Roman and shows us to an ante-chamber while prayers are being said.

My most vivid memory from St Anne's is the scent. Tomato and garlic. Maybe spaghetti Bolognese? Has the nun learnt more than quotations from the Bible during her Roman stay?

The Roman Iraqi comes and sits with us when Mass is over. She speaks about St Peter's, about grace and mercy. She tells us that at night many Iraqis come and sleep in their basement. – They think they will be safe here. Muslims come too, she confides in us. – They think our songs are beautiful.

– So you found us, Father Albert says when he enters the

room. As if he knows how I've searched for him. The old man leads me up to the third floor, to his office. Aliya lets me go alone.

– Iraq will burn, he says gloomily as he sits down at his desk by the window. – Everything around us is seething. The Shias are mobilising, the Kurds are mobilising, the fundamentalists are mobilising. Christians are increasingly frightened. Up until now we have been spared Islamists in Iraq. This is the work of the bombs.

His office is full of religious symbols: crucifixes, carvings of Jesus, paintings, but first and foremost books cover the walls. He himself is writing a work on the history of Christians in Iraq. He has little time for writing; most of his days are spent travelling around talking to people.

– It is the work of the bombs, he repeats. – So many killed, so many maimed. Why must they kill so many innocents? That is why hatred takes root in people's hearts. I was all for toppling Saddam, he was an evil man, but not in this way. I do not understand Bush. All I see is that he is destroying this country.

Father Albert asks me to leave. It is not good if neighbours see foreigners staying too long.

– God bless you, he says, before I find my way down the stairs.

Jamal-with-no-fingernails has been allocated an office beside the suicide bombers' recruitment office. There I run into Aage from Norwegian TV2 who is settling his account. I am renewing my press card. The long queue snakes away.

– We're off tomorrow morning, Aage says.

Hearing that gives me a shiver. I do not like people leaving, it makes it more frightening to stay. Fredrik and Aage are off with a few other cars the next morning.

I play with the thought. Leave behind the fear, the bombs, the war. Go home. What is in store for us?

The Americans will soon be outside Baghdad. No doubt the ground war will be terrible. They might fight street by street.

That night I scribble down in my diary:

Things are hotting up here

incredibly exciting

but,

if I don't want to be here any longer,

I'll have to decide now.

As though the book will answer me. I wish I could leave, but I can't. The next morning I drop in on Fredrik and Aage to wish them a safe journey. They wish me good luck and give me the key to their room; now Aliya will be on the same floor as me – that will make life easier.

The Americans are now inside the red circle and we speculate about the possibility of chemical attacks. Wherever I go I take my gasmask with me – but usually leave it in the boot of Amir's car when I return. The topic of conversation among journalists is always the same: Where are the Americans?

We are told that they have taken the airport. An ABC correspondent, who accompanied the troops from Kuwait, claims that he is reporting from the runway at Saddam International Airport, twenty kilometres from the centre of Baghdad.

– That's American propaganda, Aliya whispers. – Don't listen to them.

– But they reported it on the BBC. You always used to listen to the BBC?

– Yes, and they're always lying.

Later on in the day al-Sahhaf reports that the Americans are not at Saddam Airport, and that if they ever try to take it the airport will become their graveyard. That same afternoon a coach trip is arranged out to the airport. None of the reporters see any Americans, but as they are leaving fighting suddenly breaks out. A Reuters reporter misses the bus and is forced to take cover as the bullets whistle over her head.

Those of us who missed the airport tour stand on the flagstones outside the hotel and gape. Andrew from the BBC asks us what we are doing. When I tell him about the day's meagre pickings, he says: – You guys do your little stories. I am working on some serious stuff.

Serious stuff; who can find that, in barricaded Baghdad?

I am at a loss. My head buzzes with rumours, lies and half truths. What should I write about? Again I find myself inside a bubble. If I had been twenty kilometres outside of town I would have known something, but not here. Afternoon is approaching and I give up. For the first time I send an email to my editors with the title: 'Nothing from Baghdad today'. I am at the epicentre of the world's attention and can find nothing to write about.

My legs feel like lead when I descend the stairs to make my live report for Norwegian TV news. What to say? I have trawled page after page of agency reports: Reuters, AP and AFP. What do they actually say? It is nearly seven. I drag myself over to the camera, the 'snail' is stuck in my ear and I hear the voice of the producer. She sees me on the screen in the Marienlyst control room and I greet her through the black eye of the camera.

— How are you, Åsne?

— Fine, I hear myself say, a bit too high-pitched, a bit too happy.

— Oh, you've disappeared.

— The lights have gone, I answer.

The evening is dark around us. It appears that the electricity has gone all over town. What has happened? A few blacked-out seconds pass before the camera crew are able to start the generator and my white floodlight returns.

The theme tune to the news programme crackles like a mechanical echo from Oslo to Baghdad, and Einar Lunde's voice is in my ear.

— We hear that electricity has failed all over Baghdad. What is the reason?

Possible causes flit through my head. Have the electricity works been bombed? All at once? Is it sabotage? Have the Iraqis themselves turned it off? To conceal troop movements perhaps? Or chemical gas canisters?

— We do not know the reason for the Baghdad black-out, but in all likelihood the Iraqis themselves have turned the electricity off, I answer. The fact is that no bombs have fallen since the morning.

The next day, while driving around the empty streets with Aliya, I suddenly remember it is Friday and I suggest we go and hear what the mullah in Abu Hanifa mosque has to say. Neither of us is wearing a head-scarf, and we are too far away from the hotel to return, so we try to find a shop. Everything is closed. The ceremony is about to begin; people are streaming into the mosque.

— What about knocking on a door and asking if we might borrow one? I suggest.

— That's not possible, says Aliya.

— Why not?

— Why not? OK. Wait here.

A few moments later she is back with two shawls.

The mosque is overflowing. Anyone unable to get in sits outside.

— I pray to Allah for my children, for Baghdad, for the soldiers at the front, one woman says. Her tears flow. It's the stress, the fear, the strain, she explains.

The mosque is divided into two: a large area for men and a smaller one for women. The atmosphere is charged. Serious faces look to the mullah, who is standing on a platform at the end of the room. He calls the Americans barbarians.

— Their aggression has shown how they hate the Arab world. This is a dirty war. Houses fall down over our heads. Babies die in their mothers' arms. Missiles are fired at holy places.

The Arab countries, and in particular Saudi Arabia, come in for some harsh criticism too. The mullah accuses them of betraying Iraq and selling themselves to the USA. — They have eased the way for the enemy. Arabs who support the killing of Iraqi Muslims by the Americans deserve a place in hell. We pray to Allah that the inhabitants of these countries will rise up in rebellion against their leaders.

Usually the mullah speaks once before the general prayer. Now he interrupts his speech several times and calls on the congregation to pray. He finishes with a last request: Do not listen to the traitors' broadcasts. They try to enfeeble our will to resist, and whoever gives you erroneous information is a sinner.

Outside the mosque the topic of conversation is the same as the day before: Where are the Americans?

— When someone said that the airport had been taken last night, I went down into the basement and prayed before I went to bed. I was quite sure I would wake up in an occupied city. The roads would be blocked and American tanks would be trundling around the streets, a young woman says. — But when I woke it was absolutely quiet. I thought, maybe Baghdad is still free. Maybe Allah heard my prayer.

Aliya and I return the shawls. Now I insist on accompanying her. A young girl opens the door. In the half light behind her we catch sight of an old stooped woman. Rukaya lives alone with her five children in a small house opposite the enormous mosque. Today her children are on their way to her brother's funeral. — He died of shock last night, his heart stopped beating during one of the intensive attacks, Rukaya says. She doesn't dare attend. She can't get herself to leave the house. — He was younger than me, she sighs. — I feel that I am dying myself.

Her daughter tries to persuade her. — You are no more at risk from a bomb there than you are at home, she says.

The slender woman has not left her house since the bombs started falling over Baghdad two weeks earlier. — When we lost electricity last night I nearly fell out of bed I was shaking so much. I knew this was serious. I can't eat, can't sleep, can't think. These bangs are destroying me.

Rukaya's little house is filled with flowers. One entire wall is decorated with roses, tulips, sunflowers, vines of pleated lilies, in fibre, plastic, silk. On postcards, paintings, in vases. Pink, red, yellow, white, mauve, blue. Lace rugs are draped over the sofa and chair, every detail in the house polished and painstakingly looked after.

Rukaya lost her husband in the war between Iran and Iraq. — He arrived home in a coffin, completely burnt. Black as coal, those who saw him said. I myself couldn't bear to look at him. I wanted to remember him the way he was when he was alive.

Three of her sisters also lost husbands in the war against Iran. One of them never found out what happened to her spouse; he is still listed as missing.

Five years after her husband burnt to death, her oldest son was sent to the war against Kuwait. He was killed before he had been there a week.

— My life could have been happy. We were happy! But the wars have ruined everything, robbed me of those I loved. I'm incapable of anything now; I can't clean, I can't tidy up, all I do is sit and read the Koran, Rukaya says softly.

She has no more space for the scars of war.

One morning Aliya appears nervous.
— Miss Hosna, you must be careful.
— What do you mean?
— They're watching you.
— What do you mean, watching me?
— You must be careful when you send your reports. I'm sure you know what I mean. I thought I needed to say this to you now.

Aliya wants to end the conversation there and start the day's work. But I corner her. Does she mean me in particular or everyone in general? What has actually been said, and about whom?

— You must promise not to tell anyone, but Kadim asked me what your views are. Of course I said that you always tell the truth. And that you hate war. He said that several of the journalists will have to leave Baghdad now; there are too many of you. He's making out a list today. But if you're thrown out you just need to go to Amman for a week, get a new visa and return – like last time.

– Aliya, the war will be over in a week. Go to Amman now? That's absolutely crazy. The Americans control the roads out of Baghdad. Ever since Ali the martyr struck they shoot at all approaching cars.

– Oh, I see.

Aliya thinks for a while. – I'll talk to him, she says.

That same afternoon a list appears. My name stands out. 'Must depart immediately', it says.

I march straight in to see Kadim.

– Are you throwing me out?

– Yes.

– Why?

– There are too many of you – we have no control.

– Is it something I've done? Or not done? Is it because I don't show up for the bus tours? Because I don't come to all the press conferences?

– You must leave.

– Can we come to an arrangement, like before?

Kadim shoos me out of his office. – You must leave tomorrow morning.

– Tomorrow morning? Please give me one more day so I can get hold of a driver and pay my bills.

– OK.

I have one day's grace to wriggle out of this.

What is it all about? Is he just flexing his muscles now that we no longer need him; there are no interviews to apply for, no wish to travel anywhere. The Ministry of Information has had its day, so now it's trying to cash in on us, I think. I ask Aliya for her opinion.

She says: – Whatever happens, hide behind my back.
When the Americans come I will hide behind yours.

Unexpectedly, the situation changes to my advantage. The
words 'Expulsion postponed' suddenly appear on a scrap of
paper. Is this the first sign that the press centre is about to
unravel? One bureaucrat has no idea what the other is
doing. Is the Ministry on shaky ground?

To all intents and purposes the press centre continues to
exercise control over us. We are obliged to ask permission
for even the smallest detail, and it is increasingly difficult to
go anywhere without a minder. Not that I want to go out
alone; Aliya provides some kind of safety, after all. Every
day we are hounded around on to the buses, out sightseeing. I play truant.

We listen for hours on end to the Information Minister's
talks about Iraqi strength and American cowardice. One
day he speaks about pillaging by the British soldiers.

– In Basra they stole milk powder and infants' milk from
the shops, he says.

Concealed smiles all around the room.

As always, Aliya takes notes.

– Do you really think British soldiers robbed the shops
of baby milk? I ask her afterwards.

– Of course.

– But what would they do with all that milk?

– For their tea.

As long as I have known Aliya she has trusted implicitly
in the Information Minister. Studiously she writes down
the number of enemy tanks and helicopters captured and
destroyed by the heroic Iraqi forces, including the number
of cowardly American soldiers killed.

She might be a loyal supporter of the regime but she

is also one of the bravest interpreters. I am lucky to have her. When the bombing started most interpreters just evaporated. They quite simply did not turn up. Aliya chose to stay with me, in spite of the fact that it became increasingly difficult for her to negotiate her way through bombed-out Baghdad to see her family. She takes me to places no one dares visit, finds food when every shop is closed, accompanies me when most people stay at home.

As the invasion forces close in on Baghdad the city's inhabitants entertain a frustrating mix of fear, anticipation and rumours. They try to get up-to-date news through a profusion of channels, but the reports are contradictory. Someone has heard something from a cousin en route from Damascus. Someone else has been informed by a relative in Mosul. A third has been listening to the BBC in Arabic. A fourth has been watching Iraqi television for hours on end. A fifth has been listening to Iranian radio, a sixth to the *Voice of America*. The seventh person mixes it all up in his head in one confusing porridge.

To gauge what is really going on is like trying to solve a jigsaw puzzle in which the pieces originate from different boxes and several are missing.

I have been nagging Aliya for some time to take me to visit a normal family.

— No one dares have anything to do with foreigners, she says.

— I would love to know what the ordinary Iraqi is thinking at the moment. Do they know that the Americans are about to take their city?

— But they're not, Aliya objects.

— I'm interested in what the people of Baghdad think.

— You can ask me.

— Yes, Aliya, but I can't write about you. We work together. We try to find stories together. Uncover things, OK?

The next day Aliya has found me a family, a family from her own neighbourhood. They live a short way from her own street — this way her neighbours will not talk. And if we are stopped by the police we have to say that we are just visiting her family.

Hanan sits with her children in the living room. It is light and modern. The interior is pastel coloured, the ornaments of glass. On the wall hangs a faded copy of the Mona Lisa. No one knows what to believe about the war.

— *I cannot believe that they are only a few kilometres away from Baghdad. That's just propaganda. They're not even holding a single village. They're just rushing around the desert and shooting from time to time, says teenager Isam, a car mechanic. He listens to national and international radio broadcasts but has taken his stand — trusting in the Iraqi media. This gives confidence to most Iraqis: a tiny assurance in everyday life; a feeling that the Americans won't take Baghdad.*

His sister Reem has not adopted the same viewpoint.

— *I hear the Americans have surrounded Karbala. But I don't know whether it's true and I don't think they have taken Basra, says the twenty-year-old, who is studying mathematics at Baghdad University.*

— *Iraqi forces confuse them and they are forced back through the desert, her older sister Huda says, an engineering student.*

Hanan does not know what to believe.

— *The last I heard from the BBC was that they had crossed the red line. But what is the red line? she asks.*

— *I think it's thirty kilometres from Baghdad, her daughter answers.* — *Iraq has warned them not to cross this line and that if they do we'll teach them a lesson. She mimics official propa-*

ganda-speak, *like Iraqis do when they are unsure of what to
say.*

— *Oh dear, I'm so confused, says Reem.* — *Everyone says something different all the time.*

She sighs. Mona Lisa smiles her inscrutable smile from her plastic frame on the wall.

Reem and Hanan have both attended a university-sponsored
defence course. They have learnt self-defence and how to use a
Kalashnikov. But they have no plans to join the fighting should the
ground forces invade Baghdad.

— *We'll just sit and wait, says Reem.*

— *We have nowhere to go; the war will pursue us wherever we
are, so we might as well stay at home.*

But in the bedrooms their bags are packed with personal items,
some clothes, a small soap, a roll of paper and a few treasured
items.

— *Just in case, says the mother.* — *Just in case we have to leave.*

The family belongs to Baghdad's shrinking middle class and so
far has not had problems procuring food, water and fuel. One room
is stacked high with food, paraffin, oil, washing-powder and
soap. — *We can cope for many months yet.*

It is not hunger the little family is fighting, but boredom. They
dare not leave their district, school is closed, university is closed,
shops are open for just a few hours every day.

— *It's as though life has stopped, Reem sighs.* — *We just sit here.
Waiting. I have hardly any contact with my friends. I miss university. But I haven't got the strength to look at my textbooks, they
make me sad.*

The telephone rings. In spite of the bombing, telephones still
work in certain areas. Reem gets up, and returns sadder than
ever. — *It was Jenin. They're going. Her father wants to take them
to some relatives in the country. They have packed and are only
waiting for their uncle to come and get them.*

The mother and sister listen stiffly as Reem recounts the con-versation. No one says anything when she has finished.

— *The Gulf War was worse, the mother says in the end. Or rather, the bombing was worse. Then we lost water and electricity on the first day. Day to day life was more difficult.*

She also thinks she knows why they have not bombed the water and electricity plants.

— *It's thanks to the human shields who have flocked to Iraq. They protect the buildings with their bodies, says Hanan.*

Thus a new piece of the tangled information puzzle is in place. From yet another box.

— He can see the lights from Baghdad!

Remy is excited. He has just been talking to his good friend Laurent via the satellite telephone. Laurent is trav-elling with one of the American units and has been south of Baghdad for a few days. Remy has only now been able to get in touch with him.

— He thinks they are moving again tomorrow. Let's hope so.

While Remy looks forward to the ground war, I dread it. Remy lives life to the full when it is exploding around him. He would not admit it, but he enjoys war. He loves danger. Between wars he wanders melancholically around Paris; he lives in bars at night and sleeps during the day. Bosnia, Rwanda, Somalia, Afghanistan: that is Remy's life. Now he is getting bored in Baghdad.

— I should go out to them, he says.

— Are you mad? Cross the front? You might as well commit suicide here and now.

The following evening I phone Laurent myself to hear where he is.

— We are standing by a bridge outside Baghdad, but as I don't have a proper map I don't know which one. Have you got a shower when I arrive? I haven't washed in two weeks.

I do not have the heart to tell him the hotel is without water. Laurent has been accompanying a unit from Kuwait; he joined them the day I arrived in Baghdad. Now, three weeks on, he has some gruesome stories to tell.

— They are petrified and shoot before they think. One day they killed two little boys who were walking on the roadside. Suddenly they were lying on the ground. One time an old man was crossing the road. The Americans shot a warning shot but he did not react. They shot again but he continued to walk on. Then they picked him off and just left him lying in the road. When we arrive at a village they shoot in the air to warn people, a sign that they must go inside. If people don't react they shoot to kill. One day when we approached a village we spied several men standing next to a cluster of houses. American logic runs along the lines: 'If we shoot and they run, they are civilians.' So if they don't hide they are soldiers. Hence they shot and killed a woman in a field on the outskirts of the village. Everyone ran for cover. In other words: They were civilians. The Americans claim that fewer people are killed in this way. It is better to kill someone at once, in order to make people understand that they must stay inside, than to drive through an unknown village where someone might be a suicide bomber.

Laurent is sitting on the edge of the camp talking into his Thuraya. His unit might get the order to attack at any moment. He says he has learnt a lot about the strategy of the invading force.

— The American battle thesis is: 1. Protect yourselves. 2. Win the war. Their fear makes them dangerous. Today they shot at a father who was leading his son and daughter by the hand. The father was not hit but both the children were mortally wounded. The Americans just wanted to drive on, but I couldn't take it any longer. I screamed at the driver. – What the hell! You can't just drive on and let them bleed to death. I was so angry he had to stop. I got one of the cars to turn round and we drove them to a field hospital. I don't know any more – we had to leave. I'm quite sure the little girl died, she had lost so much blood, was nearly unconscious when we got there.

Laurent sighs. The telephone line is silent.

– They cry at night.

– Who?

– The soldiers. I'm sure lots of them will have problems. Only a few do the actual shooting. As though they enjoy it. No one is punished. I have never before seen such trigger-happy soldiers, Laurent says. He has covered wars all over the world for the last twenty years. A bullet smashed his knee in Gaza a few years back and has left him with a limp. His trip to Iraq is the first one since the accident.

– I'm looking forward to the shower, Laurent says on a lighter note, to conclude the conversation. – And a glass.

Yves reaches Baghdad before him. A man with a long beard and wearing the dirtiest of clothes enters the reception area. I walk straight past him when he grabs my arm.

– Mademoiselle, he says, and laughs. Do you remember me?

Of course I remember Yves. He was one of the funniest people I met in Afghanistan. Meek as a lamb and with a ringing laugh. It was impossible not to laugh with him. His big passion was weapons. He knew the names of the weapons systems of all the world's armies. It gave him great pleasure to discover the weapon and calibre used, according to sound, smell and strength. He travels the world reporting for the French weapons magazine *Raids*.

In Afghanistan I most remember him for the heart-rending conversations he held with his mother. He had no satellite telephone; he just travelled around with a laptop and wrote down everything when he got home. So he would borrow my phone.

— Maman! *C'est moi*. I'm alive. All is well. Really. Don't be frightened, Maman. All is fine. Oh, Maman, don't cry, oh. Your birthday? No, I didn't forget it, but I'm in the mountains in Afghanistan, they don't have telephones. Now? I've borrowed one. I'll phone tomorrow. It's expensive, Maman. I'm just borrowing one. I must put the phone down. *Oui*, Maman, I'll be home soon.

Now here he is, in reception.

— I've driven from Kuwait, he says.

— From Kuwait? Through the front?

— It appears so. I lost sight of my unit; suddenly I was ahead of them.

He had driven his own car in tandem with the American forces. When he lost them he was arrested by the Iraqi police and brought to Hotel Palestine. Here Uday took care of him. He confiscated his car keys, laptop, camera and passport and placed him under house arrest. Yves was given a room and strict instructions not to leave the hotel.

When I meet him in reception his clothes are hanging in shreds, they look as though they have been rolled in sand and then in oil.

— Do you know where I can get my clothes washed? he asks.

Washed? The hotel is without water. My water bottles wouldn't tackle that much dirt.

I spot the solution a few yards away. Amir. He is the same size as Yves. His mother has packed him off with masses of clothes, like Yves' mother would like to have done. I ask if he can spare a few pieces for Yves. He can, and soon Yves is sitting in my room, washed and delighted in Amir's clothes.

— Do you have vodka?

Yves empties his glass and starts to talk. About the journey, the Americans, how he got lost. In the Dora area, on the outskirts of Baghdad. The Americans rolled in with their columns of tanks. The Iraqis replied with artillery from positions by the road side. The Iraqis managed to hit an Abrams, one of the enormous American tanks, with a rocket-propelled grenade. It stopped completely and the soldiers inside sought refuge in another tank. One soldier was killed, two injured.

— The smoke lay black all over the area, from the burning Abrams and the Iraqi tank. The column turned and that's when I got lost and found myself in Baghdad. But can you imagine, an Abrams. They left it! Never in the history of America, in the history of the American army, has an Abrams been left behind during a battle. Never!

When the Americans pulled out they bombed the tanks. No one will be able to pick over the remains. Yves has fallen silent. He drains another glass.

— This is the worst sort of warfare I have ever witnessed. Those columns are columns from hell. Every unit advances accompanied by about fifty vehicles. First the Abrams, then the Bradleys and the Amtracks for the troops, then the Miclick mine-detectors, and lastly a Humvee equipped with a loud-speaker telling people to stay inside. This column shoots at anything that moves. They don't even wait for orders. There is obviously no punishment or sanction for killing civilians. That might have made them think and not act like cowboys. I've even seen them shoot cows. They love firing away with 25mm cannonballs at

portraits of Saddam Hussein. They're still taking revenge
for 9/11. They talk a lot about that, but there's no shooting
discipline, it's up to themselves, boys of twenty. I don't
blame them; I would have done the same when I was
twenty.

Actually, Yves did exactly the same when he was twenty.
He was a mercenary in the South African army and fought
on the side of apartheid. But Yves has come to terms with
his past.

– They are frightened, and suffering losses makes them
more frightened. That spurs them on. It's their command-
ers who are responsible, Yves sighs. – It was awful when
we got to Mahmudiya, a village south of Baghdad. The
Americans attacked the village because air surveillance
showed that several tanks were hidden there. According to
the villagers, more than two hundred people were killed.
Of course the Iraqis shouldn't have put tanks in the midst
of civilians, but still. The Americans were taking no chances
and shot wildly into the village to try and destroy it.
Between Mahmudiya and Baghdad I saw many wrecked
cars with all the passengers dead. I saw them shoot through
the open window of a house.

– They're forgetting one thing, Yves says, looking out
through the taped balcony door. – The battle for hearts. He
empties his glass. – That too must be won.

He falls into deep thought. I point to the balcony. The
NERA aerial is erected, the one he knows so well.

– Do you want to phone home?

On 5 April I also have to write home. Not to maman,
but to my editor in Norway who is fretting about all that
might happen to me. *Aftenposten*'s chief editor, Einar Hanseid,
says that if it were possible he would come and fetch me. I

need to send him a calming mail. That means a bit of self-examination, to ascertain why I still choose to stay.

Dear Editor,
I am very grateful for your concern and the moral responsibility you feel. I regret the worry I am causing you.

I share both the worry and fear that something might happen. But I still feel safe enough. There are more than one hundred western journalists here, and I promise I will not approach the frontline whenever it reaches our street corners.

Of course I have considered leaving several times, but I just cannot make myself do it. I cannot pack my bags and go; it is as if this whole story has fastened itself in my brain. Of course I could pull myself together and say, Åsne, this is too dangerous, but I just cannot. Anyhow, now it is not safe to leave either. But do not think that I have not considered it carefully. I have come to realise that this is my life: to travel here, cover the war, the suffering, the events. I can't leave until I know what will happen.

But please do know that I feel no pressure whatsoever from anyone to stay, except from myself. I feel no obligation to stay in spite of my large circle of readers. Eight European newspapers print my articles and I feel accountable to them – after all, I am here for them. But the moment I feel I want to leave, I will. The moment I am frightened, or uncertain, I will leave, assuming it is safe to do so.

Anyhow, the buck stops with me, as you have encouraged me to leave and would pull me out if you could. In other words, you have no moral responsibility, although I know you feel you do.

Apologies for my late reply, but I have been very busy.

Best wishes from Åsne

PS. Per Kristian, the bit about the working conditions you wanted me to write is inappropriate at the moment. Now that the Americans are at the doorsteps of Baghdad, I would prefer to write about that.

The war marches on. Bombs fall all night and all morning. Direction southeast, direction airport.

From the central command in Qatar come reports that the troops are advancing on Baghdad, while the Iraqi Information Minister obstinately insists they have got lost in the desert.

Thousands of inhabitants try to flee the neighbourhood around the airport. The Americans are soon to be seen outside their windows.

It is as though Baghdad is afraid to breathe. The broad avenues are deserted, only the skeletons of the market stalls remain, and rows of shut-up shops glare at the few passers-by.

Haidar stands on the street, fidgeting, a pistol hanging out of his pocket. He has a large graze on his forehead and scratches on his arm. He is talking to his friends. They have been sent by their mothers to buy bread. Haidar is twelve and attends primary school. But all of them are closed and Haidar and his friends have other things to do.

— I am responsible for the purchase of food for the family, Haidar says, self-consciously pleased. He enjoys himself in the queue, which winds from the road, up the steps and into the shop, smelling of freshly baked bread. At the far end of the room the baker, quick as lightning, rolls the pitta dough into a ball, throws it on to a long shovel and pushes it into the open oven. After a few seconds it is done, taken out and heaved onto the counter where it is picked up and, still steaming, stuffed into a bag.

— We have never seen queues like these, says one of the bakers. — People have to drive many kilometres to get bread. We stay open as long as we can. After all, people have to eat.

Haidar fumbles with his mother's housekeeping money. — Actually, the war is not too bad. I have more freedom now, I don't have to go to school, I play football every day, shop, and then we play soldiers.

— Soldiers?

— Yes, we play Israelis and Palestinians, he says, and shows me his toy pistol.

— Don't you play Americans and Iraqis?

Haidar shakes his head. Maybe the war between America and Iraq is too serious to play. Haidar has seen pictures of mutilated children and has listened to his parents' worried conversations. Should they stay or should they go?

Anyway, how can you play at being a bomber?

Near the bread shop in Baghdad's Karada neighbourhood are two rusty old bangers. The wrecks are loaded with bags, water containers and food. Blankets and mattresses are rolled into big balls on the roof.

— We can't bear it any longer, says Maysun Najib. — The children can't sleep at night, they cry and are petrified. We have lost electricity and water so we're locking up and leaving.

— *Where are you going?*

— *We haven't made up our minds yet. We haven't really any-where to go to. We have relatives in Mosul but we don't know if the road is safe. A neighbour's car was hit by shrapnel as he returned from Mosul yesterday. Those who were sitting in the front seat have wounds all over their bodies; our neighbour in the back seat was hit in the hand. But I still think it's safer to go there than to remain here. The fighting might start tonight. When we have finished packing we're going to the bus stop to ask the drivers. They'll tell us the best way out of Baghdad*, Maysun sighs. Some of her chil-dren run around her legs; she has got five between 6 and 18. They are happy to be going on a journey, a journey into the unknown. North, east, west — they're leaving regardless.

Baghdad's inhabitants felt that the war was drawing nearer this morning, when the crackle of machine-guns and the thud of heavy artillery replaced the boom of the night bombs. This is one of the reasons many families have decided to flee. The motorways out of Baghdad are jam-packed with overloaded cars, the major-ity full of women and children.

The presence of the soldiers has changed the atmosphere in town. Lorries laden with heavily armed soldiers drive around the deserted streets. Now and again they fire in the air, as if to cele-brate the fact that the battle for Baghdad's streets is about to start. They wave their weapons and make V-signs to passers-by. Several tanks are lined up by the motorways, ready to advance. Cars tow mobile cannons and there are large concentrations of troops around Baghdad. At important junctions soldiers are lined up and green-clad men drive pick-ups. Several of the town's parks have been turned into camps with trenches, positions and barracks.

Ahmed sits on a stool in Sadoun Street and watches the work-ers cement up his hotel. 'Atlas Hotel and Restaurant' reads a neon sign over the entrance. A revolving glass door has been turned into a wall. The windows on the first floor have been carefully *bricked up; only a tiny sliver of window remains until the whole house is sealed in.*

— It's best like that, says Ahmed, sadly. — Now not a single bullet will get through.

— The airport has been taken, the Americans report for the second day in a row.

— Yes, they took it, but we have recaptured it, retorts the Information Minister. — They won't survive the night, he adds and reiterates that Iraq will use unconventional weapons. He calls it a 'mission of sacrifice'. The statement leads us to frenzied speculation and we stare even harder at the bearded faces in reception.

At nightfall the town is quiet — too quiet. I cannot sleep. Where is the bombing? Poison gas makes no sound, no boom. I wait and wish for the explosions. At least then we know where the war is. My skin tingles. My body tingles. I toss and turn in the dirty sheets, then pad out to the balcony. The guards are also quiet, staring up at the sky. Restless, sleepless, waiting.

Finally sleep overcomes the frightening silence. But only for a few hours. I wake at daybreak, not to dull thuds or explosions, but to something sharper, closer. Mortars, small rockets, grenades, bursts of machine-gun fire. Bullets fly through the air. Street fighting! It has started. My stomach knots. I close my eyes, try to push it away. Curiosity forces me out of bed and I creep over to the window.

There! On the other side of the Tigris I spot American tanks. By the Presidential palace! The Americans have taken Baghdad during the night. They have entered the heart of the city. Explosions spread like wildfire round the palace as the third infantry division advances. From the window I see Iraqi guards running for their lives along the river bank, some of them in their underwear. Some jump into the river. Another ammunitions depot explodes.

Two Iraqi soldiers give themselves up, hands held over their heads. They are forced to the ground, face down. One of them turns round. He is shot by an American soldier. The Iraqi jerks in convulsions and lies lifeless on the ground.

It is Monday, 7 April. It is nearing 7am and I am scheduled to broadcast for Swedish TV. Bewildered, I look towards the soldiers and tanks on the opposite bank, then down to the guards on my side. They are still wearing their Baath Party uniforms.

I stop for a moment and pull something from behind my bedside table. It has been there since the very first night when I realised I could not sleep wearing a bulletproof vest. For the first time I put it on. So far, as long as danger has arrived with rockets and bombs I have figured that a bulletproof vest would not make much difference. But now, with the battle raging all around, it might be wise to start wearing it.

'Good morning, this is Stockholm, can you hear us?'

The noise around me is deafening. It is difficult to hear what the anchorman is saying. Sometimes I have to ask him to repeat a question, or try to second-guess him.

– The battle for Baghdad has started. There has been heavy fighting going on for the last two hours – artillery, cannons, grenades. Bombs have hit central Baghdad. I can see over to the other side of the river where there are several fires. We have seen . . . from the hotel we see American tanks capturing Saddam Hussein's Presidential palace. They are shooting . . .

It is difficult to hold a clear thought during the constant shelling. STV's anchorman, Morgan Olofsson, who I know from my time in Moscow, translates and explains my Norwegian phrases to the Swedish public.

– Where else, as far as you can see, or know, are there American troops?

– They have surrounded Baghdad. As far as we know they have occupied the southern and eastern parts. Where most of the inhabitants live, downtown, there has been no fighting. The various coalition forces have different tasks, some the Presidential palace, others the ministries, and yet others military installations. This is where the battles are raging now and which we can hear . . .

A machine-gun volley can be heard close by.

The feature in 'Morning Report' is supposed to last a few minutes. I hear the editor tell Morgan – 'Delay the weather'.

– To those of you who are waiting for the weather forecast, we will delay it for a moment, Morgan tells the public. Then he returns to me. As I talk, I hear the editor say: 'Skip the weather'.

– The fighting has now lasted for two hours – very intense, continuous . . . also machine-gun fire. Which indicates that the fighting is only a couple of hundred metres away. That implies that it might be the Special Forces. They have been in Baghdad for some time, undercover and now—

The blast is so strong that I fear my eardrums will burst. Hell. I lose my thread. Swoosh. Bang. Another crash.

—and now taking over central parts of Baghdad.

I should take cover, I think. More explosions. Behind the hotel, maybe? Whoosh. But you can't do that in the middle of a live broadcast. 'Skip the sport', I hear the editor say. I continue. It will upset the public if I just disappear. Boom! I'm no longer thinking, I'm flying. It is as if a missile has landed right by me. The air pressure tosses me around, throws me to the ground; I am behind the hotel in a single leap. The cameraman is running too, like everyone else. Smoke pours from the river bank. Has a missile struck our side of the Tigris? On the other side of the parking lot? An error?

The machine-gun fire continues to crackle.

In Stockholm Morgan tries to calm the viewers. – There we lost Åsne Seierstad – you might have heard the explosions in the background.

The camera continues to record from its tripod, while the cameraman has taken cover with me.

– Here are pictures from downtown Baghdad, Morgan continues, slightly doubtful. – On the other side of the river they are battling for the Presidential palace, a large complex where American soldiers have gained entry. Some journalists have sought refuge during the fighting . . . Åsne, you might be able to hear us, I do not want you to attempt to get up, but if you can hear us, you might let us know what is going on.

Morgan is quiet for a few seconds before he continues. – We'll wait and see.

I have two things on my mind. The gaping camera filming into the empty void. And the frightened viewers. I have to return to 'Morning Report'.

– It sounds as though she might be returning, I thought I heard them talking. We are watching live pictures from Baghdad this morning where the fighting for the capital has started.

The cameraman and I look at each other; without speaking we agree to continue the transmission. He returns to the camera and I run over to the stool I was standing on, replace the plug in my ear, adjust the microphone and look into the camera.

– And we have Åsne Seierstad on the screen again. We lost her for a moment while she took refuge from the fighting that is going on nearby. Åsne, maybe you can hear me now. What is going on?

– Eh, it is difficult to tell, impossible to know where the bombs drop, from where the missiles are coming, or the shooting. But actually . . .

I swallow; there is sand in my mouth.

. . . I think, however, that the majority of Baghdad's citizens will stay indoors today. The bullets are whizzing around people's houses and the only thing to do is to stay at home and wait until it is all over.

– Where are you standing? And what is that we see behind you?

I turn round to have a look.

– Oh, that! That is a statue of Saddam Hussein. We'll have to wait and see how long it will stand. I hear the American soldiers like to shoot at pictures of Saddam Hussein. But now on the other side of the Tigris . . .

There are no soldiers on 'our' side of the Tigris yet. The city streets are deserted, a few cars visible. Soldiers loaf about, perplexed, watching the fighting taking place on the other side of the river; their helmets are inadequate, their faces anxious.

Kadim convenes an impromptu meeting on the roof of the hotel. This is to be al-Sahhaf's legendary press conference, where his parallel sense of reality is seriously exposed.

– I apologise for having woken you up this morning with these shots. But I want to let you know that we have forced back the enemy and you can now rest, he says.

On the other side of the river, American tanks are positioned outside the palace. – They will all find their grave in Baghdad. We have strangled the American army and taught them a lesson, an historic lesson. I cannot understand why they send their soldiers over here in order to commit suicide, he says. – When they say they have taken our palaces, they are lying. They cheat.

– But look at the other side of the river! Those are the Americans' tanks! a reporter from the BBC says.

– There are no Americans in Baghdad, al-Sahhaf emphasises.

The very moment al-Sahhaf tells us that there are no Americans in Baghdad, the shooting subsides. He smiles, brushes an imaginary fly away with his hand and slides off down the steep stairs like an eel.

That is the last we see of him until several weeks later he pops up on Abu Dhabi TV and describes his life as the Iraqi Information Minister. He is also the last high-ranking official to have any contact with us – the Foreign Minister has long been conspicuous by his absence, as have the Defence Minister and Deputy Prime Minister, Tariq Aziz.

'An Iraqi Donald Rumsfeld', the *New York Times* correspondent calls him. 'Mixing fact and fiction.'

When al-Sahhaf has gone, the shooting picks up again. A yellowish-grey carpet of sand and smoke from the oil fires lies heavily over the town. Bombing is audible in the distance, but the Presidential palace is hardly discernible. Visibility is down to a couple of hundred metres. The flashes from the missiles split the sky and we hear planes flying low over the city.

Bloody battles are raging on the other side of the river. Charred bodies in burnt-out cars are abandoned on bridges and by the roadside. Some of the car doors are open; the fleeing passengers got no further before being caught in the fatal crossfire. Now they lie dead beside their cars. To the west of the Tigris bullets whistle round houses and heavy artillery booms. Metal shards hit palm trees like hail.

Shattered tree trunks reach towards the sky. Thick, black, oily smoke rises from destroyed tanks. Slashed Iraqi uniforms lie in the streets; the soldiers tore them off in a last-ditch effort to survive, deserting in the heat of battle. Dead soldiers lie among the bloody pieces of clothing.

A soldier from an American unit tells me later how he drove past Iraqi soldiers writhing in their death throes. Behind the tanks' armour-plating they had passed by the dying, the dead. He had seen soldiers on the slopes above the river, lifeless, half in, half out of the water. He had met men waving white rags and T-shirts, indicating their surrender. Still they were shot. Earlier in the campaign the Americans had experienced Iraqi soldiers waving white flags, en route to surrender, then suddenly opening fire.

While the battles continue on the west bank of the Tigris, people are sipping hot tea at the pavement cafés on the east bank. Every table is taken at Mazin, an oft-frequented corner establishment. Some men make room for Aliya and me. As usual Amir will not leave the car. This very morning a friend has told him that there are thieves and robbers everywhere and that a driver has been shot and killed because he would not give up his car.

Here on the east bank Iraqi police still patrol the streets. Behind the increasingly flat sandbags men with guns are positioned. They are slender and young. Around them on the ground lies the sand that has trickled out of the bags.

Two men in green Baath Party uniforms sit at the neighbouring table. Their glasses have just been filled with hot golden tea. Their growth of beard is days old, in addition to the usual moustache. One of the men is heavily built, the other slight.

— Can we talk to them? I whisper to Aliya.

— No, are you mad, she hisses, and looks the other way.

— Why not?

— Because. One does not speak to men in uniform. Especially not Baath Party members.

— But all Iraqis are collective members of the Party. Including you. You've said that yourself, I object.

— Don't talk like that or I'll leave.

— OK, I say.

Addressing the men, I smile apologetically and say *al Salamu aleikum*. Now she has to translate.

As they answer my greeting they are served large pieces of grilled lamb.

— Would you like a taste? the broad-shouldered one asks.

Aliya is about to decline, but I poke her and say loudly: *Shukran* — thank you. They extend their arms and we are suddenly sharing lunch with the Baathists. The well-built one, whose moustache is also the blackest, heaps warm pieces of meat on a pitta bread, adds chopped onions and serves. Then they strike up a conversation between themselves, and ignore us, eating their food. I let them talk and wonder when I might interrupt. I feel like an intruder; I am an intruder.

When the meal is nearing its end I ask them what they think of the war.

— This is a state of emergency. I patrol the town night and day, haven't slept for three days, haven't seen my family, the sturdy one says, whose name is Abu Saif. The thin one nods affirmatively. — Look, I eat lunch in a lousy café, spend the night on a mattress in a school, drink water when I can. I must defend my city, maintain law and order, the Baathist continues. Not angry, not aggressive, just resigned.

— The Americans have already taken parts of Baghdad. Do you think they'll take the whole town?

— We believe in our leader and therefore we are invincible. We will fight with heart and soul, says Abu Saif with the same combination of acquiescence and resolve that characterises people who have learnt set phrases by heart. He stares ahead while devouring the last bit of pitta bread. I dare not interrupt him and sit in silence.

— Can I ask you something? he says suddenly. I nod.

— If we turned the picture around, how would you react if Iraqi forces attacked your country? If we tried to kill your president to install our leaders and our system? How would you react if we cut off your electricity, water, and killed your neighbours?

Abu Saif looks sternly at me while Aliya translates his questions. When he has finished asking, he snorts, wipes his mouth with the back of his hand, gets up, bows and leaves.

The entire café has witnessed the episode. Now they turn away and continue their conversations. Aliya says we need to go.

We get as far as the shop next door, a bakery. There are two long queues, one for men, the other for women. It is not seemly that men and women stand in the same queue, Aliya explains.

The faces of the majority of people are drawn.

Only one face laughs, one open and curious gaze alone follows me. She appears to be the only one who has had a good night's sleep, the only one who is enjoying the stormy spring day to the full, the only one unaffected by the bombs.

— I hope this will all be over before she is old enough to understand, the mother of seven-month-old Zina sighs, while Zina herself continues to smile.

*

– I think she might have lost her husband, Aliya whispers.
– Or her son, maybe. She's calling for someone called Hamid. It might also be her brother.

A woman is sitting on the ground, wrapped in a long, black shawl. She is calling the same name again and again. She holds a child in her arms. The child clambers unaffected over her, too young to understand what has happened. The little girl is dressed in a dirty-white ragged dress. The mother pays no heed to her but continues to moan. In the court-yard outside al-Kindi hospital, doctors, nurses, patients and relatives pass her by. The victims today are victims of crossfire rather than bombing.

We leave the woman in peace, and never find out who Hamid is or what has happened to him. The woman's face has frozen into a terrible expression, as if it has looked into hell.

A car door opens. Three boys lie side by side on the cold, rough metal floor. Two men carry them out. They wear thin shorts and shirts, spattered with blood. All three are dead. The mother and grandmother stand by, howl-ing. – My sons, my sons, the mother cries.

This is the second time I have witnessed the death of three brothers. The boys are not even taken into the hos-pital, but straight to the little house where the death certificates are dispensed. All comes to a standstill when the boys are carried away; all is quiet except for Alexandra and Jerome taking photographs. Suddenly a group of men attack them. They set to and beat Jerome and frail Alexandra who are eventually saved by some doctors.

– Keep away, the doctors say to the two photogra-phers. – These people are in shock. They have lost their family. Show some respect.

The photographers withdraw to the entrance where we stand, waiting to get in. The attackers remain, glowering at us. White, western, the enemy.

The photographers leave. Throughout the day a steady stream of dead and wounded arrive, in ambulances, taxis, cars and on foot. A man drives up with his dying wife in the back seat. Her skirt is saturated with blood. Not a sound escapes her mouth as they carry her in. Her eyes are already in the hereafter.

We are denied access to the hospital. While we wait we watch several men being carried in. It appears they have been wounded in battle. Are the military hospitals already overcrowded?

We sneak in and thus see what we should not have seen: wounded soldiers.

The floor is splashed with blood. I see bodies with bullet holes in stomachs, legs, neck, arms. Some have started to hallucinate. Others howl. Painkilling medicine has run out.

— How many soldiers have you admitted today? I ask a doctor.

— There are no soldiers here, the doctor says.

— But they are wearing uniforms?

— I see no uniforms, he says, and pushes me out. — You must go now, do you hear?

In the courtyard friends of the wounded stand, resting on their Kalashnikovs. Not all are in uniform; some are volunteers. They look worried; some are smoking, nobody pays attention to us.

— This is our worst day so far, says one of the doctors. — Missiles, rockets, bullets and cannons. Never have we taken in so many wounded in one day. And the Americans call this introducing democracy!

The young doctor, who is fluent in English, is

interrupted by a shout: Water is back, the water is back!

The doctor hurries over to the tap to wash his hands. Baghdad's largest hospital has been without water since morning. They might lose it again at any moment. There has been no electricity either, and when the generator went so did the light and all the equipment that is dependent on power.

The patients lie in beds without sheets, in their bloody clothes. The place swarms with flies, on the patients, in the beds, on the dead. The air is stale in death's ante-room; the temperature in Baghdad is thirty-five degrees.

At 1am I take my place in front of the camera to deliver the night's last report. I am on the hotel roof, in Reuters' spot. Next to me is Ulrich from ZDF, Giovanna from RAI, Michel from French TF1, Abu Dhabi TV is a little further away, the BBC in the corner. Each talks to his or her camera. The questions materialise in our ears. I am reporting to Dutch TV, and in spite of not knowing the owner of the voice, I feel a connection with these Dutch people; it is as if they pull me towards home. They see me, and their voices are caring. That is a help.

When I am done I walk into Paul's tent. He is Reuters' supervisor, and the coordinator of pictures from Iraq to TV stations all over the world. In addition he is responsible for the live cameras. Like Josh, Yves and Timothy, he is ex-army. He served with the Green Jackets in Northern Ireland for many years and is one of those I keep bumping into in the world's hot spots.

In the tent, pictures whirr on the monitors and I watch fascinated. Soldiers, battles, tanks rushing across sand dunes, the American flag on top of the Presidential palace. The war in close-up. Events I have not seen myself, only heard about.

Paul stretches out on his stool, fit, quick, supple, restless, in his mid-thirties. He appears tired. Owing to security risks Reuters has cut down heavily on manpower. For Paul that means a duty of sixteen hours, divided between the office on the fifteenth floor and the tent on the roof.

— What sort of a life is this? he says. Paul rarely shows his gloomy side.

A brutal wind fights with the tent canvas, making it difficult to hear what Paul is saying. When it drops he continues.

— My life has become the world's wars. I'm away for months at a time. But I just can't stay at home; I suppose this is my life.

I understand exactly what he is saying.

— Enough is enough. When this is over I'm going to stay at home. Find a girl, work at the Reuters office in London. Or I'll destroy myself. If they had sent someone to relieve me I would have left on the spot. Now I have to stay to the end.

Paul yawns. It becomes increasingly difficult to sit upright in the chair. The pictures flicker over the screen. My eyelids will not stay open; the canvas flaps.

— All I wish for now is a good night's sleep, Paul says.

I nod.

— I'll pop into your office tomorrow to take a proper look at the recordings, I say.

It's strange to be so close to the fighting, yet so far away. — All we know is what is happening at the hotel and at the Presidential palace across the river, I say.

— Well, that's something at least, Paul laughs and gives me a hug. — It'll be over in a couple of days, I promise you. Then we can go home and start living.

I leave Paul in the gale on the roof. He has an hour to go, waiting for some pictures.

*

A strange sound wakes me in the middle of the night. It lulls me in and out of sleep. Darkness embraces me, as does the curious, light sound. It is gentle, like a memory from carefree days. The trickle of water. Drip, drip, drip.

It's raining.

When day breaks I am woken anew. I peep out of the window to see whether the view might have changed during the night. In the morning twilight all I see is rain; raindrops pregnant with desert sand fall heavy to the ground, leaving yellow-brown blotches wherever they land. I try to sleep. I am exhausted but my body is full of adrenalin and won't let me have more than a few hours sleep. I peer out of the window again. The rain has cleared; the sun is forcing its way through the clouds, pushing them to the side. It could have been a beautiful morning.

The battles start with a bang just after 5am. Booms are heard from every direction, the building vibrates and window panes shatter many hundreds of metres away. Fire from heavy artillery shakes Baghdad out of its slumber. The bombers circle menacingly before dropping their cargo. The bombs seem to hover in the air for a moment before descending, and then, boom, hit the target. Buildings explode, some are levelled to the ground. Once again grey smoke rises heavenward.

Only some curious young boys dare show themselves. Their eyes are turned towards the sky, the planes, the fire-balls. They watch seriously. No sensation seeking, no excited faces. I myself am too frightened to venture out. I sit in my room, exhausted, sick with the lack of sleep. Soon I must report to the wide-awake Swedes.

Like the previous day, the most serious fighting is centred around the Presidential palace. The republican guard is trying to recapture it. They fight with mortar and machine-guns. The American answer is immediate, strong and precise. Following a night given over to the sound of raindrops the air attack starts at full strength, tanks and artillery batteries attacking from the ground. Baghdad residents suddenly catch an unknown sound in the air, the intense chatter of small cannonballs, followed by an ear-piercing braking sound. A10 aircraft are flying low, peppering Iraqi positions. The planes dispense 4,000 130mm bullets a minute and are called 'tank killers'. This is the first time this type of plane has been used in a centre of town.

Now war is not only raging by the Presidential palace. Parallel to the fierce attack on the administration quarters, fighting has also broken out southeast of the town. Several marine units have crossed the Tigris during the night and are approaching the commercial district, the markets and the residential quarters.

The streets around the hotel are deserted. Aliya phones from 716, a few rooms away, and asks about the plan for the day. I hesitate. I have no plan. I do not dare go out.

– I'm writing, I say.

– OK, I'm in my room if you need me, Aliya answers. Tough Aliya, staying with me, not knowing how her family is faring. She cannot phone them, the telephones are out of action. She cannot go and see them as that would mean crossing the front.

In spite of Saddam Hussein's countless requests to take up arms and fight, Baghdad's inhabitants do exactly the opposite. They lock their doors, bolt the windows and wait for the war to end.

Outside a man with a cigarette trolley stops by a puddle. He leans the trolley against the pavement and lights up.

I consider going up to Paul in 1502 to take a look at the

pictures Reuters have snapped during the course of the morning. With their lenses they can see far more than I can from my balcony. As I am on my way out the door the phone rings. It is Tim.

– The water is back!

Excellent. Now I can fill the bath. I also fill about thirty hoarded bottles. My room is a pigsty, there is nowhere to dispose of rubbish. Some just throw rubbish bags into the corridors, as though they will disappear by themselves.

After the water ritual is over I have no energy left to ascend to the fifteenth floor. Anyway, if I wait they might have some more pictures.

To pretend that I am actually doing something I open my mail. The first one has the title 'War chariot' and is from Per Egil Hegge, *Aftenposten*'s senior correspondent.

> Brothers and sisters,
> This is rather overdue – but on the other hand it
> is never too late. We must eliminate the word
> tank meaning war chariot. In Norwegian a tank is
> a milk tank, or a petrol tank. Åsne in particular
> uses the word tank; for all her good qualities her
> military vocabulary is weak and this must be
> changed in her manuscripts.
> Per Egil

The next email is also from *Aftenposten* and signed Per A. Christiansen. He rattles off all the different spellings of Iraq's Minister of Information: Mohammad Said Al-Sahaf, Muhammed Said al-Sahaf, Mohammad Said al-Sahhaf, Muhammed Saeed al-Sahaf, Mohammed Saeed al-Sahaf, Muhammed Saeed Sahaf, Mohammad Saeed al-Sahaf, Mohammed Saeed al.Shahaf, Muhammad Saeed as-Sahaf,

Mohammed Saeed a-Sahaf. He suggests we should agree on one version.

I reply that I prefer Muhammed Said al-Sahhaf. As I press the send button there is an almighty crash, the windows rattle and the building shakes violently. That was close. I instinctively glance at my watch. One minute to twelve. Still feeling the swaying hotel in my body I cross over to the window. Have they hit the Air Force HQ nearby – or was it even closer? I see nothing from the balcony and continue to concentrate on *Aftenposten*'s linguistic usage. Arabic names can be transcribed in endless ways; one must only stick to one. And from now on I will use the word war chariot and not tank.

The telephone rings. It's Tim again. Has the electricity returned, I wonder.

– The hotel is hit. The hotel is hit. Get out! It might collapse!

I stiffen for a fraction of a second, holding the receiver in my hand. Then I rush out. Should I have taken the computer? The telephone? No, I just run. Everyone is running, the stairs are full of people, rushing down, out to the back garden, through the reception, out the glass doors, away from the hotel complex. The building is still standing. Will it fall?

Someone suddenly calls. – Reuters is hit! Reuters' office is hit!

They are carried out of the lift in blood-soaked blankets. There are no stretchers, no first aid. A jeep, its back doors open, stands by the front door to take away the wounded. Another car drives up. More bloody blankets. They are carried out in long bundles. We cannot see who lies in them. It takes a long time before they are brought down; they wait vital minutes for the sluggish lift and lose a lot of blood.

Josh walks towards me. He is crying, staggering.

— My friends! he cries. — I was there, I saw it all. Taras on the floor, Paul on the floor. The office is all smashed up.

— Paul, I ask. — Do you . . . do you know anything about him?

— I don't know, I don't know. There was nothing I could do.

Josh's face is red, he shakes, looks away, walks off. Josh the soldier. The satellite guy. Like Paul. When the cars drive off we remain outside the hotel. Puzzled.

A crushed camera lies on the floor in 1502. Bits of concrete and metal shards swim in pools of blood.

Why was the hotel targeted?

From HQ in Qatar a message is sent to the effect that soldiers on the bridge had been shot at from the hotel and that they had replied to the shooting in self-defence. It makes me shiver. What if the Iraqis start to use Palestine as a point of departure for the defence of Baghdad? We know there are anti-aircraft guns on the roofs around us. If they now place soldiers and weapons on the roof, maybe in the garden, in the stairwells, in our rooms, what we most fear will come true — we will be hostages.

That same morning, Tarek Ayob, the reporter for the Arabic TV channel al-Jazeera, was killed as he was about to deliver his report. He was on the roof of the channel's office, a stone's throw from the Information Ministry, when a missile annihilated the generator a couple of yards away. It exploded and the metal shards cut up his body. He died instantly, while the programme's anchorman, on the other side of the Persian Gulf, sat watching.

— These attacks are not accidental, is Robert Fisk's opinion. — Al-Jazeera has been targeted three times in as many years. First in Kabul, then in Basra and now here. They say it is mistaken identity, but they know what they are doing. Journalists are among the American's targets.

Uday hurries past, swiftly, lightly. Jean Paul asks him what has happened.

— People die in wars. Surely you know that, Uday says breezily before turning into his office.

A thin column of smoke streams from the room on the fifteenth floor, windows are shattered on several floors. The missile hit the balcony balustrade, concrete and glass rushed in.

Uncertain, I stand there. The hotel framework has not been hit. I return to my room. As I let myself in the telephone is ringing. It is Bjørn Hansen at NRK.

— Are you OK?

— I'm OK.

I hadn't thought about the fact that the news from Hotel Palestine would reach home, that the agencies would spread the news and that someone might be worried.

— We'll put you on the morning broadcast and you can give an account of what you have seen while I phone your parents. What is their phone number?

I am put through to the studio and give a narrative of the little I know of the missile which struck.

— Are you thinking of changing hotels? Nina Owing asks.

— No, where to? We cannot stay where we want. This is the only hotel available. Battles are raging around the two others we were initially offered.

— So what will you do?

— We'll wait and see what happens.

Then the Swedes, the Danes, the Finns, the Dutch and the Canadians phone.

*

– France 3 has pictures.

Remy pops in en route to their offices on the four-teenth floor. They are editing the photos ready to send them around the world. All morning the TV crew had been following the campaign through the districts where the ministries were located side by side. For ten minutes immediately before the bang, France 3's cameras were focused on the three Abrams standing on al-Jumhuriya. The cameras captured the moment when the middle tank suddenly turned its cannon towards the hotel. A flash of light, a bang and Hotel Palestine shook. The missile hit the floor above France 3. The experienced Ukrainian cameraman Taras Protsyok was filming the three tanks from the balcony. He was hit in the stomach by concrete and glass shards, as was the Spanish cam-eraman José Couso from Telecinco. He was standing on the balcony next door and his leg was cut clean off. Three Reuters employees were hit in the face, legs and neck by shrapnel.

American HQ stubbornly insists that the tanks were fired on from the hotel. In the first briefing General Vincent Brooks says that the soldiers replied to an attack from the lobby. That would have been a physical impossi-bility. The lobby faces away from the bridge. Later the general says that was a slip of the tongue and that the tanks were attacked from a position in front of the hotel. The commander of the third infantry division's second brigade then says that the crew returned fire because they had seen the enemy's field glasses pointing at them. A dozen TV lenses and cameras had been following the fighting from the hotel balconies.

No one had seen men with weapons or heard shots fired from the building. The pictures from France 3 were proof of that. – If there had been shooting from the hotel the cameras would have caught the sound, says the photographer.

Hotel Palestine is a landmark in Baghdad. – They will never attack this hotel; after all, Americans live here, an Iraqi woman surrounded by her children had assured me.

But that is exactly what the Americans have done. In the subject box I write: 'Missiles against the cameras'. Someone knocks on the door. Josh stands out in the corridor, a bottle of whisky in his hand. His face is wet with sweat. And tears. He sits down on my chair and cries. Sobs. I sit on the bed.

– My friends are dead.

Josh repeats himself again and again. The big man is wet through. His face is swollen, dissolved in tears. He had been standing on the lower roof, where the cameras were positioned, when the missile hit. Everyone had dropped to the floor when they heard the whistle.

Josh had rushed up the stairs. Well trained in first aid from his army days, he'd hoped he could do something to help.

– When I arrived there was blood everywhere. I rushed and got my first-aid kit. Bandages, I called. Bandages! We must stop the flow of blood. But they just continued to carry them out to the lift, into the lift. It took ages. They lost more and more blood. I couldn't do anything. They died in my arms. I had my first-aid kit but I could do nothing. Nothing. Helpless, helpless, helpless.

Josh shakes. His tears flow. He has forgotten the glass of whisky in front of him.

– Taras died on the way to hospital, José a bit later. Paul will be OK, and the two others. I should have bandaged them. But I just couldn't get at them. I could have saved them!

– Josh. It is not your fault that they died. They died because of the missiles; American missiles.

I try to comfort him. Desperate eyes look at me. I walk round the table and put my arms around him, worried that he might break down altogether, that he will not last the course. We remain sitting by the round table. Until today Josh has been the comforter and encourager. Now it is my turn. For a long time I sit and stroke his back. It is late afternoon, twilight is approaching. I have written no more than the title. To catch the deadline I will have to continue. But my friend is sitting here. I say carefully: – Josh, just stay here. But I . . . I'm sorry, I must start to write. Sorry.

He is staring vacantly at me.

– Do stay here while I write, I say again, and realise how hollow it sounds.

– No, I'll go now. We have a transmission.

The big man gets up and leaves. The technician. The voice in the ear of the reporter during live broadcasts. The voice that connects studio to reporter. The backroom boy who no one sees, no one hails, who never achieves fame and honour. Who suffers all that we suffer, the same dangers, the same traumas, but who never reports them. He has to store them in his head while he adjusts the satellite in order that the signal might reach the London studio and in order that someone else might vent their impressions.

When I have sent the story I prepare to report for the TV news. I dig the helmet out of the cupboard. White, hard, heavy. I put it on for the first time and hurry down the stairs.

– The helmet is crooked, says the technician and tightens the strap. We start the transmission.

– The whole building shook, I tell Christian Borch of

News Night. Bloody blankets . . . smashed cameras . . . three killed . . . tanks shooting . . . memorial . . . shock . . .

— What is the situation in Baghdad this evening?

— Planes circle overhead . . . bombing in the distance . . . the battles continue.

Out of the corner of my eye I spot David reporting from his position to Sky News. We both talk about what we have seen, heard and experienced, me in Norwegian, he in his polished Queen's English. It pours out of us. We transform the incident into short, concise sentences.

— We will leave you there, Åsne Seierstad in Baghdad.

As though synchronised, David and I take out the earpieces.

— That's really cute, David calls from his position.

— What?

— White! It's white!

— What?

— Your helmet. It suits your golden locks!

Some helmets are navy blue. Some green, some black.

— Yours is the only white one, he compliments me.

I look over at Josh. He stares hard in the other direction. Now that the transmission has come to an end he sits down on a stool and lights a cigarette.

The spotlights on the roof are pointing at us. Everywhere else is pitch-black. It feels unreal, like being on a floodlit ship. The roof is like a sparkling deck, surrounded by glowing lanterns. We don't know what the surrounding darkness hides. Nor what our surroundings will look like when we wake in the morning. Where will we be then? What will the view be? A new sensation grips me and settles in my stomach — dread.

*

Next morning the rats have deserted the sinking ship. Uday, Kadim, Mohsen – all gone. Gone too are the men who sat and chain-smoked behind the table with the cardboard sign. Gone are the uniformed Baath Party men. Gone are the guards, the police.

The hotel manager paces the reception. – We have been left to our own devices, without guards, without weapons.

The toughest among us have already been out. They report that the Americans have taken Saddam City, that they are being received like heroes, with flowers and flags, that looting has started in the wake of the Americans' entry.

Over the whole city police and security guards have vanished into thin air. Armed gangs roam the streets, smash windows, loot shops, schools, public buildings. But they are, to a certain extent, cautious, there is no talk of mass-looting – yet. The roads around the hotel are deserted.

– They'll be here soon, they'll be here soon, the hotel manager chants. – They know that journalists live here, that they are unarmed, that they have masses of money. Thousands of dollars. Like mobile treasure troves – unprotected. Woe betide us, they'll be here soon.

He advises us to hide computers, telephones and money. Remy helps me to find a hiding place. In the tiny corridor between my room and the bathroom some roof tiles are loose. He dismantles them and shoves everything in. Now what?

I remain on the ship. I dare not venture into town. I can't risk being caught in crossfire. Having heard Yves' remarks, the most foolhardy thing to do would be to drive around with Amir. The Americans might think we are suicide bombers. I sit on my bed and twiddle my thumbs, trying hard to convince myself that one does not go into a town where an invading army are fighting their way to the centre; where one does not know where the frontline is. I walk out onto the balcony. Deliver a report of all I haven't seen, just heard. The only thing I have seen is that the Iraqi soldiers have disappeared. Today, the more daring become my private news agencies. I dawdle around the hotel, popping out to the rumour-mongers on the flag-stones outside.

— Mohsen tried to leave the hotel in Yves' car. But Yves had let the tyres down!

— Portuguese TV has been beaten up in Sadoun Street. They took everything!

— That happened to Sanja too!

— Who?

— The Bulgarian. The one who is making a documentary.

— Uday went around the rooms yesterday collecting money. He threatened to throw people out if they didn't pay!

— That devil never got anything from me!

— He collected thousands of dollars.

— Both airports have been taken.

— My interpreter is gone.

— And my driver.

— There's no one serving breakfast this morning. I'm dying for a glass of tea.

— Uday's Arab horses have been let loose. They're running around in the streets.

— Did you hear that? The shots are coming nearer.

— Hm.

— Al-Kindi is full of wounded. Every minute new ones arrive. With shrapnel sticking out of their backs, their heads!

— Helicopters!

— Towards the centre of town!

— Saddam's *fedain* have taken refuge in the Air Ministry.

— The army has fled to Tikrit!

— Most of them have deserted!

— *Mammamia, sono stanchissimo!*

Lorenzo is even sweatier than he normally is following his spell on the stairs. He tears off his bulletproof vest.

— What's happening? I ask

— *Hai fame? Ti dirò tutto.*

Lorenzo pulls me with him and dishes up both pasta and his stories.

— *Finito! Lo spettacolo e finito!* What would you like?

In his room on the ninth floor he looks helplessly around his food store. A few seconds later he chops cucumber, an onion, opens a tin of tuna fish, garnishes with pepper and arranges the meal on a plate.

— Antipasti?

A tin of artichokes, God only knows from where, is divided between our plates.

— Where have you been today? he asks.

— Nowhere.

— Haven't you been out? But this is where history is being made! Today!

— I am too frightened.

— Madonna!

— Well, tell me then!

Lorenzo has been to Saddam City. He recounts how people embraced both him and the Americans. — First they were all clapping. Then they realised their hands could be used for other things. Looting exploded. They grabbed anything they could find. From shops, restaurants, houses, kiosks and public buildings. Nothing was too small to leave behind. Electric cables, paper baskets, fans, pots and pans, lamps. A weapons' depot was emptied. I saw children carrying five to six Kalashnikovs all at once. Eventually nearly everyone was carrying a weapon with which they danced around. Then the mood changed. There we were, with our cameras, belts stuffed with dollars, nice cars, helmets and bulletproof vests. And no weapons. Suddenly my interpreter says: 'Let's go.' Not a second too soon.

— Was there no fighting?

— No, it appears that Saddam's soldiers have deserted the city. The Baath Party offices are being plundered. Any party members left will be beaten up.

— And the Americans?

— They'll no doubt come this way. Hopefully before the looters! Lorenzo laughs. — No one can predict the Americans' moves. They do what they like. To win the war!

How could I have been such a coward? On this important day I sat in my bedroom, biting my nails, while the drama was being played out all over town. Amir and Aliya were happy that I stayed at home, but I am cross with myself. As if that was not enough, I am still frightened. I feel like a wimp, while Lorenzo delivers numerous reports to Italian radio and TV — in crescendo.

A strange sound enters our world. It sounds like thunder. Like an approaching storm. Pealing, rumbling, scraping. It grows, snorting, angry.

We steal out onto the balcony.

— The Americans!

A column of tanks rumbles down one of the main streets. Huge, they occupy the whole area. Slowly, reverently, the first Abrams roll into Paradise Square. One after another they follow on. Roaring, they circle around inside the square.

It is like watching an opera from the upper circle. An opera nearing *il gran finale*. We watch spellbound, bewitched by the drama unfolding before our eyes, until we awake from the spell and wish to be part of the scene. We leave our vantage points, abandon the balconies and rush down the stairs, Lorenzo at a gallop, me waltzing on his heels. Down on Paradise Square we stand, gaping. An extraordinary sight, these Americans, like extras in a war film. All the safety equipment makes them look enormous. Stiff and concentrated, they roll over the rotunda, weapons pointing in all directions, ready to shoot, ready to attack. This is unknown territory; no one knows where the enemy might hide.

It is not in Paradise Square. When the first tank has circled the whole roundabout it stops. All the tanks follow suit. In no time they are in control of the entire square.

The faces of the soldiers are unmistakably American. Big, broad, well-fed. Some blond, some dark, some black. The American look.

– It's over. The war is over, I think.

A knot dissolves and something flows inside me. I call out to one of the passing tanks.

– Thank you for coming!

I want to swallow the words as they escape my mouth. But I have been so afraid . . .

Aliya has come down. She stares stiffly ahead. Her lips are tightly squeezed, her shoulders hunched. Distrust shines from her eyes. Without looking at me she comes and stands by my side.

After a while some young men gather around the statue in the centre of the square. Someone with a large sledge-hammer tries to knock it down. Others pull themselves up and place a rope round its neck. They push and pull. But it stands firm; the granite plinth alone is several metres high.

– Down with Saddam. Thank you Bush!

Actually I have never given the statue much thought. Never looked at it closely. It has always been there, in the background, when I deliver my TV reports, and I have passed it on my way out to town and on my return. Only today, as it is being attacked, do I really see it. It is like a statue of Stalin, unapproachable, cold and paternal all at once, with a hand pointing, leading towards the future.

The statue, raised a year earlier on 28 April 2002 to celebrate Saddam's sixty-fifth birthday, stands firm. The hammering reminds me of the Lilliputs in Gulliver's travels. The marines from *Charlie* company come to the rescue, eager for destruction. A chain is placed around the dictator's head. One end of the chain is fastened to an American tank which rolls backwards. The statue doesn't move. The tank pulls harder. The statue stands firm. The soldiers try again. The statue moves forwards slightly, but remains erect.

The tank takes a run, we hear a creak, but Saddam remains standing. A few marines climb up and fasten an American flag to his head. The mob near the statue shout jubilantly. Those outside the crowd freeze slightly. Saddam is blindfolded and gagged.

– We are in Iraq, not America, one man standing beside me says. He stares fixedly at the drama in front of him.

– We are the ones who should have got rid of Saddam. But look, we let them do it, another sighs. – We are cowards; we should have voiced our opinions, face to face, not pull down statues now that he has fallen.

– At last we can say what we want, a third intervenes. – That man has blood on his hands; he is a tyrant, he strangled us.

They disagree. At last a political discussion is being heard in the streets of Baghdad. Some applaud, others resist.

– This is an insult, the first man says. – The American flag must not fly in Baghdad.

As though *Charlie* company have heard the voices at the far end of the square, an Iraqi flag appears and is placed on the statue's head, the Stars and Stripes is removed. Many heave a sigh of relief; the men around the statue perform a dance.

– Shias, one of the men snorts. – They are all Shias. Listen how they invoke Imam Hussein.

An elderly man watches the drama developing in the square. A little boy is standing beside him on a concrete wall. The man's face is pitted with scars and he looks on, as if petrified.

– I never thought the regime would fall this quickly, he says when woken from his reverie. – It has ruined my life. Now it has gone.

The man puts his arms around the boy. He looks like his grandfather, but the boy is his son, the man is only forty.

– The war has aged me, he says, as though reading my thoughts. – It has sucked the vigour out of me. All these wars started by our president. When I was seventeen I was sent to fight Iran, eight years of hell. Three years later the Gulf War started. I was nearly killed when a missile struck a few yards away. That's how I got these scars. He touches the cuts by his lips, over his eyes, on his cheek. He pulls up his shirt and exposes many more.

– But the deepest wounds are here, he says, and points to his heart. – My two youngest brothers were killed in the Gulf War. One was mown down by bullets from an American tank, another died during one of the big battles in the desert. I escaped and walked on foot from Kuwait to Baghdad. When I got home I had nothing, no money, no shoes, my clothes were hanging in shreds. I was alive but my life had been taken from me. I gave twenty years to the Iraqi army. Years that gave me nothing but pain.

The Abrams revs up, pulls hard. The statue groans; the tank pulls, Saddam roars and creaks and moans, then falls over and lies horizontal next to the plinth. The group around the statue explode in wild jubilation.

When the man she has revered as virtually divine pitches forwards and falls to the ground, Aliya turns away. It is disgraceful the way the statue falls, broken in two by the brutal forces of an American tank.

The war-weary soldier smiles a wan smile. The lustreless eyes shine for a short moment. Then he pulls the little boy closer.

Amir has witnessed the drama from the bonnet of his car. Tears flow down his cheeks. He regards the fallen Saddam indignantly.

– This is my country, he says. – Iraq is my country! It shall not be ruled by Americans.

Abbas stands beside him. He too is crying. Tears of joy. – I am so happy. At last! At last we are free! At last we can start living! I love America.

– What right have they? Aliya whispers. What right have they?

After

Baghdad is shrouded in a fog of words. The words break out, are snapped up and burrow into people's minds. They churn around and force other words out, which in turn flutter into other ears. These words turn into sentences that have not been spoken for decades. They form hateful declarations and embittered conversations, exclamations of happiness and thanksgiving. They turn into embraces, maybe even kisses.

In this giddy new existence words are spoken that could once have sent you to prison. Words that could have seen you tortured. Words that could have put a bullet in your neck. Words that could have robbed you of everything.

Now they crash into each other like waves. Elated. Surprised. Hesitant. Bitter. They are shouted out loud or sobbed through tears.

One word is *liberated*, another is *freedom*. One word is *invaded*, another is *occupied*. Hatred. Revenge. Dictatorship. Saddam. Devil. Finally.

— We are free! Thank you Mister Bush! A young boy shouts in Saddam City.

— *Allahu Akbar!* God is Great! chants a mullah in the mosque.

— We will drive the infidel occupiers out; this from a sinister type with a ragged beard.

What Saddam Hussein thinks few get to hear. But George Bush's words fly over the Atlantic: Our victory in Iraq is certain.

Once upon a time there were two friends. They lived under the governance of Saddam Hussein. Brothers, they called themselves, and they mumbled when they spoke. Dictatorship reigned in Baghdad, fear ruled.

Then came a war.

The friends stood side by side when the statue fell. They both cried. One's cheek was wet with sadness, the other's shone with tears of gladness.

Then followed the words. One insisted the country was invaded, the other that it was liberated.

— *We do not deserve this humiliation, Amir said through clenched teeth.*

— *This is the happiest day of my life, Abbas shouted with joy.*

The two friends looked at each other through their tears.

They were the two sides of the face of Baghdad. Amir was a Sunni. His brothers had enrolled in the Baath Party and in the militia designed to defend Baghdad against intruders. Abbas was a Shia. Many of his relatives had not yet been released from the dungeons. They might never be found.

In the first frothy hours after the collapse, they still had a lot in common. None of them had liked the ruler.

— *A bad president, one whispered.*

— *A bloody tyrant, the other shouted.*

His presence no longer cast a shadow over the population. The only ones in hiding now were the dictator himself and his henchmen.

The two friends strove to find common ground, they tried to patch together the bitter feelings. But the understanding was short-lived. They each remained opposite sides of the city's face, a face which appeared increasingly distorted.

— Look at these looters, these dogs, Amir snorted with a stiff jaw. Abbas held his tongue.

— I'm not saying it because I'm a Sunni, but these Shias are the symbol of dirt, anarchy, chaos.

— The Shias are not alone in looting, Abbas answered.

— Soon there will be a civil war, Amir maintained. — Because we cannot just stand and watch the Shias ruin our country.

— Amir is not talking like that because he's a Sunni, and I'm not happy about the country having been liberated because I'm a Shia, of course not, Abbas interrupted sarcastically.

— We used to have order, fixed points in our existence. Of course our dictator was strict, but our people need a firm hand. A strong man. If not, we'll capsize and descend into madness.

Amir looked around, indignant. — Now we do not know who is in charge, what the future holds. We know nothing anymore.

The other didn't see uncertainty, but adventure, the possibilities. Abbas, who had known prison, hopelessness and fear, had started to dream.

— The future, freedom, democracy, that's just lies, Amir grunted.

— The future, freedom, democracy, we can build that, Abbas argued.

The two friends had a girlfriend. If they were the two sides of Baghdad's face, she was the city's heart. When the ruler was downed, she too fell, into a coma. It wasn't that she collapsed or *fainted; she remained upright, but a curtain descended over her thoughts and feelings.*

She never cried. People in a coma do not cry, they just exist. It was like that with Aliya too. When the two friends started quarrelling she disappeared into her room, lay down on her bed with her clothes on and fell asleep. No one said goodnight to her. In fact, no one noticed that she had gone. They were too consumed with shouting words and constructing new sentences. She knew that the fair-haired girl would be talking to camera after camera into the small hours. No one needed her this evening.

Late the next morning, a few rooms away, the fair-haired girl slept. Exhausted, she was lulled to sleep by the drone of tanks. No one heard the shots at night, or the planes shrieking overhead, en route to new battlefields.

Sisters, they had called themselves, when they had promised to protect each other. Shakra and Samra. Light and dark.

— Hide behind my back now, the dark one had said. — Then I'll hide behind yours when . . .

Baghdad's heart had locked itself behind closed doors. She was hurt, humiliated. When the sun rose there was a knock on her door. The knocking made her flinch. Before opening she tried to protect herself by appearing hard, cold, sharp.

— Good morning, how are you?

— Fine.

— You don't look fine.

— Oh.

The fair-haired girl picked at her heart.

— What do you think about Saddam's fall?

— I have no opinion.

She twisted the knife.

— But how do you feel?

— I have no feelings.

The intruder was merciless.

— But are you angry, unhappy, happy?

— Please do not ask any more questions.

Sisters, they had called themselves, when they had promised to protect each other. They stood looking at each other. The intruder removed the knife and gave the heart of Baghdad a kiss. The embrace was short. The wounded sister withdrew.

— I must take some time off to visit my family today, Aliya says.

— Of course, any time. Amir is outside. Would you like to go now?

— No, I can wait.

— You can go now if you like.

— No. Let's work.

Amir is waiting in the parking lot, but not in his usual place. Now the car is outside the American barrier. The tanks have taken his place. Amir is silent, Aliya is silent. Big boys in bulletproof vests occupy the reception, the stairwell, the corridors, the exit, their city.

Sadoun Street, which runs parallel to the Tigris, one block away from the bank, is seething with men pushing carts, cars and crates. A lorry is parked on the pavement. Fastened to it is a chain, which is attached to the bars of the door of Rafidain — The Two Rivers — savings bank. The car groans and pulls, the bars give way. The door inside is smashed in with an axe. The mob rush into the bank. A few moments later they stream out again.

— A bomb, a bomb, they cry, and run over to the other side of the road.

There they stand, waiting.

— The guy who shouted 'bomb' wanted the money for himself!

The rabble run into the bank again – and return empty-handed.

– They took it all when they fled. The scoundrels! The vaults are empty!

The journey through the streets of Baghdad uncovers more of the same. Shops, restaurants, hotels, ministries and public buildings are emptied of anything of value. Even the city's hospitals are the victims of plunder.

Outside the Ministry of Immigration horses pulling huge carts are waiting. Computers, TV sets, electric fans, desks, office chairs, packets of writing paper, a mirror, cups and plates are snatched up.

– We have lived for thirty years under a regime which took everything from us, freedom, purchasing power, choice. Now people feel they have the right to steal some of it back. As if that can make up for what they have lost. But they are stealing from their own people, not from the regime – that has fled. And what is a dusty ventilation fan against ten years of lost life?

The man talking regards me with sad eyes. He is dressed in threadbare clothes that once were smart. – Anyhow, it won't work, there's no electricity.

Aliya translates automatically, without spirit, without feeling. Amir leans against the bonnet of the car and shakes his head. It is more important than ever to keep an eye on it.

– They said they were opening the doors to freedom and they have opened those to chaos instead, he exclaims bitterly.

A strange spectacle passes us. A horse pulls a cart, which is pulling a car, which is hauling a wagon to which yet another horse is tied. A gang of men, women and children stumble excitedly after the procession, an entire family on the make.

Amid the chaos some American soldiers arrive. They walk determinedly towards a building, guns pointing in all directions.

— Weapons were stored here, explains the sergeant, Nicholas. — In the centre of town. When we arrived people were helping themselves. Now we have the place under control.

Inside the building crates containing guns, bullets, cartridges and pistols are stacked up. Some are marked in Latin, others in Cyrillic, yet others in Arabic.

Nicholas volunteers to show us other weapons' caches. The patrol stops by a sports club. The swimming pool is empty of water, but full of sandbags. Grenades are stored in the weight-lifting room. Carefully placed between trampolines and shelves full of starting blocks are a dozen two-metre long missiles.

— Air-to-air, the sergeant says. — They have tried to tinker with them. Iraq has no air force so they have tried to convert them into ground-to-air missiles.

Nicholas is sweating. The sun shines relentlessly on his red neck. The Americans have been ordered never to take off their heavy safety equipment.

— We heard them moving things at night and were petrified they were weapons which would make us targets for bombers, says a boy hanging around outside. He is a basketball player and made diligent use of the sports arena. Before the war.

Now the sports complex is empty. Anything of value has been looted, pictures of Saddam Hussein smashed. A few dirty shirts have been chucked into a corner, handwritten results lists trampled underfoot.

Aliya sorts through the rubbish, translates lists, diplomas and half-burnt letters of homage to Saddam. I no longer ask how she feels. It's an untimely question. Use your loaf, I chide myself.

Weapons have been hoarded in the buildings next door too. In one of the rooms over one thousand rifles are stacked side by side. During the early morning people broke into the storeroom.

– They dropped whatever they were carrying when we arrived, Nicholas says. – We could do nothing but let them go.

One room is full of mobile anti-aircraft missiles, another holds crates of ammunition. – These are awesome, says Nicholas, and holds up some small, black bullets. – They dig into the body, whirl around and produce horrible internal bleeding.

He puts them down. – These are for 14.5mm machine-guns, he says, and points to some others. The entire wall is covered in shelves holding dirty boxes marked 'Teargas – Product of Jordan'.

The weapons were meant to be handed out to people to fight the Americans. But in the end neither army, militia, special forces or the neighbourhoods were ready to defend the city.

– We discovered a large cache of grenades yesterday. We dug a hole in the ground and buried them. Now they are ten metres down. So that's pretty safe, says the sergeant.

A couple of soldiers keep strict guard over the storeroom, but they do nothing to prevent the looting of the neighbouring building, one of the Baath Party's local offices. While the Americans stand watching with loaded guns, the masses remove everything of value. They smile and laugh at the soldiers, who stare fixedly ahead behind dark sunglasses.

— We are an invasion force, not an occupying army. People ask for protection but we are not the police. We are here to put an end to Saddam Hussein's regime, we are here to rid the country of weapons of mass destruction, but there are not enough of us to give them the security they desire. We don't even have enough troops to guard the weapons' depots. Several we have had to bolt up and leave.

Some women approach us and watch Nicholas attentively as he is talking.

— I fear the night, Khadija, a mother of five, says, watching the looting. — All day people have robbed shops and public buildings. Tonight maybe the time has come for private houses. It is your responsibility, she says to the sergeant. — You have driven the police and security forces out of town. Now you'll have to protect us.

— This is anarchy, an elderly man nearby takes up the thread. — Society has collapsed and Bush is to blame. You cannot leave us in the lurch now, hand us over to the bandits.

A deranged woman runs up and throws herself into the arms of the soldier.

— We are frightened, she cries.

— We'll do our best, Nicholas answers gruffly and pushes her away. The woman stiffens. She assesses the sergeant through narrow eyes, then she turns on her heel and leaves. Nicholas lost a supporter there. Many more will join her.

Three young men, their hands bound behind their backs, are hauled through the gates to the hospital in the district once called Saddam City. When the dictator fell the district was renamed al-Sadr. A seething mass surrounds the hospital, some carrying weapons, others without. It is from here that the million inhabitants of the district are ruled, the only public building in use.

— Suicide bombers, someone shouts. The mob crowds around the prey, the three men look up at them, scared stiff. They were discovered wearing explosives trying to negotiate a roadblock, the rumours spread. — And they were in possession of several grenades.

— They are Saddam's men, says an onlooker. — They have come to kill, not to defend us.

The men are led into the hospital's courtyard. A man pulls out a long sabre and follows them. Two others walk behind with pistols. — They are from Syria, they are terrorists.

Several curious spectators tag along but are brutally pushed away.

— We'll lock them in the hospital and the Americans can take care of them, says a self-proclaimed security guard.

But there are hardly any Americans in al-Sadr. Chaos rules. The hospital has been taken over by a sheik — a holy man.

— I have erected four barriers around the hospital, says Sheik Said Ali al-Musawi. — This is the only hospital in town that has not been looted. Doctors have abandoned the other ones, the patients have been moved. Everything of value has disappeared; that is not going to happen here.

The sheik is both happy and uncertain about recent events. — I am glad that Saddam Hussein has gone. If he were standing in front of me now I would cut off his arms and legs. Then I'd watch him die slowly. Make sure he suffered an awful death. He deserves that after what he has done to us.

For nine years Said Ali al-Musawi was incarcerated in a four by four metre cell in the infamous Abu Ghraib prison in Baghdad. — I was arrested in 1994, accused of leading a group which wanted to overthrow the president. They tortured me to make me confess. They tied my arms behind my back and hung me up, beat me with sticks and cables, gave me electric shocks. They threatened to kill my wife. My cell was painted red so the light would stab my eyes. I never saw the sun, never felt the fresh air, for nine years, he says *bitterly. — The torture continued for years, because I had nothing to confess.*

Said Ali al-Musawi was released from prison in October last year, when Saddam Hussein, with the elections in mind, set thousands of prisoners free.

— *But I am not so fond of the Americans either. I am an Iraqi and every inch of me is patriotic. I cannot accept that foreigners rule our country. But they helped us to get rid of the dictator and for that they deserve a 'thank you'. Under him life was worse than miserable.*

Most of the doctors left the hospital in Saddam City when the ground war started. — *There was no security here, lawlessness reigned, so they just went home,* Chief Physician Mowaffak Gorjea says. *But twenty-two out of one hundred and twenty remain. The best stayed.*

The hospital has been without water and power for some days. Now water has returned, but the hospital is dependent on its three generators. — *One is broken. If one more breaks down we have had it. All the equipment is several decades old. I don't know how long it will last,* says the doctor. — *I know I could have saved many patients if the equipment had been better,* he sighs.

In a room on the third floor lies Ali. Ali's world has been reduced to four walls, a sheet, a dirty polyester blanket and a towel. He lies stretched out on the bed. Above him an iron hoop has been constructed over which a brown and white-patterned blanket has been spread. Ali's body needs air, nothing must cover it. His aunt sits beside the twelve-year-old. She waves the flies away continuously; they must not settle on his scarred body.

His stomach and chest are covered in red, brown, yellow, black and white crusts. Every bit of skin, from his neck down to his hips, was burnt when the missile struck his house.

— *His condition is critical,* says the chief physician. — *Thirty-five percent of the body has third degree burns, of what is left of his* body, that is. If he had still had arms it would have been more than fifty percent. If he remains here I'm afraid he'll die. Infections, infections. . .

The missile hit Ali's home ten days earlier, in the middle of the night. His mother, who was five months pregnant, his father and little brother were killed instantly. Ali's blanket caught fire and his arms were so badly burnt that they had to be amputated. He was the only one to survive.

We stand some way off looking at him. We do not know what to say. Ali himself breaks the silence.

— I want my hands back.

The voice is weak and slightly grating. His lips quiver when he talks. The hospital has no painkillers. His thoughts might be worse than the wounds.

— They were all killed. Mummy, Daddy, my little brother, and all the friends in my street. Four houses were destroyed, he says. — I never want to go back, there's nothing left.

Ali is quiet again. He is too tired to talk. He asks his aunt to fix a towel to the metal bars and place it round his neck. That way he won't see his burnt body. The arm stumps disappear under the towel.

— Can I have my hands back? Ali asks yet again.

I want to go home; I can't take it any more.

It is unbearable to look into Ali's eyes. I have to turn away, I do not want him to see me cry.

Aliya remains there, talking quietly to him. In a tender voice she says something in Arabic.

I walk over to the window to pull myself together. The sky is grey with smoke from the fires.

I cannot leave yet. I have to find out more about life under Saddam. The worst atrocities took place here, in Saddam

City. We stop at random, get out of the car, knock on a door and present ourselves. We want to know if anyone in the neighbourhood has relatives who disappeared under Saddam.

Yes, they have. The father disappeared one day. He left for work and never returned. The brother disappeared too, and two cousins.

We sit down on a threadbare mat.

It was in the spring of 1980. When the husband failed to show up at home his wife had gone to his place of work. There they had asked her to go to the police. She went, but the bureaucrat behind the counter had just shrugged his shoulders.

– I know nothing.

The second time she went he said there was no point asking more.

The third time he had hissed: – If you come again, your sons and brothers will disappear the same way.

She never returned.

We listen to her in the darkened room. A small window emits three rays of light; none of the lamps work. Several neighbours sit listening. I shiver. The room is chilly; the change from the burning sun on the street outside is considerable.

– Maybe he lives in a subterranean cellar, the wife says, her voice faltering. The daughters, little girls when their father disappeared, look doubtfully at us. The men stare into space.

More neighbours join us. They all have stories to tell. In the 1980s the Shia Muslims were subject to a wave of arrests: Saddam Hussein feared potential rebellion, and that the Shias supported the regime in Iran. His suppression was especially aimed at the illicit religious Dawa Party. Saddam worried about the might of the mullahs, and the mere act of belonging to a certain mosque or carrying out religious duties was enough to send anyone to the torture chamber.

I try to interview every person in the blacked-out room, but become confused. In time everyone talks over each other and about each other's stories. They add details to their neighbours' tales, and Aliya is only able to present a fraction of what is being said. While she translates the storyteller continues to talk. The family ties are also unclear. Who is a brother, a cousin, a son or a nephew? I lose the thread but get the essence. The incarnation of evil.

It appears that everyone in the little back street is present. They sit on the floor, stand along the wall, slouch in the doorway, listen from the hall.

– Can you help us find them? an old lady asks. Two of her sons disappeared en route to the mosque one day.

I look at her.

– I don't think I can find them, but I can write about them. About the injustice you have suffered.

– But can you help us to find them? she asks again.

– I don't think so. I'm sorry.

Disappointment shines from the eyes of the black-clad woman. She doesn't say another word.

Some of the men have themselves experienced prison. Low-voiced, they talk about the torture they witnessed. Aliya translates mechanically. This is a reality she knew nothing about. Growing up in Baghdad's middle class, in a safe and apolitical Sunni Muslim family, she was isolated from the Shias in Saddam City. I remember her fear of travelling here before the war.

The dust in the room hovers in the three shafts of light. On the walls are pictures of the missing husband and sons; beside them two pictures of the Shia Muslims' holy men,

Hussein and Ali. One picture catches my attention. The Virgin Mary with child.

— Ask why they have that picture, I say to Aliya.

Aliya asks.

— They say because it is beautiful.

— But it's Jesus and Mary. That's a Christian picture.

— I won't translate that, Aliya says without looking at me. — It's there because it's pretty. Is that OK for you? Is there anything else? Can we go now?

On the way home we hardly speak. All our strength has been sucked out. The next day we continue the search.

Some did their calculations with dots, others with lines. The tiny cells are full of inscriptions — by the floor, along the door and up towards the roof. In these dark rooms, where no light ever pene-trated, prisoners tried to survey their existence by scratching a dot or a line in the wall at the beginning of each day.

Sometimes there were six to a cell, others were alone in the miserly square metres. Some cells are painted red to prevent the eyes from ever getting any rest. In others the red has been painted over with white. Where prisoners have scraped away the white paint, the red colour has appeared, as if they wrote in blood.

'Don't despair, Allah will support you', is written in the blood-red letters. 'I give my heart to Saddam Hussein. May Allah protect me'. 'To my beloved children Safar, Ali and Marwa, 19.7.1990' is cut into one wall. In all directions, across the endless dots and lines, cockroaches scuttle, quick as lightning.

We are in one of the interrogation centres of the secret police — Mukhabarat. Political prisoners were incarcerated here, in al-Hakimiya in Baghdad's Zuwiya district. Immediately before the bombing started the prisoners were moved, no one knows where to.

Desperate relatives now visit the prisons to seek information about their loved ones, or at least to look for signs on the walls. The day before, a group of relatives had tried to break open a large door with axes and iron bars. They thought it might lead to an underground prison.

— It is rumoured that there is a subterranean section here. Perhaps they were buried alive when the guards left, maybe they're still breathing down there, says Mudaffar, who is looking for his brother. Adnan was arrested three years ago. Mudaffar pauses between blows to the door. — One day they came to the shop and took him. Said he was an enemy of society. We know nothing, only that they took him here.

Jabir is trying to find traces of his father. He was arrested in 1994, accused of conspiring against the regime. The young boy is one of the few who knows where his father is. The family were asked to come and fetch the body. The secret police told them he had died of a heart attack. They at least have a grave to visit. — But I want to see where he lived, Jabir says. — Every day, all these years, I have been thinking of how he suffered.

Jabir walks through the narrow passages with a torch. There are no windows, no ventilation. The cells stink of excrement, vomit, mould. Several of the cells appear to have been abandoned in haste, right after the prisoners were fed. In some cells two eggs remain on a plate, in others only the shell is left. There are neither blankets nor pillows, only a drain in the floor.

The interrogations took place at the end of the passage. Blindfolds and cloth to tie hands and feet, electric cables and pipes lie scattered around the room. The interrogation room is chaotic; the prison has been looted during the course of the last few days. Drawers have been turned upside down and paper strewn on the floor. A cupboard with tapes has been emptied; only the covers remain. Journals have been trampled into the ground. A woman's shoe lies among the rubbish; a man shudders when he sees it.

In the courtyard in front of the prison, Sabab stands with his hands in his pockets and looks up at the building. — I was here for three months and was one of the few let out. I was accused of belonging to a political group I had not even heard of. I never thought I would survive. They tied my arms, hung me from a fan in the roof and spun me round until I fainted. They beat me with sticks. Gave me electric shocks. They broke both my arms. I never thought I would get out, he says.

— The majority of those brought here were never released. Some were hanged and buried in mass graves, others were thrown in front of their family's door in the middle of the night, one man relates; he will not divulge his name. Like many others he fears that the old regime is not yet finished.

Outside Baghdad is the dreaded Abu Ghraib prison. The high walls are covered with portraits of Saddam Hussein. These are now riddled with bullet holes, in his eyes, his nose. On some the whole face has disappeared. The walls are punctured with gaps caused by exploding bombs and missiles. Inside are many square kilometres of prison complex. Factory-like buildings house rows of naked cells. Each building contains a food hall with concrete benches and tables. The only colour is a portrait of Saddam Hussein at the end of the room. The president is smiling and smoking a cigar.

People come to Abu Ghraib too, to look for their loved ones, even though the prison was virtually emptied when Saddam Hussein proclaimed his amnesty last autumn.

One man roves around, from cell to cell, through passage after passage. He is looking for the secret basement where he thinks his brother is being held. — Abbas has been missing for eighteen years. He was twenty when the secret police came and took him from the university. They accused him of being a member of Dawa, Najib explains. — When we inquired, all they said was that it would be best for him if we never mentioned him again. If we ever returned to ask about him we too would be imprisoned. My mother has cried *for eighteen years; for eighteen years we have been wondering where he is. I shall find him now, he says determinedly, and walks through cells, dining halls and looted offices. In search of the entrance to the secret basement.*

Instead he finds something else. In one of the buildings he enters a bare room. Some stairs ascend to a concrete plateau which covers half the floor space. Two lengths of rope are suspended from the roof, two nooses lie on the floor. Under the bits of rope is an opening. On each side of the opening are two trapdoors, and between them a bolt which can be pushed down in order to open them. Anyone with a noose around their neck will hang.

Najib hurries out into the sun. He glances into another passage of small cells: the death row. Here prisoners waited for their execution.

— I must find the secret entrance. Abbas is there, I am absolutely sure, says Najib, and walks on.

We leave Najib and Abu Ghraib prison, reading the inscription over the doorway on our way out:

There is no life without the sun.

There is no dignity without Saddam Hussein.

In a puddle outside the gate I tread on a rope. Hiding in the wet sand are some photographs, a toothbrush, a flaky tube. The rope is coiled up. It is the same type of rope as those that dangled from the roof in the execution room; the only room where there was no portrait of Saddam Hussein.

We can hardly get into the hotel. The Americans have erected so many checkpoints that it takes an eternity to pass through them. First there is an outside barrier. Behind this is a sea of Iraqi men — seeking work, demonstrating, or simply curious. We force our way through the crowd by means of our press card, the yellow one I paid thousands of dollars to renew just a few days before the war. Thereafter we stand in a queue to be frisked and have our bags and pockets checked.

The last barrier is immediately in front of the hotel. The press card is produced again. We are frisked again. Aliya stiffens when a large American man checks her waist for explosives. Anger surges inside me.

– Should you not have female soldiers to search women? I ask.

– We do.

– I can't see any.

– They're on the other side.

So the female entrance is on the other side. I tell Aliya we will use that next time.

In the lobby a smiling American welcomes us. He wants to talk. We don't. The reception area is packed. The hotel is overflowing with journalists from Amman and Kuwait who waited for the fall of Saddam. Janine is among them. She approaches us in flowing desert robes and embraces us.

The women's team is united again.

The five missing journalists were found, after eight days in Abu Ghraib prison. They had been interrogated, threatened, accused of spying. At night they heard the other prisoners being beaten.

They were freed and sent to Jordan.

On the way back from Abu Ghraib we had passed several corpses. Uniformed, half-naked, civilian. Some were already black with decay. Somewhere, someone was waiting for them.

In the car I had thought about Ali's face, soft and

beautiful, like the face of a fairy. Like Fatima on the cold bench in the mosque.

Towards evening I descend from my room to make my TV reports. I wear the bulletproof vest. In spite of the rumbling tanks outside the situation is more dangerous than ever. Anyone might be in possession of weapons. In the floodlight in front of the cameras we are sitting ducks.

I exit through the back door in the basement to avoid the steaming reception. Cameras and mobile transmission cars take up every available space in front of the hotel. I zigzag my way to my position in the garden. A few bearded types lie coiled in the grass: the warriors from reception! The ones with the martyr missions! Extraordinary. They are spreading themselves under the noses of the Americans. I speculate about what they might be hiding under their ample shirts.

I mount the stand in front of the camera and report looting, torture chambers, and the inhabitants' growing opposition to the invasion army.

On my return I scowl at the men in the grass. They take no notice of me. I'll bring Aliya down and have a talk to them, I think. Find out what they are doing here, why they did not flee with Saddam's soldiers. Perhaps they want to continue fighting, as guerrilla soldiers or suicide bombers? What better place than Hotel Palestine, not so much for a couple of hundred western journalists, but for an equally large number of American soldiers. I wonder how the guys in the garden got through the barriers. Maybe they have just never left.

En route to my room I pop up to Lorenzo to borrow a cable. He is in a radiant mood. Proudly he displays the day's loot: blindfolds in an orange material, others in leather, and a rope.

– Picked up at the prison, he says.

I look at him, appalled.

– From the torture chambers?

– *Si, bella*.

I feel I have been shipwrecked, washed up on a rotting beach. I can hardly stand up. Nauseous, I turn and walk to the door.

Nabil has opened his restaurant again and has put tables out in the garden. He tells me he was not in time to send his wife and twins away. When he at last made up his mind to do so there were no longer any planes flying, and his wife refused to take the babies on a fourteen-hour drive to Syria.

– There are queues, chaos, bandits, she said.

Instead they ensconced themselves in their 400-metre square luxury home and sat tight.

All the tables are taken and we ask if we can order something.

– No food, only beer, Nabil laughs. Earlier there was food and no beer.

– We have no power, so no food. No fridge, no heat.

Behind Nabil's happy countenance, bitterness lurks in his eyes. He sits down beside us.

– Was it necessary to kill so many? Was it necessary to bomb residential areas? Shoot people in the street?

He lifts a lukewarm beer to his mouth but does not drink.

– Oh yes, the dictator has fallen. Oh yes, as a restaurateur and businessman it will be possible to enter into good contracts. Maybe the economy will blossom after so many years of isolation. But it was a dirty war. In spite of the American army's superiority, they behaved like savages. My heart bleeds for Iraq, Nabil sighs. – And I also fear the

Shias. I understand they are picking themselves up now, they suffered a lot under Saddam. But I do not want to live in a fundamentalist country. I hated Saddam but between you and me, he protected us Christians. Thanks to Saddam Hussein our life in Iraq was a good one, thanks to him I'm a rich man. Now I'm frightened, says Nabil, and finally takes a deep gulp of the beer.

The artists' café Shahbendar has also reopened. I look for Isam, the candid literature critic, but cannot find him. Instead I spot my artist friends, Haidar and Rafik, who discuss passionately. Samir is still in Syria. The painters agree on two things: That Iraq has been liberated and that they do not like the Americans. They smile. Sip their lemon tea and look reasonably happy and unconcerned.

— When I was seven I went on a boat on the Tigris with my parents, Haidar says. — I pointed at the Presidential palace and asked what it was. My parents regarded each other with horror and told me severely that I must never again point at that building. A bit later I protested when we learnt something at school about Iraq's history. My teacher was horrified and demanded that I never again open my mouth in class. So when I was seven I understood that we were not free, that we lived in danger. I learnt how to behave like a good Iraqi – in other words, to lie. Always and everywhere. I have been a liar ever since.

Haidar drinks his tea and purses his lips as if the tea no longer tastes good. He pulls on his cigarette. Even this appears to taste bitter.

— The tyrant has gone and I need lie no longer. But for thirty years I have lived under the skin of a liar. Now I must free myself.

*

— He talked on the radio today, Aliya says one morning.

— Someone has seen him in town, she says in the evening.

— He'll be back on his birthday to kill all Americans, she continues the next day.

— He's only hiding, the revenge will be sweet, she assures me.

But the days pass and Saddam does not return.

Before leaving Baghdad I want to see it, the palace on the opposite bank. I have stared at it so often; it was where the first bombs over Baghdad fell, where the hardest battles were fought, where the republican guard and the volunteers stood their ground the longest, and where I spotted the first American tanks. I have pondered over the building at daybreak, at night, during the sandstorms. It is the first thing I see every morning. The Presidential palace.

— Aren't you excited? I ask Aliya.

She shakes her head.

— Don't you wonder how your president lived?

— He lived many places.

We stop well short of the barbed wire by the entrance; we do not want to be mistaken for suicide bombers. Soldiers aim their guns at us, the tank cannons point in our direction. Amir parks the car, while Janine, Aliya and I wave our hands in the air and carefully approach the first barrier. The soldier who moves towards us does not lower his gun before we show him our press passes.

— Those are no good, the soldier says, pointing to my and Aliya's yellow cards. — You need a press card from HQ.

— But that's in Qatar, I protest.

— You can get them in Kuwait too, the soldier answers.

— But we have not been in the Gulf, we have been here, I stutter.

– Sorry guys, turn back.

– But . . .

– Turn back!

– I was here before you, I shout, and realise how idiotic I sound. We have survived their bombs and missiles, fought Iraqi bureaucracy, censure, fear and stress. We have lived without power and water, and then some pipsqueak from the American marines tells us what we can and cannot do.

I glance over at Aliya. Her face betrays nothing. Yet she must be cross, denied access in her own city by an American pimple-face.

Janine tries a soft voice. She has the correct card from Kuwait.

– Can't you let them in on my pass? she tries, ingratiatingly.

– Those two, never, says the soldier.

One of his superiors comes to our rescue, a large American I had spoken to at the hotel the night before.

– Come with me, he says, and asks us to jump into his Humvee.

Aliya refuses.

It appears the limit has been reached: an American vehicle.

– Well, we don't really need you in there, I say. – Everyone speaks English in Saddam's palace these days.

The insult could hardly have been worse.

Aliya stands still. She struggles with her conscience, her anger, the humiliation, her curiosity. The latter wins and she jumps in behind the driver.

The destruction is total. Some buildings have been virtually pulverised; trees have been uprooted. Bombs, missiles, tanks, grenades, cannons, bullets of every calibre were used in the battle for the palace.

— The battle lasted eight hours, says the officer. — It was a long day.

We drive past an American tank; a small black pennant with a skull flies in the wind, the platoon's emblem.

— Not all the bodies have been removed, he warns.

The officer points to some corpses by the road. Civilians. — Several arrived when the battle was as good as over. They hid rocket launchers behind their backs, aimed and shot. None of us were hit. But they were. We were prepared for street battles and our young soldiers went through tough training. But the Iraqis just ran and hid.

He stops by the next gate and hands us over to George, a black American from Harlem, New York. George smiles broadly and shakes our hands with a strong fist.

— Would you care for some sightseeing?

We follow the soldier over a carpet of cartridge cases. Past orange groves, fields and scorched gardens. It seems nobody has taken care of the place in a while. This spring, only the soldiers have kept house. The area, which covers several square kilometres, was the strategic heart of Saddam Hussein's system. The palace was like a town — the presidential town — with an HQ, elite forces' barracks, buildings belonging to the secret services, reception halls, and last but not least, the president's private apartments.

— There are 258 rooms, says George.

We step into the hall. It is a Babylonian version of Louis XIV's Versailles: hall upon hall, marbled floors and brocaded walls. Our footsteps echo. Most of the furniture has been removed, and what remains can only be described as imitation baroque, gilded plastic. The bedrooms have different types of beds — mahogany, white painted chipboard, gilded décor, ornate patterns or carvings.

In Uday's palaces the Americans found pornographic films, crates of champagne, whisky and rum, designer clothing, billiard tables, a Jacuzzi and a mass of private photographs and weapons. Saddam's cupboards are empty. Most of his belongings were moved long before the war.

Some of the halls have been transformed into HQs for the new rulers. On the tables are satellite telephones, computers and coffee cups. Generators have been erected to provide power. A notice on a partition wall says: 'Freedom is never for free. The price must be paid in blood. Give me freedom or give me death. We will never forget September 11th'.

George points and explains, opens doors, shines the torch up stairs. All the while he tries to strike up a conversation with Aliya.

– Look how your president wallowed in luxury while you lived in shit, he says.

– Hm, says Aliya.

– It's crazy, George continues.

– Hm.

– Your president waltzed around under crystal chandeliers while you guys didn't even have clean water!

– Hm.

– He spent your money.

– Hm.

– Your money. He stole from his people. This palace should have belonged to the people. It was built with your money!

– Hm.

– You had no freedom. He tortured prisoners, gassed his own people, while at the same time sitting on a golden throne. Aren't you mad? George asks.

Now not even a hm escapes from Aliya. She falls behind

and lets the wiry Harlem boy walk on. She stops and asks if we want her to translate the plaques on the walls.

– They commemorate all the wars Iraq has won, from the time of Babylon up to the present day.

When she has translated the plaque that represents the victory over the Americans in the Gulf War of 1991, she continues to read from the ceiling. There Allah's ninety-nine names are inscribed in black on gold. Aliya reads – The Beneficent, the Merciful, the Gracious, the King, the Holy, He Who Gives Peace, He Who Gives Faith, the Protector, the Mighty, the Compeller, the Majestic, the Creator.

George and Janine continue on. I stay and listen to Aliya, who is chanting softly.

– The Maker, The Bestower of Form, the Forgiver, the Subduer, the Bestower, the Provider, the Opener, the All-Knowing, the Withholder, the Expander, the Abaser, the Exalter, the Bestower of Honour, the Humiliator, the All-Hearing, the All-Seeing, the Judge, the Just, the Gentle, the All-Aware, the Forbearing, the Incomparably Great, the Forgiving, the Appreciative, the Most High, the Most Great, the Preserver, the Sustainer, the Reckoner, the Revered, the Generous, the Watchful, the Responsive, the All-Encompassing, the Wise, the Loving One, the Most Glorious, the Resurrector, the Witness, the Truth, the Ultimate Trustee, the Most Strong, the Firm One, the Protector, the All-Praised, the Reckoner, the Originator, the Restorer to Life, the Giver of Life, the Causer of Death, the Ever-Living, the Self-Existing by Whom all Subsists, the Self-Sufficient, the Glorified, the One, the Eternally Besought, the Omnipotent, the Powerful, the Expediter, the Delayer, the First, the Last, the Manifest, the Hidden, the Governor, the Most Exalted, the Benign, the Granter and Accepter of Repentance, the Lord of Retribution, the Pardoner, the Most

Kind, the Owner of the Kingdom, the Possessor of Majesty and Honour, the Just, the Gatherer, the All-Sufficient, the Enricher, the Preventer of Harm, the Afflicter, the Benefiter, the Light, the Guide, the Originator, the Everlasting, the Ultimate Inheritor, the Guide, the Patient One . . .

Allah's ninety ninth name is the Patient One.

When Aliya has finished she looks at me.

– Only Allah knows the hundredth name.

Then she trots after the others.

What did it feel like to be bombed, George asks when we catch him up. Aliya opens her mouth for the first time.

– We are used to it.

– I see, says George. – I mean, I understand.

He has stopped on one of the balconies and is looking out over an orange grove.

– What do the Iraqis really think about us? Are they pleased to be rid of Saddam Hussein?

Aliya does not answer. She stares straight ahead.

Even George is quiet.

After some brooding, he says:

– Well, I understand that you don't like us. I would not have liked us if I were you. I mean if I were an Iraqi. I would fight us. For sure.

On a stretcher in an American base lies Paul from Reuters. He is covered in wounds and bandages, has gashes on cheeks, nose, arms, chest, side, hips, and down to his legs.

– My testicles are still intact, he jokes to a colleague who is visiting.

Samia, a Reuters' correspondent, lies in the same base. Her face is cut. Shrapnel penetrated her head and still sits there. The surgeon tried to remove it but failed.

Josh has resigned. He is exhausted and tired of the war.

His feet are suffering from suppurating blisters, and his back has second degree burns from sweating in the bullet-proof vest while running at full speed up and down from the roof, carrying petrol cans to fill the generator.

But the greatest wounds are inside him. He has had enough. New Sky personnel have taken over. Four of them live in his room.

— I'm moving to Australia, he says when I meet him in the noisy reception area.

— To Australia?

— Yes, I have had enough of this madness for now. Come and see me there. We are leaving tomorrow morning.

David rushes past and bids farewell on the run.

— See you next time, he calls, as if we were to meet at a golf tournament.

Antonia leaves. And Giovanna and Stefan. Aliya is still quiet. Amir is increasingly sad, while Abbas has more energy every time we meet. I drag myself around.

One evening the 'martyrs' by the live points get on my nerves to such a degree that I ask the Americans to do something.

— They lie around on the grass among us all, I moan. — Who are they? What are they doing here?

— That's what we were wondering, says the NCO with whom I am talking.

— They look like suicide bombers.

— They surely do.

The next evening they have disappeared. A raid was conducted in the hotel to find out whether 'undesirable elements' were hiding there. It had been planned by the highest authority and had nothing to do with my complaints.

The foreign warriors had been let down by everyone who had welcomed them. By Saddam who had promised to award them, by his sons who had disappeared without a trace, by the republican guard who had changed into civilian clothes, by their own government who wanted nothing to do with them. And lastly by me, who had always been terrified of them.

September 11th. Always uttered as a matter of course, as if it explained everything. Every time I speak to a soldier, without fail he mentions that date. In spite of their doubts about the war, their argument in the end comes down to: You know, September 11th.

Most of them want to return home, after months in the desert. The soldiers I meet are possibly naïve, with a strong belief that Americans can do what they want, but they are a more diverse group than I had expected.

Outside the hotel in the dark between the tanks I meet a young soldier. He shines his torch on me.

— Where are you from?

— Norway. And you?

— Massachusetts.

The generators hum around us. People hasten past with cameras. Some privates sit on a concrete block and smoke. We make small talk; this soldier is also not as simple as I, in my European arrogance, had assumed. After a while he manoeuvres himself into existential waters.

— I do not know whether this war is right, he says. — I was thinking, out there in the desert, about what we are doing. I am against terrorism, but what have these Iraqis to do with terrorism?

The soldier glances over to his friends on the concrete.

— I think it's all because of the oil. Have you seen? Chaos.

The only ministry we are protecting is the Oil Ministry. The others are looted and torched. When we are out on patrol I notice that the Iraqis are hostile towards us, their faces bitter. We are no longer welcome. What do you think?

– Well, what people tell me is that they hope you won't stay long.

– That's what I hope too, the soldier sighs. – I want to go home. I want to leave the army. This is the dumbest thing I've ever done.

– What will you do?

– I want to be an opera singer.

– Wow.

– I have a good voice. My parents have always been sceptical, but I think they would prefer that to my staying in the army. I want to take lessons in Italy. Do you know what my dream is?

I shake my head. The boy regards me determinedly, but his eyes are worried.

– To sing *Otello*. At La Scala in Milan.

– Fruit cocktail or pineapple?

Timothy holds two tins in the air. My last dessert with Channel 4.

– Do you know, Kadim was the boss, the producer Paul tells us. Paul speaks fluent Arabic and has all the latest news about the press centre's evaporated heroes. Uday was only allegedly the boss, while Kadim actually belonged to the inner core of intelligence. – He was put there to keep an eye on Uday, Paul says. – It was always like that, the boss was never the top man. Sometimes the accountant was boss, sometimes the secretary. All were assessed and watched, to make sure no one got too much personal

power. Power was with the regime. Kadim could get Uday
sacked, not vice versa.

Now they are all gone anyway.

— We leave in a few days, Lindsay says. — There's room
in the car if you want to come.

I jump at the offer without hesitation. A dozen cars will
make up a convoy, with an escort from former soldiers of
the British Special Forces. Some of the TV companies have
engaged them to protect personnel between Amman and
Baghdad.

Out!

I must just do one thing before I leave.

Visit some of Baghdad's families.

The newsreels might show looting and demonstrations,
but that is only a small part of the truth. The majority sit at
home wondering what is happening.

*The doorbell hardly stops ringing in Muayad's house. Small cups
of strong coffee and endless cigarettes are consumed in the family's
overfurnished sitting room. It is a room which bears the hallmarks
of war. The tape which protected the windows against bombing has
still not been taken off. The sheets that covered the furniture when
the family left town are still there. Valuables which were packed in
suitcases and hidden have not yet been taken out.*

*What has changed most is the conversation. — We have not
spoken freely since 1967, says the neighbour Ahmed, a flight
engineer. — We have feared our neighbours, our friends, even our
own thoughts, he says. Fear has been part of my body, always
crushing, always present.*

*— It still lies in wait, says his wife, Iman. — I won't feel safe
until I see Saddam Hussein's corpse.*

*Ahmed and Iman stayed at home during the bombing. — When
the first bombs fell we cheered. Every night we went to bed, praying*

for more bombs, bigger bombs, they laugh. — We thought they were taking too long and despaired when it dragged out, Ahmed says. — But now at last the Americans are here and I hope they stay. If they leave us there'll be civil war. They need to stay for a couple of years. If we choose our own leader it will be the same old story: Bloodbath.

Muayad removed his family from Baghdad during the bombing, to his mother in the country. — *I have three daughters and this side of town was not safe,* he says about the Adamiya district. The professor of political science is not quite as happy about the American presence as his friends in the house next door. — *I am a nationalist, a pan-Arab. They have saved us from dictatorship and thank God for that. But we do not wish to become the fifty-first state. We want to rule ourselves, choose our own leaders.*

— *The Americans have killed so many civilians. They have shot Iraqis in the face,* his daughter Dora remarks. — *What sort of liberation is that? I'm frightened of the Americans.*

Dora lost one of her best friends during the bombing, when shrapnel flew in through his bedroom window. She didn't hear about it until the war was over and now she has been mourning for several days.

— *It felt like being on the* Titanic. *Everyone made their farewells in the days before the bombing started. Our hearts were black with fear.*

— *My roof has twelve bullet holes,* says Muayad, and we follow him out to have a look. — *There were several* fedain *forces in the area; they were Saddam's most loyal soldiers, and fierce fighting developed. When we returned, dead soldiers were lying in the streets.*

Muayad thinks that only a limited number of Iraqis really welcome the Americans. — *They smile when they come face to face, but spit when they turn their backs,* the professor says about the Iraqi attitude to the soldiers. Like many, he thinks the Americans desired *the chaos which now reigns in Baghdad. — After a week of looting and unrest we will scream for law and order and they can suppress us, brutally.*

Iman thinks Muayad is exaggerating. — *Of course it matters when people are killed, but that is the price we must pay and it is not too high. Remember the fear that has disappeared and the fact that we can sit here and disagree, that is important.*

The group of friends know many who were imprisoned or disappeared during Saddam Hussein's reign. A third neighbour, Yasser, who has just qualified as a computer engineer, tells the story of a school friend who made a joke about Saddam Hussein during break.

— *The next day he failed to turn up at school, and the day after. After a week we went to his house to check up and the whole family had gone. Mukhabarat had come in the evening and taken them. They never returned,* says Yasser. He still remembers the fateful joke.

One day Saddam Hussein decided that anyone who wanted could leave Iraq and settle abroad. Large queues formed outside the passport office. The president got to hear about it and decided to go and have a look for himself. He put on an old tunic and a false beard. He queued up and when he got to the front of the queue he asked for a passport. Then he tore off his beard so everyone could see who he was.

— '*I want to leave too,*' he said, and the civil servant issued him with a passport. When he turned round to leave he realised that the entire queue had evaporated. '*Where are they all?*' he asked.

— '*When they saw that you were leaving they decided to stay in Iraq,*' said the man.

Iman too has a story about how little was needed to get reported.

— *A journalist who worked for a ladies' magazine once passed a non-flattering remark about Saddam Hussein's wife's dress sense. Two of her colleagues overheard the remark. A few hours later the police came and took her. The next morning her parents found her* outside their front door. Her body was black and blue from being beaten and she had been burnt with cigarettes; her tongue had been cut out, Iman says.

— Do you understand? The two women who overheard the comment were themselves terrified. Both were frightened that the other would inform on them if they did not report what they had heard. Maybe they were being tested? We could trust no one. We had to be careful what we said to our own children. They might denounce us at school. Teachers were obliged to inform on children who said anything suspicious and the headmaster had to convey it further down the line.

— Every school day started thus: Long live our President Saddam Hussein, Maha, a primary school teacher, says.

— What will we do now, and how will we spend all those hours we used to teach the children about Saddam's life, his virtues and achievements?

No one answers Maha. The discussion continues about the past. It is too early to give much thought to the future.

— What I'm most ashamed of, says Walid, a businessman — is that we lost our courage. After thirty-five years of oppression we have turned into a race of wimps. We should have got rid of the dictator ourselves, not waited for the Americans to do it, he sighs. — I myself was never imprisoned, but we were tortured mentally by the all-pervading fear. We could only whisper, one to the other, and even that was dangerous.

Walid's crime was to install a satellite TV at his home. — Everything was permissible if one only paid for it, he says. — The Baath Party official who supervised our road would appear at regular intervals. He needed to be blackmailed to keep his mouth shut. Two days ago he was there again. He asked for protection and wanted to live with me, a return favour for not having informed on me. What a cheek! I declined. — I owe you nothing, I said, and asked him to leave.

Walid rises up in anger and tears some dinar notes from his pocket. — Look, he's even in my pocket, he snorts, and points to the picture of Saddam Hussein on the bank note. He reaches out for a pen and scribbles black crosses over the fallen leader's face. — I'm trying to rid myself of a ghost, a dark cloud, a gruesome reminder of the past, he says, then folds the notes and stuffs them back into his pocket. — The fear must leave my body.

Amir and Abbas talk to others rather than to each other. They even stand alone rather than talk to each other. One is sad, the other euphoric.

Every time they meet, Abbas asks: And how's your Saddam?

Every time Amir answers: Fine, thank you, and how are your Americans?

The exchange of words is increasingly hostile. One day Amir is leaning against the bonnet of his car when Abbas passes by. Abbas throws his head back and exclaims:

— One day he will have to answer for what he did to us. And his errand boys too.

— One day we will rid ourselves of the Americans and their flunkies.

They glare at each other. Abbas turns on his heel and walks away. Those are the last words they exchange.

On the one hundred and first night Aliya wants to sleep in my room. We have not really talked properly since the statue of Saddam was toppled. The wind plays gently through the open window. We each lie under a dirty grey blanket. I am off the next morning.

I glance over at Aliya. Ten days ago her world was turned on its head and her old illusions crushed. These ten days she has not eaten, not slept. She has worked mechanically but avoided personal conversations. She has passed on the joy felt over the dictator's fall, but has not expressed what she felt. She has translated the desperation of relatives in the empty prisons, but has never revealed her own. She has overcome her fear of Americans, but has never shown her contempt. She has interpreted the wounded children's prayers but has never shed a tear. She has accepted derision and insult against the country she loves, against the president she believed in and admired, but she has never railed back. She has listened when people have said she is wrong, but she has never responded.

Then it is the one hundred and first night. Aliya curls up in my bed.

— Do you know, she says, mostly to herself, looking up at the ceiling. The palm trees are rustling outside the window. A rush of cold air makes her pull the blanket around her body. She closes her mouth and lies still, staring into the dark room. The Americans' searchlights ensure that the room is never really dark. She draws her breath and forces herself to continue.

— People say *he* never cared about us.

Just that. No more.

The breeze outside the window picks up.

Aliya coughs, a dry cough, as though she has more to say but the words are pushed back. She is still for a long time before continuing.

— They say he only cared about himself, she says, in wonder.

The white floodlight shines through the wispy tulle and makes thin shadows. A sudden breeze over the Tigris forms a tiny whirlwind. It floats through the balcony doors and makes the curtains dance.

I'm profoundly convinced that the only antidote that can make the reader forget the perpetual I's the author will be writing, is a perfect sincerity

Stendhal, *Souvenirs d'Egotisme*, 1832

Discussion Questions for Reading Groups

1. In the first part of the author's stay in Iraq, before the war has started, Åsne can't get people to talk to her openly. It's just too dangerous for anyone to reveal their real opinions. As Åsne says, "the problem was elementary: no one said anything." (p.1) "I am here to find dissidents, a secret uprising, gagged intellectuals, Saddam's opponents. I am here to point out human rights violations, expose oppression. And I'm reduced to being a tourist." (p.26) How does Åsne get around this seemingly insurmountable problem? Discuss whether you agree that Åsne is correct in feeling that she is performing a service by getting these stories out. Is her quest an essential one?

2. If someone does reveal an honest opinion, Åsne faces a moral dilemma: quote them, thus possibly endangering their lives, or just leave them out of the article. When talking to a group of college students, Åsne is surprised

when one of them admits that no one says what they really think. "When I write my small piece about the farewell lunch I wonder whether or not to include the boy's comments. I add them, then cross them out. Someone might find him. Someone might have seen him." (p. 59) What is Åsne's responsibility to the people who talk to her vs. the importance of bringing the truth (as she sees it) to hundreds of readers in another country? Is it fair or ethical for Åsne to even try to get an honest response, given that a moment's honesty could ruin someone's life?

3. Even among highly competitive war reporters, the women journalists are very solicitous of each other. Åsne reports, "the women excel at looking after each other." (p. 209) Does this merely reflect the fact that women are socialized to be caregivers and nurturers— or is there something about being in a life-threatening environment that causes the women to band together? Discuss the ways men and women in the same very cut-throat field might react differently to this situation.

4. In the early twentieth century, the famous travel writer Gertrude Bell wrote that the most important thing to have when traveling among Arabs is an ample supply of patience. Åsne certainly found this to be true in dealing with the various ministries, minders, and bureaucracies that governed Iraqi life. What other qualities or personality traits help Åsne succeed in this difficult and frustrating assignment? Was this her secret in getting into and then extending her stay in Iraq? Patience is a quality that women are expected to develop and attain— in this one way, is being female an advantage for Åsne?

5. Like all the other journalists in Iraq before the war starts, Åsne's work is intensely monitored and scrutinized by the Ministry of Information and its employees, including Åsne's driver and translator. Considering that Åsne can't honestly report what she sees and that everything published in Norway or transmitted to Scandinavia is censored, why is it so important for Åsne to stay in Iraq? Is she accomplishing anything when she can only deliver a small part of the real story? Is this one of the reasons she wanted to write this story as a book? How are books different than news journalism?

6. Are there any occasions when you think Åsne may have been manipulated by the Ministry of Information? What do you think of the accusations made by some politicians that the reporting from Iraq aided "the enemy"? Is Åsne ever complicit in the Ministry's propaganda campaign?

7. Despite the frustrations, hardships, and outright danger of working in Baghdad, Åsne is desperate to stay in Iraq and witness the war up close. What compels Åsne to stay when so many other journalists—especially given the threat of chemical warfare, regular bombs and missiles, and being taken hostage and used as human shields—are happy to leave before the war breaks out?

8. Åsne is Western, yet not a citizen of one of the big powers like the United States or Britain. How does the fact that she's from a relatively powerless country affect her life as a journalist in Iraq? If she were from the United States, would people have seen her as the enemy and been even less forthcoming? Being a woman and having a female interpreter, was Åsne able to have more

contact with Iraqi women? Might they have been less afraid of her than they would have been of a male reporter?

9. Åsne doesn't get to talk to many "ordinary" people, and when she does, what they say is filtered through a government-appointed interpreter, with the interviewee usually terrified of getting into trouble. Even so, Åsne does manage to occasionally convey to her readers back home a sense of what life is like on the eve of the war. The profusion of rumors, the lack of real information, the indecision about whether to escape to neighboring cities or countries, and the uncertainty of everyday life all come through in Åsne's writings. How does she manage to cobble together a realistic picture of life in Baghdad given the restraints under which she has to work? Or is her portrayal of Iraqis, by definition, biased and slanted?

10. One of the saddest and most moving stories in *A Hundred and One Days* involves Ali, the twelve-year-old boy whose house was hit by an American missile that killed his mother, father, and brother, and covered him in burns, ultimately requiring the amputation of his arms. Seeing this tragedy pushes Åsne over the edge—"I want to go home. I can't take it any more" (p.296) she says after seeing Ali. Yet she still can't bring herself to leave. Now that people are finally free to talk about their lives under Saddam, Åsne wants to document the atrocities, to write about them. Has Åsne become too close to her story? Does she have the detachment that a journalist is supposed to maintain? If she has become too involved, does it affect the way

she works or writes? Is Åsne unusual in her level of involvement? Can being subjective and reacting as a human being, a woman, help a journalist connect to the people she is writing about? Discuss.

11. Before the war started, assuming Iraq will win, Åsne's translator, Aliya, blithely offered to defend Åsne: "You are my sister," Aliya says. "If anyone attacks you I will protect you with my body. . . . You are my fair sister and I am your dark one." (p. 166) After the war has started, Aliya continues working for Åsne but seems to have totally shut down, while Åsne finds the situation exciting and compelling. Discuss how their different upbringings affect their different reactions to the war. Discuss what Aliya's story means in the context of the larger picture of Iraq's people. Few would argue that forcing Saddam from the country is a bad thing, but has it been a completely good thing?

12. In just 101 days—a mere three months—Åsne has witnessed cataclysmic events: the fall of a brutal dictatorship, a horrific war, the deaths of friends, and the wounding and killing of innocent Iraqis. "In . . . ten years as a journalist reporting from war and conflict zones," reports Åsne, "I have never worked under more difficult conditions" (p. 1), yet she also found the experience "incredibly exciting" (p. 231). How do you think this experience in Iraq affected her life?